The FINANCIAL GUIDE To DIVORCE SETTLEMENT

Helping Your Clients Make Sound Financial Decisions

CAROL ANN WILSON

This publication is designed to provide general information prepared by professionals in regard to subject matter covered. It is sold with the understanding that the authors are not engaged in rendering legal, accounting or other professional service. Although written by professionals, this publication should not be utilized as a substitute for professional service in specific situations. If legal advice or other expert assistance is required the service of a professional should be sought.

ISBN 0-9626790-4-6

Printed in the United States

Published by ICDP Publishing
6396 Gunpark Drive, Suite W
Boulder, CO 80301
303-527-3429
800-875-1760

To my husband of six years, Bill Fullmer,
who showed me that there is life after divorce.

FOREWORD

It is an unfortunate truth that divorce is a fact of life in the United States. As a matter of fact, the U.S. has a higher rate of divorce than any other industrial country. Since the dissolution of marriages is an everyday event, any way that the process can be made easier is of great interest to attorneys who practice in this area. As attorneys, we continue to search for products to make life easier for our clients, and we occasionally come upon a book that will shorten the divorce process. This particular book, the *Financial Guide to Divorce Settlement*, is one of those products that eases the painful financial dissolution of a marriage.

Information is the most important resource in a fair and equitable settlement. Without information and a knowledge of the financial pot, the process cannot be fair. Consequently, finding a book such as *The Financial Guide to Divorce Settlement* makes the discovery process that much easier.

A few years ago, I began using Divorce Plan™ software created by Carol Ann Wilson and Quantum Financial Inc. This software enables lawyers to project different financial scenarios, as well as predict the impact of the settlement decision years down the road. This particular software was and still is the best product of its kind to help professionals enable their clients to reach more equitable settlements. Now Wilson has taken the next step. Building upon the strengths of the software, she has written a book to enhance its use.

The process of divorce is more than simply dividing assets. Planning for the future is also an intricate part of the process. Just like the words "And they lived happily ever after" is not always the end of the story in a marriage, the divorce decree is not the end of the process for litigants. Planning for the future and understanding the impact of a settlement is equally important. *The Financial Guide to Divorce Settlement* explains the process and the impact on the future of each litigant. The financial planner can utilize this book to help his or her client through the maze of financial decisions. More importantly, the book discusses and illustrates the ramifications of each of these decisions on the client's future.

Interestingly enough, in addition to a sound financial analysis, Ms. Wilson offers a groundbreaking suggestion: professionals should work together to help clients through the divorce process. This notion of teamwork among attorneys, financial planners, and mediators may seem unique, but with the changing attitudes toward litigation through the courts, it appears to be on the cutting edge of the changes in the divorce arena.

Having spent a number of years trying to develop programs to cut down on the divorce rate, I continue to realize that divorce will be with us for a long time. There is no way to make everyone happy. Given that fact, easing the process for those people going through it ought to be part of our arsenal. Additionally, anything that will help professionals work together to ease the divorce process is to be greatly admired. This book gives a road map to financial solutions, and a way for professionals to work together in the best interest of the client. Hopefully, it also aids the professional as constructively as possible in easing a couple's transition from being married to being single again. The *Financial Guide to Divorce Settlement* provides the framework for this to happen. Utilization of the Guide in conjunction with the Divorce Plan software is greatly recommended.

Lynne Z. Gold-Bikin, Esquire
Past Chair of the American Bar Association
Family Law Section, and Fellow of
the American and International
Academy of Matrimonial Lawyers

PREFACE

"Divorce is often the biggest psychological crisis of an individual's life: that is, unless a child or spouse has died. On the stress 'Richter scale' divorce is in the top three."—Dr. Judith Briles, author of *Dollars and Sense of Divorce* and *Money Sense*.

In the late 1980s, I was hired by a woman from Connecticut who was getting divorced. She wanted me to represent her in court. As an expert witness, with my charts and graphs, I would be able to show why she should get the property and maintenance award she was requesting. I flew to Connecticut armed with my reports.

When we walked into the courtroom, the husband's attorney said to the judge, "Your Honor, we request a continuance so that we can find our own expert witness to rebut Ms. Wilson's testimony."

My client's attorney's response was, "Your Honor, there are no other experts like Ms. Wilson. She is the only one in the United States."

I thought to myself, "Wow! Why should this judge listen to me if I'm the only one out there?" So, right then, I decided to start teaching other financial planners how to develop the same expertise I have.

The notion of using my financial planning training to aid in equitable divorce settlements first came to me back in 1985. As a financial planner, I met with several women after their divorces were final. They seemed to be in severe financial trouble. I couldn't understand why, if the assets had been divided evenly, they should be having such financial problems. From these encounters, I developed the Divorce Plan(software, which clearly showed me that *equal is not always equitable.*

I started gathering facts, reading books, attending legal education classes, talking to attorneys, and speaking to hundreds of people who had been through divorce. It became evident to me that something was wrong with the system that couples go through when they get divorced.

I believed there was the possibility of an equitable settlement that would help *preserve financial security after divorce*. That became my theme song.

After several years of specializing in this niche, I heard it said that my work in this area had changed family law in Colorado. Attorneys were crafting more equitable settlements, and judges were handing down different rulings.

Well! If *I* could do it in Colorado, then others could do it in other states and *we* could make a difference. That was an exciting thought.

After the experience in Connecticut, I felt that if other financial planners all over the nation were doing the same thing—presenting data that showed the financial results of any given settlement—it would become an accepted, credible profession. It would become easier for all financial planners' expertise to be accepted in court. We would present data that would help people reach reasonable settlements. In turn, judges could—and would—make clearer decisions.

After handling 500 to 600 divorce cases and appearing over 100 times as an expert witness in court, and after speaking and teaching for several years, I saw the need to put all this information in one place. You are holding it—*The Financial Guide to Divorce Settlement*. My only regret is that it wasn't in my hands when I started down the road in 1983 as a financial planner. I know it will be helpful and useful to you.

Carol Ann Wilson
6395 Gunpark Drive, Suite W
Boulder, CO 80301
800-875-1760
e-mail: InstCDP@aol.com
http://www.InstituteCDP.com

ACKNOWLEDGMENTS

To Amy Ost, my publishing editor, who knew better than I did that I had this book in me;

To Judith Briles, a friend and mentor, to whom I am so indebted that I can never repay all the help she has given me;

To Kara Stewart, my copy editor, who made my work look good;

To Alan Gappinger, who has always been there to answer questions and give clarification;

To Barbara Stark, Helen Stone, Ed Schilling, Ann Mygatt, Christine Coates, Michael Caplan and Gail Heinzman for their contributions;

And to my husband, Bill Fullmer, whose understanding and support has been instrumental in the writing of this book.

TABLE OF CONTENTS

CHAPTER 1

The New Divorce Niche

Most people enter marriage believing in the words "till death do us part." They know their marriage will last forever; it will be one of the successful unions. They will beat the divorce odds. And they do, for a while. Then something happens and they realize that they may become one of the divorce statistics.

Divorce isn't something that happens to "other people" anymore. In fact, there are about 1.2 million divorces every year in the United States. That's at least 2.4 million people who must face the challenges a breakup can cause—not counting their children, in-laws, relatives, and friends.

From the U.S. Department of Health and Human Services, Centers for Disease Control and Prevention, National Center for Health Statistics, we have these numbers: In 1997, there were 2,384,000 marriages and 1,163,000 divorces for a 49% divorce rate. In 1998, there were 2,244,000 marriages and 1,135,000 divorces for a 51% divorce rate. (It seems that the divorce rate is staying right at the 50% level.)

Given the fact that divorce can and does happen, the solution is often not to prevent divorce but to help the process and the settlement be as equitable and as painless as possible. This has created a real market niche for professionals who are needed in all phases of the divorce process.

THE WIFE'S POINT OF VIEW

The higher the income of the family, the wider the financial gap between divorced partners. The reason? Even though society is changing, most couples still invest in the husband's career while the wife's job takes second place. And if the marriage lasted a long time, the wife has lost at least a decade of career growth. Although recent changes have started to alter this pattern, most divorcing couples began their marriages in this traditional format. Divorcing men and women simply do not have equal income-producing potential. Instead, women who have spent 20 or 30 years in traditional marriages find themselves out in the cold with minimal marketable skills and minimal real job prospects.

The courts often ignore this crucial issue when dividing marital property. Most lawyers and judges try to provide equitable divorce settlements for both parties. However, without a comprehensive financial analysis, many wives end up in dire financial straits despite legislation designed to provide fair divorce settlements. A number of factors can contribute to an imbalance in a divorce settlement; however, one fundamental fact prevails: *a traditional married couple's lifestyle is usually based on the husband's income.* We define "traditional marriage" as one in which the wife has either never worked or earns much less than her husband.

In dividing marital property, courts traditionally have overlooked one major asset of a marriage: the husband's career and the assets associated with it. These include his:

- salary
- stock options
- health insurance
- life insurance
- disability insurance
- vacation pay
- sick pay
- education and training
- seniority and networking
- potential earning power

Unfortunately, many courts don't recognize career assets as property. In creating an equitable financial settlement, it is important to remember that *prop-*

erty is divided just once, but career assets continue to produce income regularly for years.

The courts assume equal independence from both partners. Sometimes the court will award rehabilitative maintenance to ease a spouse into the work force. But the courts base these settlements on the assumption—often false—that both spouses can be equally self-sufficient. In reality, *marriage creates economic inequality.*

Research on divorce found that the most important issue women is *survival.* They are terrified of becoming "bag ladies"! Yet this fear isn't as irrational as it may sound. In the late 1980s, several states set up task forces to study gender bias in the courts. For example, in Colorado, one section of the task force was charged with the area of divorce. It studied cases taken directly from the court files. The parameters were that (1) the marriage have lasted 12 years or longer, (2) the case be decided by a judge as opposed to being settled out of court (the task force wanted to see the results of what the judges were doing), and (3) there was a minimum of $10,000 in positive net worth.[1]

Out of 28 cases, the average length of marriage was 20.5 years. At the time of divorce, the average age of the wife was 44, the husband, 45. Eleven of the 28 families had net assets of less than $50,000 at the time of divorce and ten had net assets of $100,000 or more.[2]

Figure 1-1 is a graph which shows the results of this study. It is a composite of the 28 cases, showing the average net worth of husband and wife at the time of the divorce (based on the court-ordered property division) and the projected change in net worth for each of them. At the time of the court order, the wife's average net worth is slightly greater than the husband's, because she is usually allocated less of the marital debt. Within four years of the divorce, however, the wife's projected net worth declines by 25 percent while the husband's nearly doubles. Within eight years of the divorce, the wife will have a negative net worth while the husband's projected net worth is approximately $200,000.[3]

In gathering data, besides looking at the court files, the Colorado task force interviewed many divorced men and women. One women told her story about the maintenance award after 38 years of marriage during which she was not employed. The judge ordered her husband to pay her $300 per month for two years. He awarded the house, appraised at $160,000, to the wife, and all the other assets, including a retirement fund, to the husband, saying, "Mother has been out of the work force, and if we gave her all that money she wouldn't know how to handle it."[4]

Another woman told the Colorado task force that she had been awarded a tractor as part of the property settlement but her ex-husband refused to

FIGURE 1-1

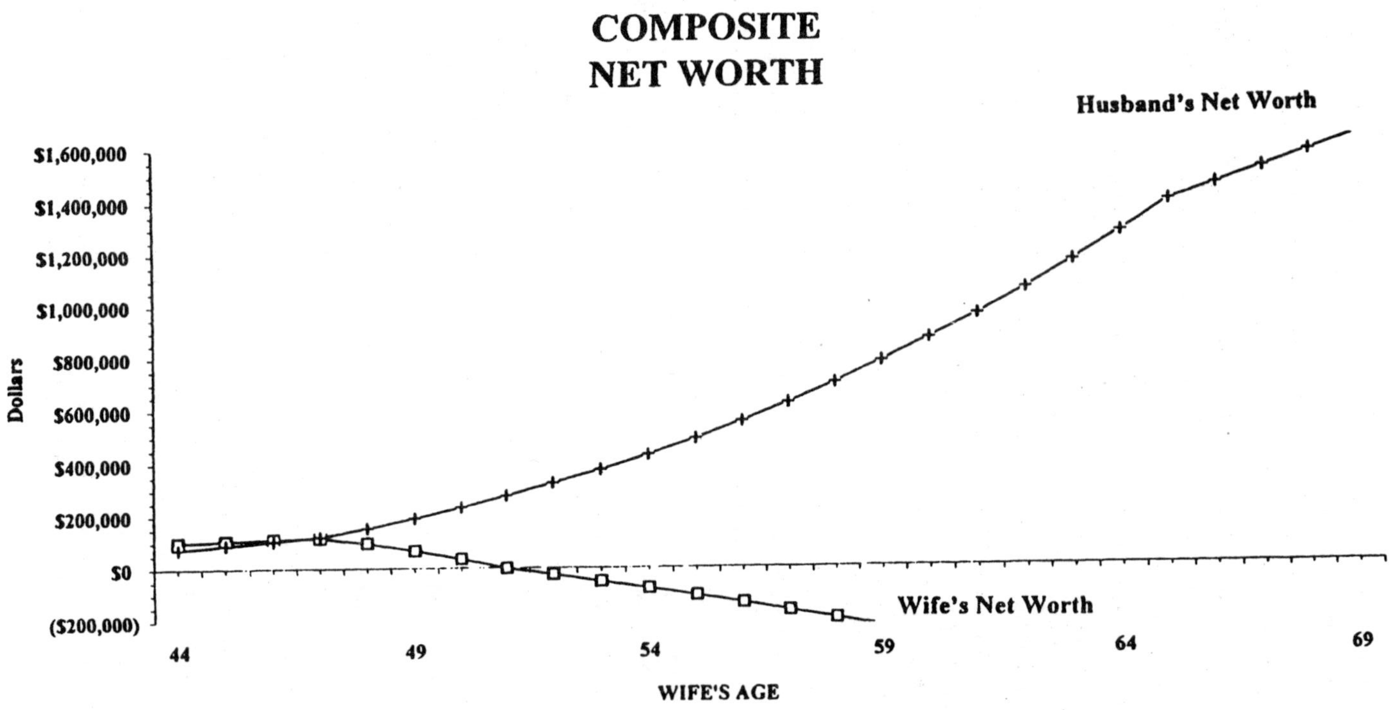
COMPOSITE
NET WORTH
Husband's Net Worth
Wife's Net Worth
Dollars
$1,600,000
$1,400,000
$1,200,000
$1,000,000
$800,000
$600,000
$400,000
$200,000
$0
($200,000)
44
49
54
59
64
69
WIFE'S AGE

deliver it. She had tried for four years to get the original order enforced, without success. One district judge gave her former husband permission to continue using the tractor. When her lawyer objected, the judge asked her what she was going to do with the tractor.[5]

A 1997 report from the Business and Professional Women's Foundation has gathered together the following statistics:

The Washington State Task Force on Gender and Justice in the Courts found that only 10% of all wives being divorced were awarded maintenance and the average amount was $432 per month for an average length of 2.6 years. The national average as of spring 1986 had 15 percent of wives receiving an average of $329 per month.[6]

1. The average woman loses approximately $420,000 over a lifetime due to unequal pay practices.
2. Women on average can expect to live 19 years into retirement while men can expect to live 15 years.
3. Only 39% of all working women and fewer than 17% of part-time working women are covered by a pension plan.
4. Only 20% of all widows receive a survivor pension, which is usually only 50% of what their husband's benefits had been.
5. Fewer than one-fourth of divorced women age 62 and older receive any employer-sponsored pension income, whether from their own or their ex-husband's past work. Often, divorced women are left with no share of their ex-husband's pension, even after a long marriage.
6. In 1995, women comprised only 58% of the total elderly population but comprised 74% of the elderly poor. Older women are twice as likely as older men to be poor, and nearly 40% of older women living alone live in or near poverty level.
7. Of all unmarried women age 65 and older, 40% rely on Social Security for 90% or more of their household income.
8. The U.S. has the greatest percentage of elderly women in poverty of all the major industrialized nations.

THE HUSBAND'S POINT OF VIEW

The awakening of the men's movement in this country is providing insight into the pain that men experience. The divorce process is a common source of much of that pain. Surprisingly, in many cases it is the man—not the woman—who is paralyzed by emotions. Feeling terribly victimized, men sometimes conclude that courts agree with the cynical saying, "What's his is theirs and what's hers is hers."

Men have several very real concerns. The number one concern for fathers with young children is how the divorce will affect their relationship with their children. Even though we hear about fathers who abandon their children after divorce, this is not the prevailing behavior. During divorce, men fight for the right to participate in the lives of their children. Only if denied that right do they sometimes walk away in frustration and discontinue child support payments.

Fathers dread their lack of control in the divorce situation and fear the court's power to decree the most intimate details of their relationship with children. The fact that a man and woman no longer get along with each other does not mean that a father loves his children less. In fact, in many cases going through a divorce takes the father through an educational process that brings him closer to his own hidden emotions—paving the way toward a warmer and more participative role as a dad.

After the issue of children, another concern is the prospect of paying life-time alimony to his ex-wife. No one wants to be tied into that possibility. Men want an end to the payments. They believe they cannot get on with their own lives as long as they have to pay out a large portion of their income to someone who is no longer a part of their life. They see this as keeping the relationship going with no possibility of relief. They really do not understand why, when a relationship is at an end, they should have an obligation to support this person indefinitely.

Having to pay out large sums in the first few years after a divorce for things like child support, alimony, attorney's fees (both his and hers), as well as property settlement, means that a man's discretionary income may suffer greatly. He frequently feels that he has been "taken to the cleaners" and that he is doomed to pay for the divorce forever. In some cases, he may be right. But statistics show that in the vast majority of cases, the financial effects of divorce are relatively short-lived. Men can take solace in the fact that their earning potential is almost always higher than the ex-wife's and they will eventually be financially better off than the ex-wife.

A critical concern to men is sharing their pensions. A man feels he earned the pension and he should not have to share it with anyone. It's interesting that, in many cases, the man will agree to a 50/50 property split and give the wife other assets in exchange for keeping his pension— "just don't touch my pension!" It becomes an extremely emotional issue that can steer a man in the wrong direction!

A concern for the self-employed man is his business. If it has significant value, this can be an area of great concern for both sides. All too often it is the only asset of real value and since it cannot be divided, paying the wife her half of the value can be a real problem. Sometimes this is solved with a property settlement note.

A universal concern is a perception that the deck is stacked against men from the beginning because of pressures from a press sympathetic toward women. Men feel that they are made to pay the price for a minority of husbands and fathers who ignore their responsibilities. It is the experience of many men that they are "assumed guilty" for the breakup of the marriage—and that they must pay in order to atone for this sin.

The Colorado task force received a few complaints from men who felt they had been victims of gender bias in awards of spousal maintenance or child support. For example, one man stated, "The purpose of maintenance is to sustain the weaker of the parties, when that one has contributed to the rise of the union by sacrifice of career or education, until such time that the weaker one becomes established and self-sufficient. In my case the wife was the direct cause of the financial problems of the union and should not be rewarded for that. This lady has no intention to re-train, or have a career."[7]

IS AN EQUITABLE DIVORCE SETTLEMENT POSSIBLE?

Divorce often has a devastating impact on everyone involved. While some couples effect a "civilized" divorce and can remain semi-friends, many couples go through World War III which, especially if they end up in court, can have a permanently damaging result on the rest of their lives.

Can something be done to lessen the negative impact of divorce? Are equitable settlements really possible? Yes.

However, few judges and attorneys are financial experts. Financial analysis of the outcome of possible settlements is complex and requires substantial experience. When legal expertise is not matched with sophisticated financial projections, an apparently equal division of property can leave the lower- or non-earning spouse destitute within a few years.

Contrary to popular belief, arranging a settlement that benefits the lower-earning spouse does not necessarily have to harm the higher-earning spouse. In addition, even though a lower standard of living may be anticipated, it does not have to be dramatically lowered for either spouse.

Although it is impossible to predict the future, sophisticated software methodology can be used to forecast the eventual financial outcome of specific divorce settlements. Such software allows judges, lawyers, and divorcing couples to compare the outcome of various suggested settlements. The Divorce Plan™ software program can be used to test different scenarios, such as higher or longer-lasting maintenance, disproportionate property division, and reduced standards of living.

With available software, along with professionals versed in the intricacies of putting together equitable final settlements and experts dedicated to helping couples avoid the court battle, a more humane result can be accomplished. This book provides the tools to getting a broad-based understanding of how to do this.

NOTES

1. Colorado Supreme Court Task Force on Gender Bias In The Courts. 1990.
2. Colorado Supreme Court Task Force on Gender Bias In The Courts. 1990.
3. Colorado Supreme Court Task Force on Gender Bias In The Courts. 1990.
4. Colorado Supreme Court Task Force on Gender Bias In The Courts. 1990.
5. Colorado Supreme Court Task Force on Gender Bias In The Courts. 1990.
6. Washington State Task Force on Gender and Justice In The Courts. 1989.
7. Colorado Supreme Court Task Force on Gender Bias In The Courts. 1990.

CHAPTER 2

The Financial Advisor's Role

THE AFTERMATH OF DIVORCE: A PARABLE

After her divorce, Joyce went to a financial planner to see how to best reposition her assets. Together, they decided to do a total financial plan for her. During the planning session, it became apparent that during her marriage her husband had done all of the investing. He chose all of the investments, made all the decisions, and invested all the money.

At divorce time, he said, "Let's just split everything 50/50. You take this half of the investments and I will take that half. Is that okay?"

Joyce answered, "Well, I guess that sounds pretty fair. That is okay with me."

Unfortunately, there was something she did not know or understand. Neither did her attorney, and neither did the judge. They didn't realize that Joyce was getting half of the investments with *all* the tax recapture. Her 50/50 split cost her an additional $18,000 in taxes. If Joyce had seen a financial planner *before* the divorce was final, she would have been in a better position to formulate a more equitable settlement.

This parable has an unfortunate ending, but pre-divorce financial counseling can help people going through divorce arrive at a fair settlement for all involved.

Who do people turn to for such assistance? When people think about getting divorced, the first professional that comes to mind is an attorney. Typically, a financial advisor whether it be their CPA, their financial planner, or a Certified Divorce Planner isn't thought about until later. Unfortunately, too much later.

Financial problems can tear a marriage apart and are often the primary cause that eventually leads to divorce. If couples can't solve their financial problems during the marriage, why do they think they will be able to agree on the financial issues of divorce?

They have questions like:

- How do we value our property?
- Who gets what property?
- What are the tax issues?
- How do we divide retirement funds and future pensions?
- How will the lower-earning spouse survive?
- What kind of additional help or support does that person need?
- Who gets the house?
- Will that person have to pay capital gains tax?
- Who gets the children?
- Who will pay for college, for summer camp, for orthodontia for the children?
- What happens if a paying ex-spouse dies?

Many attorneys also struggle with the intricate financial details that concern tax issues, IRS rulings, capital gains, dividing pensions, and the like. The attorneys attended law school to become expert in the law, not to become financial experts. Fortunately, however, many attorneys are aware of their shortcomings in financial expertise and are willing to get help from a financial expert. That's where you, the financial planner, come in. Some attorneys try to do it all themselves and many of them have made serious blunders.

WHAT IS THE FINANCIAL PLANNER'S ROLE?

There are many titles for a financial expert: Certified Public Accountant (CPA), financial planner, Certified Financial Planner (CFP), Chartered Financial Consultant (ChFC), economist, accountant, and Certified Divorce Planner (CDP).

A Certified Divorce Planner is a new type of professional. This person is often a Certified Financial Planner who has taken additional intensive training to become skilled in working with people in divorce, becoming part of the divorce team with the attorney, dealing with all the financial issues in each case, and appearing as an expert witness if needed. This designation and training is given by the Institute for Certified Divorce Planners.[1]

The role of a financial planner, as opposed to a generic financial expert, is to help people achieve their financial goals regardless of whether they are divorcing or happily married. After deciding what the goals are, the next step is to look at what needs to be done to achieve those goals. These goals can be from one year to 50 years in the future. Looking that far into the future requires certain assumptions about income, expenses, inflation, interest rates, return on investments, and retirement needs. After the assumptions are made and plugged in, the scenario needs to be reviewed on a regular basis to see if they are still on track.

In other words, the financial planner looks at financial results in the future based on certain assumptions made today. Conversely, the CPA typically looks at the details of the scenario as it is today and makes no future projections. These ideologies can certainly be blended for the best interest of the client.

Each person in the midst of divorce is understandably concerned about their financial future and how the decisions they make today are going to affect their future. It behooves them to make some educated guesses as to what the future will hold based on what their final decisions are today.

A financial planner is well-versed in interviewing clients to find out what their future goals are, when they want to retire, how much risk they are willing to take with their investments, what kind of a living style they want, what kind of education they want for their children, and so on.

Certified Financial Planners, on the other hand, are also trained in tax issues, estate planning, retirement planning, investment planning, insurance planning, cash flows, and budgeting. What better professional to have involved to help a spouse reach a reasonable settlement that will come closest to reaching both their goals.

Few win in a divorce. It seems that no matter how much money there is, each spouse has to adjust their standard of living after the divorce to make things work out. But there are solutions that can be reached which will minimize the potentially devastating effects. It is safe to assume that both of the divorcing spouses loved each other once upon a time. Hopefully, at divorce time, they have some concern about how the other will fare after the divorce.

IF THE CLIENT IS THE WIFE

In a traditional marriage where the husband has worked and the wife has stayed home to care for the children, the wife client poses concerns about having enough income to live on to continue her previous standard of living. Sometimes, this is just impossible. Many couples can't afford their standard of living with one household, let alone two, and they end up with large credit-card debt. Asking an ex-husband to pay enough to allow his ex-wife to continue her previous life style may not be realistic. After looking at the numbers, the expert should counsel the wife about expectations. Perhaps a lesson in budgeting is appropriate.

It's also important to acknowledge the high degree of emotional stress during this time. Both parties hurt. There's often anger. Territories and turfs are drawn. The financial planner can be a key facilitator in moving either or both parties toward some type of therapy or professional counseling.

Another concern for the wife is whether to go back to work or whether to train for a better job. Typically, in the traditional marriage, the wife is either not working outside the home, or she has a very low-paying job. A career counselor may be useful in testing the wife for skills and possibilities in the job market.

The wife often gets custody of the children. This has several effects that often are not considered. First, as the children get older, they really do cost more to maintain! They have more expensive hobbies: skiing, biking, musical instruments, computers, etc. They eat more. Their clothes are more expensive. They might need orthodontia. Items needed for school cost much more than a few pencils and paper. As schools cut back, parents are required to supply *all* the essentials.

Second, having custody of the children will influence what kind of job the wife gets. It will be very difficult to develop a career where, to get ahead and earn the top salary, she will have to work nights or weekends or spend time traveling. So, her primary career will likely have to be flexible to allow her to care for the children.

A third effect of having custody of the children is the emotional and psychological difficulty of dealing with children's issues and problems on a daily basis without a second parent to share in this. All parents can relate to this.

Many wives have not been involved with the financial issues during the marriage and just don't know what it will take to live comfortably. They don't know what all the assets are and which ones they should ask for. They don't know if they should take one of the rental properties and become a landlord. They don't know the effect of getting future benefits from the pension versus taking a cash payout today. There is a lot of educating that has to be done in some of these cases. Many attorneys bring in a financial expert to take part in this educating process.

IF THE CLIENT IS THE HUSBAND

Most often, the husband is very astute concerning the financial issues. He often offers to split the property evenly and give the wife some alimony so that she can get educated enough to get a good job. Sometimes, when husband and wife no longer want to be married to each other, the husband's opinion of the wife's job or potential job skills may escalate to a high degree.

The husband is concerned about losing his children. Divorcing his wife often results in divorcing his children too. The ex-wife may find it impossible to speak kindly of the ex-husband and this can affect the way the children react toward him. The ex-spouses may even move apart geographically which makes it more difficult to have a continuing sharing relationship with the children. Some attorneys urge their men clients to ask for custody of the children, whether they want them or not, to use as a bargaining tool in settling other matters such as division of property and maintenance.

Some husbands are terrified of losing their net worth. The thought of giving away half of what they have built up over the years is not acceptable to them. Other husbands, out of guilt, offer most of the assets to the ex-wife.

If the husband has been the higher-earning spouse, he typically will not ask for help from a financial consultant. He feels that he understands the financial picture more than his wife does and he doesn't understand why she hires outside experts when he has shown her a very fair way of dividing their assets. If, however, the wife is asking for more than he feels he can afford to pay, he will want reports to show that he is unable to meet her demands.

WHAT ELSE WILL THE FINANCIAL ADVISOR DO?

Many divorces involve a pension that needs to be evaluated. Financial experts are trained in figuring the present value of a pension.

Most divorcing couples own a house. A financial expert can calculate the answers to questions about the basis, the capital gains, whether it is feasible to keep the house, and who needs to buy what after the divorce is final.

When investments are involved, the financial expert can evaluate them as to their basis, the tax issues if they are sold, how risky they are to keep, what kind of return they are producing, and so on.

A financial expert will look at inflation's long-term effect on how much is needed at retirement, how much needs to be saved, how much can be spent compared to how much is earned, and so on. This can lead to good planning for the future and may be one of the most important parts of advising during the divorce process.

If a settlement cannot be reached on all of the issues, the case will probably end up in court with a judge making the final decisions. A financial expert can appear as an expert witness who shows, with reports and graphs, the result that any given settlement will have on each spouse. This information is helpful to the judge in coming to the final conclusions.

The financial expert is thus a very important part of the divorce process and should be brought in on most cases to be part of the team. There have been real liability issues in the past where the financial issues were not looked at carefully enough up front.

FINANCIAL PLANNING *DURING* THE DIVORCE

Assume John and Mary Smith are your clients. You have done a financial plan for them and all their investing. One day, John calls you and says, "Mary and I are getting divorced. I need to come in to talk to you to find out what the effect will be on me to divide those assets." What do you say to John?

Since Mary is still legally your client, you must inform John that the only way you can give information is to give it to both of them. You may not advise one over the other. And if they do not settle their case and they go to court, you will not be able to work with either one of them.

Suppose you have done a financial plan for John and Mary Smith but you have only ever dealt with John. You have never even seen Mary. When John calls you with the same dialogue, what do you say this time? Mary is still legally your client and your answer must be the same as before.

Suppose John Smith has set up his IRA with you and that is the only thing you have done for him. He is married to Mary but Mary's name does not appear as owner of any investments. What is your answer now? This time is different. Mary is not legally your client and you can meet with John and give him financial advice.

INVESTING DURING THE DIVORCE

Marge was the client. The CDP had done the Divorce Plan(spreadsheets for her and had done all the revisions with the attorney. They were all ready for court when the date was postponed for another six months.

Marge said, "I have $80,000 just sitting in a savings account earning 3½% interest. I know you can do better than that for me. Will you invest it for me?" The CDP had to tell Marge she couldn't do that at this time—for two reasons.

The first reason was that it could be construed as a conflict of interest. The CDP would be going into court to testify as an expert witness for Marge and if she was also investing her money at the same time, it might be a problem with the judge. It seemed to be more prudent to wait until the divorce was final.

The second reason was if it was shown that Marge was only getting 3½% on her money, it would indicate that she definitely needed more help. Actually, a 5 % return was shown on the spreadsheets.

While serving as an expert witness for Marge in court, the husband's attorney attacked the numbers saying that she could get at least 15% on her money because the stock market was doing so well and inferred that the CDP was pretty stupid. The answer was given that as a 64 year old woman who couldn't work, Marge needed to be conservative in her investments. If any reversals took place in the market, she would not be able to replace any losses. The judge agreed with the CDP and actually chastised the other attorney!

NOTE

1. The Institute for Certified Divorce Planners in Boulder, Colorado offers training for professionals and certifies them as a Certified Divorce Planner. The agenda includes an overview of the divorce market, tax laws of divorce, division of property, alimony, child support, pensions, being an expert witness in court, marketing these services and much more. Also included is hands-on training with the Divorce Plan(software. Phone: 800-875-1760.

CHAPTER 3

From the Attorney's Point of View

Not all attorneys are going to hire financial planners to help them present and analyze the financial data in a divorce case. They believe that they understand the financial issues without additional assistance.

Instead, the attorneys who hire financial experts want to help their clients get the most favorable results possible through settlement or as a result of a contested trial.

Don't worry that you'll never be hired by the attorney who is resistant to working with a financial planner. That is fine. In fact, you do not want to work with that kind of person. You want to work with the attorney whose objective is to help the client settle the case and if a trial is necessary, present the best evidence possible. Fortunately, there are plenty of such attorneys out there.

In this section, you will hear the opinions of two divorce lawyers—Barbara Stark and Ann Mygatt—straight from the horse's mouth, so to speak.

BARBARA STARK

The following is from Barbara Stark, J.D., a fellow of the American Academy of Matrimonial Lawyers. She is a nationally recognized speaker and frequently lectures to professional and lay audiences.

* * * *

The average rate of collection for a divorce lawyer is about 70 percent. This means that they only earn money on 70 percent of the hours they work. Understandably, there is a great deal of price pressure on their hourly fee because of all of their uncollectable bills.

Attorneys are paid generally on an hourly rate basis. As attorney fees go up, the client is more and more unwilling to pay these fees. This resistance is due not only to economic reasons, but also to clients' unwillingness to engage in the battle that these high fees may represent. Most clients do not want to go to court in the first place and they certainly don't want to use all their kid's college money on the costly aspects of the adversarial system.

It boils down to this: Two people who were unable to handle their joint finances when they were married are now divorcing and there often simply is not enough money for their current needs, much less financing some really expensive matrimonial attorney's fees.

Also, ferocious competition puts pressure on divorce lawyers' fees. Every lawyer has the pressures of increasing overhead, shrinking market share, and paying liability insurance. To meet these financial burdens, even lawyers who specialize in other forms of law will start to accept divorce cases. Economically, they cannot afford to refer those cases out anymore.

The team of the lawyer and the financial planner is really a blending of expertise. An experienced lawyer is someone who can teach you. As a financial planner, you need to come into this business knowing the divorce laws, knowing the case trends, and knowing what is going on in the courts. But as that knowledge grows, a good lawyer is going to teach you as you go through cases because you and the lawyer are going to be sharing ideas. Actually, you will develop with a good divorce lawyer a sense of mutual respect and a rhythm to the relationship, where you work together really well. That is the ideal, in terms of working with lawyers.

But there are a lot of inexperienced lawyers out there. The reason? There are simply too many lawyers. Many lawyers who hang out his or her shingle take divorce cases but do not necessarily have a high level of expertise in the economic issues. It probably will not surprise you that when attorneys come right out of law school, they have no idea how to handle a divorce case. They do not learn how to do this in law school.

Just because you are working with a lawyer, do not assume the lawyer has solid experience in the field. If you are an inexperienced financial planner working with an inexperienced lawyer, you both are going to be working your way through the case together and it may be a little bit awkward because the lawyer may rely excessively on you. The lawyer could perceive you as the expert while you perceive the lawyer as the expert. You have to keep the communication very open so that you have a feeling of where you are going as a team. But you must always remember that the lawyer is the expert in the law and is the "captain" of the team. The lawyer is the one who can pull all the information together and give legal advice.

Here's the final point to remember. If you want to build a good reputation in your community—both in court and out of court—the most important thing you have is your credibility and your integrity. You never want to lose that. There are lawyers (and financial planners, for that matter) in your community who do not have credibility and do not have integrity. Be cautious and check out the lawyers for whom you work. There will always be another case but you only have one reputation. You want to protect that reputation as carefully as you can and make sure that working with that lawyer passes the "smell test" with you. If it does not smell right, if it does not feel right, get out of the situation because it is not worth it to you in the long run.

ANN MYGATT

Ann Mygatt, J.D., (former prosecutor for the district attorneys' office in Boulder, Colorado), has been practicing in the area of family law since 1983. She had the following to say about working with lawyers.

* * * *

You, the financial planner, are extremely important in this business because we lawyers want to settle our cases. We really do not want to go to trial but sometimes it's unavoidable. If we have to go to trial, we need you as an expert witness.

As a financial planner hoping to work with lawyers, there are three things you need to know: how to work with lawyers, the legal pitfalls, and finally how to market yourself to divorce attorneys.

How to Work With Lawyers

How do Certified Divorce Planners fit into the picture of a divorce trial? More than anything else, you have to be flexible. You have to play many different roles when you work with a divorce attorney. Not only are you on the team, you are a critical member of that team. At any time during the divorce process, you may play any one or all of the following roles depending when you get the case initially.

1. Strategist Before the case is even filed, the CDP can be used as a strategist. We need to know what the financial implications of different divorce settlements are going to be.

For instance, there was a case where a woman was getting divorced after a 25-year marriage. The two daughters were just about out of college. The woman had expectations that when she became divorced from her husband—who was earning about $95,000 a year—she would essentially be taken care of for the rest of her life.

She needed to know from a financial planner what was going to happen. Even though her husband had earned a significant salary, she did not have a realistic view of what she could expect at the divorce. They did not have very much property, and they had spent almost everything they had earned during the marriage. In addition, she hadn't worked much outside the home. It was very important for her to spend time with a CDP to go over the charts that explained what she might realistically receive.

2. Mediator One often-overlooked use for a CDP is in the role of mediator. The financial planner can meet with my client a couple of times and then with both the husband and the wife together. Then we all go through the charts and the explanations of what there is in the way of assets and income, and what the future will look like. Sometimes out of that process, either with attorneys or without attorneys, the couple can come up with a mediated settlement that they both accept. If so, they won't need to have a trial in court.

3. Negotiator The role of negotiator brings to mind an amusing case. Two people had been married for about 15 or 20 years and they had spent some time in Southeast Asia. They each had an import-export business and, not surprisingly, the two greatest assets of their marriage were their businesses. They made a fair amount of money from those businesses but they were not willing to agree as to what the value was. Each said, "Your business is worth more than my business, and I want to be compensated for that." To get them to finally agree to a value, we had each person pick his or her own expert. Then, we put the experts together and said, "You come up with a number that would be fair for each of these businesses." Lo and behold, they did and the clients agreed to that valuation.

4. Client Expectations Manager I think this is probably one of the most important roles that a financial planner can take in this process. Clients sometimes need a reality check. I will send them to a financial planner and say, "Sit down and talk." These people need to know the truth. Many people come into my office with either grandiose expectations of what they can do or grandiose expectations of entitlement, and they need to be given a dose of reality. Sometimes it is easier for me to use a financial planner to help set realistic expectations than it is for me to do it myself.

5. Evidence Presenter Being an evidence presenter in a case is critical. The lawyer may assemble a number of different experts for different issues in a case, and the CDP may be there for one part of that case. But it is a very critical part and in this role you are, more than anything else, a translator. You are there to translate for people who don't fully understand the impact of financial matters, including the lawyers.

In fact, in the middle of one trial, I was cross-examining their witness. All of a sudden, I thought, "Everybody is talking gibberish. I do not understand what anybody said in the last 10 minutes." So I asked for a break, I took my expert out in the hallway and said, "Tell me what just happened. What did he just say?" The expert calmed me down and brought me back to reality. It helped a lot because the expert's skills as a translator were really good.

As attorneys, numbers and financial data are not our area of expertise, so we really depend on you, the financial planner, to translate what you know into information that makes sense. Translation was what I needed, and after about 10 minutes in the hallway, I understood. I brushed myself off, went back into the courtroom, and finished up the case.

Basically, the financial expert carried that case, and we got a great result. The reason we did is because we had someone in court who could present (1) the evidence of the wife's reasonable needs and (2) the fact that the husband had the ability to pay her maintenance and still meet his own reasonable needs. It also helped that we could show the judge exactly what the financial circumstances were now, and would be 5, 10, and 15 years from now.

6. Advisor/Trial Preparation Assistant More than anything else, a lawyer needs you to help us optimize our results to the client. You can make us look good to both the client and the judge.

The Dangers and Pitfalls of Working With Divorce Lawyers

1. Adversary System It is a fact that our courts are set up to be an adversarial system. When you are set for trial, you are at war. This means people who are involved as litigants and participants in this process are afraid. When you are dealing with people who are afraid, you are in very dangerous territory. People who are afraid are more likely to lash out, they may be irrational, and they may be looking for someone to blame if they do not get what they want.

These are things to keep in mind when you are working with divorce attorneys. Divorce lawyers are under a lot of pressure because they have the highest incidents of grievances and the highest incidents of malpractice claims than any other area of law.

You are going to be working in that arena. You cannot assume anything. You cannot assume that the judge knows anything unless it is put in evidence as a fact, and only then might the court find that there is enough evidence to find in favor of your client.

2. Pressures Within the Legal Profession One of the greatest concerns of the American Bar Association as well as the state bar associations is that professionalism and civility has declined so much in the last few years. Some of the reasons are that there are too many lawyers, not enough jobs, too much competition, and not many mentors.

As a result, a kind of a subculture of Rambo tactics and real viciousness has developed as a case escalates in an adversarial setting. It seems to come out more often with divorce and personal injury attorneys than any other kind. In fact, I have heard it said that the divorce attorneys are really the Rodney Dangerfields of the legal profession.

3. Technological Information Revolution In the last few years, attorneys have significantly changed how they run their law offices. They now have access to PCs so they can run software programs. However, most lawyers in your market are going to be like me. As an attorney, I am your client in more ways than one. I am a sole practitioner. I do not have the resources of a large law firm. I need to have somebody help me through the thicket of the technological tools that I do not have the time or the inclination to master. Though this technological information revolution confuses me, it probably is one of your greatest advantages in this business.

How to Market Yourself to a Divorce Attorney

Educating lawyers is going to be one of your greatest challenges in marketing yourself. To have the best chance for success, there a few things to keep in mind.

1. Professional Demeanor Do not show up in blue jeans or chew gum. Like it or not, first impressions count. Look professional and you will come across as more like the expert you are. This will help them have confidence in you or build confidence in you.

2. Knowledge and Competence Your knowledge and competence are what make people come back. It is your expertise that makes people want to hire you again. That special knowledge makes you necessary. You are the solution to our problem. But, a "know it all" attitude with attorneys will not be successful.

3. Common Sense Common sense involves knowing how much time, money, and effort to put into a case. You do not want to over-market yourself. Not every case needs a financial planner, and you do not want to market yourself to everyone. The effort that goes into your marketing should be consistent with that realization.

4. Flexibility You also need to be able to look at a situation when you are asked to do something and be able to jump into it where you can. You might have different levels of flexibility and you need to know your limitations. For example, some cases require calculating present value of a pension; others need a cash flow and budget analysis.

5. Visibility and Promotion You need to be visible and you need to promote yourself and your field in a way that does not threaten attorneys and their view of "market share." You need to show people how they need you and there are a lot of different ways of doing that: Network, write articles, put on small conventions or seminars for people. You can do this with an attorney, another financial planner or another expert.

I was sitting in court one Friday morning. One of the lawyers had brought in a financial planner to testify. At the end of the hearing, about five of the lawyers in the audience asked for her card because she had done a good job. She was up there promoting not only her client's case but herself and the field as well. You never know where you might meet new clients.

No matter what you are doing or where you are, always figure you might run into a client or potential clients.

6. Know Yourself The last thing to keep in mind is knowing yourself. You may not be the right financial planner for a particular client. The more you work in this field, the more you are going to know your limitations. You are going to know your strengths and your weaknesses, and how you can help people. Part of your strength as an expert is knowing when to say, "No, I cannot work on this case," and having the courage to decline a case. When you've had more experience as an expert witness, you'll know how you can help and how you can best work with that divorce lawyer in that particular case.

When you've had more experience as an expert witness, you'll know how you can help and how you can best work with that divorce lawyer in that particular case.

CHAPTER 4

Property

When looking at the property issues in divorce, the couple always asks three questions:

1. what constitutes property?
2. what is it worth?
3. how will it be divided?

In addition to those items traditionally seen as property, today's couples should take into consideration career assets.

Although each couple is different, there are some averages when it comes to property. "Most divorcing couples have household furnishings (89%), cars (71%), and some savings in the form of money in bank accounts, stocks, or bonds (61%). Almost half (46%) of the couples own or are buying a family home, which is likely to be a couple's most valuable asset. Only a small proportion of divorcing couples have a pension (24%), a business (11%), or other real estate (11%)."[1]

It has been said that most divorcing couples have a net worth of less than $20,000. If this is so, it may be that couples are investing in their careers and earning capabilities instead of their savings accounts. They may see their careers as being more valuable than tangible assets. Because future income is typically of greater value than property, the main financial issues at divorce, particularly for women and children, are those of spousal and child support.

WHAT CONSTITUTES PROPERTY?

Property includes such assets as the family home, rental property, cars, and art or antique collections. It can also include bank accounts, mutual funds, stocks and bonds, life insurance cash value, IRAs, and retirement plans. As you can see, there is virtually no limit to what can be considered property.

In some states, regardless of how property was brought to the marriage or who has title, all property of both spouses is subject to division and disposition at divorce. These states do not differentiate between marital and nonmarital (or separate) property. However, the "source" of the property (gift, inheritance, owned prior to marriage, etc.) while ignored when classifying the property, may be very important in the way in which the property is divided.

As you've seen, these different types of state are not all that different. They all follow the general idea of dividing property to achieve fairness. The difference is the starting point, and the rules each type of state uses to reach this fair result. For example, some start from the standpoint that all property is subject to division by the court, and then, depending on circumstances, give property that was owned prior to the marriage or was acquired by gift or inheritance to the parties that owned it or received it. Other states start with the notion that such property isn't subject to distribution by the court at all, and thus narrow down the issues to be decided.

However, although the laws vary from state to state, property is in most states usually divided into just two categories: separate and marital (sometimes called "community") property.

In general, separate property includes what a person

(a) brings into the marriage,
(b) inherits during the marriage, and
(c) receives as a gift during the marriage.

On the other hand, marital property is everything acquired during the marriage no matter whose name it's in. In some (but not all) states, marital property also includes the increase in value of separate property. Co-mingled separate property may also be treated as separate property.

WHAT IS IT WORTH?

The best way to explain property values and types is by examples of situations similar to those you'll encounter in your practice.

Let's look at an example. Beth and her husband are getting a divorce and live in a state with marital and separate property. Assume that when Beth got married, she had $1,000 in a savings account. During the marriage, her $1,000 earned $100 in interest and now the account is worth $1,100.

Her property is $1,000, because she kept it in her name only, and in some states, the $100 in interest goes into the pot of marital assets to be divided because that is the increase in value of her separate property. If Beth had put her husband's name on the account, she would have turned the entire account into a marital asset. She would have made a presumptive gift to the marriage.

In second or third marriages, both people may bring a house into the marriage. Suppose that Beth had a house when she got married, which she kept in her name only. At that time, the house was worth $100,000 and had a mortgage on it of $70,000, so the equity was $30,000. Now Beth is getting divorced. Today the house is worth $150,000. The mortgage is down to about $50,000. Equity has increased to $100,000.

At Marriage	At Divorce
$100,000 Value	$150,000 Value
-70,000 Mortgage	-50,000 Mortgage
$ 30,000 Equity	$100,000 Equity

The increase in value is the increase in the equity, or $70,000.

Let's reverse the situation. Assume Beth put her husband's name on the deed to the house when they got married. After all, they were going to be together for the rest of their lives. As soon as she put her husband's name on the deed, she gave what is called a "presumptive gift" to the marriage. This turned the house into a marital asset.

Now let's assume that Beth's aunt died and left her $10,000. That is an inheritance. If she put it into an account with her name only on it, then at the divorce, it is her separate property except for the increase in value. It is the same with a gift. When she received the gift or inheritance, if she put it into a joint account, she turned that money into marital property.

Beth saves $100 of her paycheck every month. She puts this $100 a month into an account with her name only, and now it is worth $2,600. At her divorce, is this money separate or marital property? It is marital property because it is acquired during the marriage, no matter whose name it's in.

When Beth got married, her husband gave her an eight-carat diamond ring. Let's assume that they are in court and she is testifying that the ring was a gift from her husband so it is her separate property. He says, "Are you kidding? I would not *give* you an eight-carat diamond. That was an investment, so therefore it is marital property." The judge decides.

What if Beth's husband had given her an $80,000 painting for her birthday? She claimed it was a gift and he claimed it was an investment and therefore should be treated as marital property. The judge could consider it an investment. Because it is not the type of thing that most people would freely give as a gift, it could be seen as an investment for the family so it could be considered marital property. But remember that you can never predict what the judge will decide.

What happens when both parties want the same item. Let's say Beth and her husband had divided all their property except for one item. They couldn't agree who was going to get the set of antique crystal that they purchased in England. They both wanted it so badly that they ended up spending $60,000 in court to decide that one issue. This may seem absurd, but it happens every day. One of the roles of a financial planner is to insert reason and logic. At $60,000, they could have each bought a set and a trip to England!

Most often, the home furnishings are not included on the list of assets because the couple simply divide the items. If they are to be valued, the typical value is what you could get if the items were sold at a garage sale.

HOW WILL PROPERTY BE DIVIDED?

What kind of state do you live in; that is, what rules of property and labeling does your state follow? There are two different types of states—community property states and equitable distribution states—and the differences are subtle. Once you know how your state handles property division, you can help your client decide which property is the husband's, the wife's, and the couple's.

Community property states first identify the property that is not subject to division of the court, which is the husband's and wife's separate property. The husband's or wife's "separate property" generally is owned before the marriage, or obtained by gift or inheritance. Everything else is "community property" and is subject to a 50/50 division. When in doubt, the state presumes the property is owned by the "community." Any property acquired in a community property state retains its community property status no matter where the couple moves.

Equitable distribution states, on the other hand, usually agree that the couple's property—"marital property"—is divided between the husband and wife *equitably*, or fairly. This does not necessarily mean 50/50. There are two types of equitable distribution states. They are differentiated by the way they identify property.

Martha and Tom

Martha and Tom have been married for 35 years. She stayed home and took care of the four children. Tom earns $150,000 per year and has started a business in the basement of their home. He expects the new business will bring in revenues after he retires. They own their home, which is worth $135,000. It is paid off. His pension has been valued at $90,000. Their savings account is $28,000, and Tom values the basement business at $75,000. Their assets total $328,000. Assuming a 50/50 property split, each would receive $164,000.

These are their assets.

House	$135,000
Pension	90,000
Savings	28,000
Business	75,000
Total	$328,000

However, splitting the property and assets down the middle is often not the most equitable division. In this case, as in many divorces, Martha wants the house. It is not unusual for the wife to have an emotional attachment to the house, especially if that is where she raised the children. Put it in her column on the property settlement worksheet.

While women often have an emotional attachment to the house, men have emotional attachments to their pension. Tom is no exception. We put the pension in his column.

Tom also says, "I have a business deal coming up soon and I am going to need cash for that deal. I must have the savings account." Put the savings account in his column.

Then Tom says, "The business in the basement is mine. You don't know what it looks like and you don't even have an idea of what I do." Put the business in his column.

Here's what the property settlement worksheet looks like.

		HER	HIM
House	$135,000	$135,000	
Pension	90,000		$ 90,000
Savings	28,000		28,000
Business	75,000		75,000
Total	$328,000	$135,000	$193,000

Her assets total $135,000 and his assets total $193,000. If we were to look at a 50/50 property split, he would owe her $29,000. Although Tom has a large income of $150,000 a year, he does not want to give up any of the business or pension or savings.

We can even out this division with a Property Settlement Note. Tom can pay Martha $29,000 over time, like a note at the bank. He can make monthly payments with current market interest. Or, he can borrow funds directly from the bank, since he has assets, including a savings account comparable to what he would owe.

A Property Settlement Note is from the payer to the payee for an agreed-upon length of time with reasonable interest. It is still considered division of property, so the payer does not deduct it from taxable income. The payee does not pay taxes on the principal—only on the interest. It is important to collateralize this note.

If there is no other asset available, it is possible to collateralize this note with a qualified pension by using a Qualified Domestic Relations Order (QDRO). If the payor defaults on the payments of a property settlement note, then the payee can start collecting pursuant to the terms of the QDRO from the pension.

Martha does not like this settlement. She says, "I want the house and I want half of your pension. We have been married for 35 years and I helped you earn that pension." Place the house ($135,000) in her column and $45,000 of the pension in each column. Then she says, "I want half of the savings account. You are not going to leave me without any cash." Put $14,000 in her column and $14,000 in Tom's column. She agrees that the business is Tom's, so $75,000 is placed in his column. The property split now looks like this:

		HER	HIM
House	$135,000	$135,000	
Pension	90,000	45,000	$ 45,000
Savings	28,000	14,000	14,000
Business	75,000		75,000
Total	$328,000	$194,000	$134,000

Her assets are valued at $194,000, his at $134,000. Martha owes Tom $30,000 to make a 50/50 property settlement. It's not that simple. She does not have a job, has arthritis, and cannot walk very well. In reality, Martha is not in good health and is unlikely she would be able to get a job that pays above the minimum-wage.

Her largest asset is the house, an illiquid asset. It is paid for, but it does not create revenues to buy groceries. She could rent out rooms for additional income, but that rarely works and it creates a different lifestyle that she may not want. How is she going to pay $30,000 to Tom? The prospects are bleak. Given that Martha is in her mid-50s, has never worked outside the home, and her largest asset is illiquid, the parties may decide that this unequal division may be considered the most equitable.

Calculating alimony comes after the property is divided. The reason for this is that alimony can be based on the amount of property received, so it is important to look first at the property division.

Dividing Marital Property and Debts

Many people try to divide each asset as they discuss it ("Your half of the house is $4,000, my half of the house is $4,000"). Since clients rarely divide the house like this, this may not be the most useful way to go about it. It may be more practical, to begin with, to list each asset as a whole under the name of the person who will keep it. For example, in the wife's column, list the marital equity in the house if she is thinking of continuing to live there. List the entire value of the husband's retirement in his column, if that is the initial inclination. An advantage to this method is that it allows the client to see the balance, or lack of it, of the initial plan as the client and his or her attorney-develop it.

If the client wants to know dollar values, they may need a third party, such as an appraiser, to help you determine them.

This is the time for the client to have a real heart-to-heart discussion with the ex-spouse and/or his or her attorney about the range of their sense of fairness and how the law would see the property division issues. Ask:

- Is the only possibility for them a 50-50 division of things by value? By number?
- Are they more interested in cash than in things?
- Will they take less than 50% if their share is all cash?
- Are they more interested in future security than in present assets?

- If they are willing to wait for a buy-out of their share, such as house or retirement, are they looking for more than 50% to compensate them for waiting?
- Are they interested in a "lopsided" agreement (more to one than the other) to compensate for the larger earnings of one of them now?
- Do they want to be "made whole"—end up where they were at the beginning of the relationship?
- Do they need to be compensated "off the top" for some contribution they made to the acquisition of property?
- Is there a possibility that any assets/investments are hidden?
- What is the law?

If you can get them to agree on a plan that meets both person's ideas of fairness, you will find you have an agreement which practically writes itself.

As you allocate the debts, decide first whether they are marital, separate, or a mix. Then agree who will pay off the balance of each. Remember that the problem of unsecured debts may be more easily handled as a budget item than division of property.

Think beyond the short term to the long-term effect of the division of assets and debts you are considering. For example, suppose one spouse gets all assets which appreciate slowly or depreciate, and which take money to maintain (home, car, furniture). Then suppose the other spouse takes all assets which increase in value or produce income (stock, retirement accounts, rental home). In such a case, even a few years after the divorce, what in the short term appeared to be a fair or equal division will look quite different. The net worth of the second spouse will far exceed the net worth of the first—and the gap will just continue to widen. It becomes your responsibility as a financial professional to accurately assemble the financial facts and assumptions for your client to fully evaluate settlement options.

EQUAL VS. EQUITABLE

Property divisions can be likened to trading. You trade assets back and forth until the couple agrees on the division. Or, in an equitable property division state, it means splitting the property equitably. It does not necessarily mean "equal"—it means "fair."

Equitable = fair, not equal.

On the other hand, the word "equality" suggests fairness and equity for all parties involved and parties can see this issue differently. What required an equal division of property may force sale of family assets, especially the family home, so that the proceeds can be divided between the two spouses. The net result can be increased dislocation and disruption, especially in the lives of minor children. This may not be fair, in that the needs and interests of the children are not considered.

A second problem of "equitable is equal" is that a 50/50 division of property may not produce equal results—or equal standards of living after the divorce—if the two spouses are unequally situated at the time of divorce. This is most evident in the situation of the older homemaker. After a marital life devoted to homemaking, she is typically without substantial skills and experience in the workplace. Most likely, she will require a greater share of the property to cushion the income loss she suffers at divorce. Rarely is she in an equal economic position at divorce.

Generally, a 50/50 division is a starting point when property is divided in an equitable division state. A major consideration can be how much separate property the client has. Let's say a client is fortunate enough to have $2 million in separate property. The marital estate totals $200,000. The $2 million separate property, may mean that a 50% division of the marital property is inequitable.

Divorce Plan™ software looks at the long-term results of any given settlement. It graphically and numerically illustrates where each party is financially when certain assumptions are used. For instance, if the charts show that the wife runs out of assets within eight years while the husband is becoming very wealthy, it may indicate an adjustment is needed in the divorce settlement agreement. It's important when factoring in assumptions, that the "what-ifs" be realistic.

CAREER ASSETS

With many couples, one spouse has significant assets tied to his or her career. These career assets include:

- life insurance
- health insurance
- disability insurance
- vacation pay

- sick pay
- Social Security benefits
- unemployment benefits
- stock options
- pension plans
- retirement savings plans.
- promotions
- job experience
- seniority
- professional contacts
- education

In many cases, a complete financial analysis may require that career assets should be considered as financial factors in arriving at an equitable settlement. However, the role of career assets in the law of your state needs to be defined by an attorney. For example, take a family in which the husband is the sole wage earner. Many times, the wife put the husband through school or helped him become established. At the same time, she abandoned or postponed her own education in the process. She may have quit her job to move from job to job with him. Together they have made the decision to spend the time and energy to build his career training with the expectation that she will share in the fruits of her investment through her husband's enhanced earning power. Over time, he has built up career assets which are part of what he earns even though they may not be paid out directly to him.

Even in two-income families, one spouse's career (usually the husband's) takes priority. Both spouses expect to share the rewards of that decision. At least, in the beginning of their marriage.

Some states even place a value on degrees such as the medical degree, the dental degree, or the law degree.

A case in 1998 involved Lorna and Gary Wendt. It was a highly publicized battle over career assets and even made the cover of *Fortune* magazine. He was the CEO of GE Capital; she was a "corporate wife."

The Wendts, married after both graduated from the University of Wisconsin, began with a net worth of $2,500. She gave up her music teacher job after her husband graduated from Harvard Business School. Lorna's Ph.T., or "Putting Hubby Through" degree, was introduced as evidence at the divorce proceedings.

At the time of divorce, he declared the marital estate to be worth $21 million and offered her $8 million as her share. She argued that the estate was worth $100 million and she wanted half—-$50 million. Her position was that his future pension benefits and stock options had been earned during their marriage. She said that her contribution as the homemaker and wife of the CEO enabled him to rise through the ranks to the top of his organization.

The Wendt case broke through the long-held belief that "enough is enough"—-that a spouse deserved enough to maintain her lifestyle—-nothing more. In a landmark decision, the judge awarded her $20 million—-far less than the $50 million she asked for, but far more than the $8 million her husband initially offered. She also received $250,000 per year in alimony!

THE FAMILY BUSINESS

Whenever one of the marital assets in a divorce is a business, there are challenges in dividing this asset. A business can be anything from dentistry, medicine or law, to real estate, or a home-based business. It can be a sole proprietorship, a partnership, or a corporation.

Value the Business

Becky and James were getting a divorce after 35 years of marriage. James owned a heavy construction business. He agreed to split the assets 50/50 and said that the CPA at work valued the business at $300,000. Becky told her attorney, "I used to keep the books in the business for James, and we took in more than a million dollars each year. Do you think it would only be worth $300,000?"

Fortunately, Becky's attorney insisted that she have the business appraised. The appraisal cost Becky $4,300, which made her very nervous to spend so much money. But the appraisal valued the company at $850,000 so her investment of $4,300 netted her $275,000 more than she would have received with the $300,000 valuation!

In a divorce situation, it is almost mandatory to have the business appraised. Becky was right to question the value of the business when it was figured by the CPA at her husband's business. There are Certified Business Appraisers (CBAs) who value businesses. To earn this designation, appraisers must pass a rigorous written exam and submit appraisals for review by a committee of experienced peers.

Dividing the Business

There are three options when deciding how to divide the business. Either one spouse keeps the business, both spouses keep the business, or they sell the business outright.

1. One Spouse Keeps the Business.
This is the most common solution and works the best for most couples.

In Becky and James' case, it was pretty clear that the business was run by James and he would keep the business and buy out Becky's interest or give her other assets of equal value. If there are no assets large enough to give her, they could write up a property settlement note and he would pay her over time. If Becky owned shares of the company, the company could buy back her shares over time.

However, care needs to be taken when buying out shares of stock. If there has been an increase in the value of the stock, Becky could be liable for capital gains tax. If James bought her shares directly, it would be considered a transfer of property "incident to divorce," which is not a taxable issue. The basis would go with the stocks and would not be recognized until the stocks were sold by James later on.

2. Both Continue to Work in the Business.
On the other hand, it is much more difficult to divide a family owned business where the husband and wife have worked next to each other every day for years. They both have emotional ties with the business. In addition, if they try to divide the business, it may kill the business. Some couples are better business partners than marriage partners, and are able to continue to work together in a business after the divorce is final. However, this won't work for everyone!

3. Sell the Business.
Another option is to sell the business and divide the profits. This way, both parties are free to look elsewhere for another business or even to retire. The problem here may be in finding a buyer. It sometimes takes years to sell a business. In the meantime, until the business is sold, decisions need to be made as to whose business it is and who runs it.

Stella and Dan owned a national franchise fast-food business. They also owned the land and the building the business was in. They had worked hard on this business together to make it a success. When they divorced, it was a difficult decision but they finally agreed that Dan would take the business and Stella would take the land and building. This decision made Stella the landlord which allowed her to control the rent that the business paid her and also how repairs and maintenance on the building should be handled. They soon realized they had made a bad decision. It cost them more money with their attorneys to hammer out a new buy-out agreement which allowed Dan to keep the business and the property, and gave Stella enough cash to move out of the area and start over in a new location.

HIDDEN ASSET CHECKLIST

The divorce process is a time of mistrust for each spouse, and right or wrong, each may accuse the other of hiding assets.

Assets are traditionally hidden in one of four ways. The person either

- denies the existence of an asset,
- transfers it to a third party,
- or claims the asset was lost or dissipated.

In addition to these, there is a new way to hide assets: creation of false debt.

It is the attorney's responsibility to organize and coordinate discovery. However, he or she may ask for your assistance. Here are some logical areas where financial expertise can help the attorney in generating the facts.

Tax returns are the first place to start in discovery to find assets. It's a good idea to go back five years. Perusal of tax returns can help especially if they reveal things about which you were unaware. The first two pages of a tax return can serve as a "table of contents," since it lists all the schedules and additional attachments to the basic return.

Important forms to review include:

- (Schedule A (itemized deductions). This shows income which produces assets.
- (Schedule B (interest and dividend deductions).
- (Schedule C (business or professional income). This form offers a place to hide assets.
- (Schedule D reports gains and losses from stocks, bonds, and real estate.

- (Schedule E shows supplemental income/loss.
- (Form 1065 reports partnership returns.
- (Form 1120 reports corporate returns.
- (Form 2119 covers the sale of a residence.
- (Form 2441 claims child-care expenses.

You need to review both federal and state tax returns, and compare all 1099s to W2s. Amended returns may also make a difference.

The following information is excerpted from *The Divorce Handbook* by James T. Friedman which is a valuable resource for financial planners assisting their clients during a divorce. Mr. Friedman is a specialist in family law. Since 1970 he has been regularly engaged in drafting family-law-related legislation on behalf of the Illinois State Bar Association, the Chicago Bar Association and the American Academy of Matrimonial Lawyers.[4]

In the course of discovery (sharing documents and financial information with the opposing side), most spouses believe that their counterpart has somehow hidden or failed to disclose the existence of certain assets. The following checklist of items to research may assist in determining the whereabouts of hidden assets or whether, in fact, they exist at all.

1. *Financial statements*: Any loans from lending institutions require sworn financial statements to be filled out. In most cases, the borrower is trying to impress the lending institution with the extent of assets and may exaggerate these. Looking back five years or so at these statements may put you on the trail of assets which are now unaccounted for, or which show valuations substantially greater than what is now claimed.

2. *Personal income-tax returns*: A review of the personal returns filed during the past five years may indicate sources of interest or dividends. The returns may also reveal unknown sources of income or loss from trusts, partnerships, or real estate holdings.

3. *Corporate tax returns*: If one spouse is the principal owner of a closely held corporation, he or she may be manipulating salary by taking loans from the corporation. Or he or she may be charging personal expenses to corporate accounts, which will later be reimbursed or charged to the officer's loan account. Corporate returns should also be checked for excessive or unnecessary retained earnings (undistributed profits). These may disguise available profit distributions or an artificially low salary level. Reimbursement of prior capital contributions or repayments of loans to the corporation may also provide hidden cash flow to your spouse.

4. *Partnership returns*: the comparison of partnership returns (IRS Forms 1065 and K1) over the years when the returns are available will indicate any sudden changes in the partnership interest or distribution. Such changes often occur at the time of a divorce and then compensating adjustments are made after the divorce is completed.

5. *Canceled checks and check registers from personal, partnership, and closed corporation accounts*: While time-consuming, it is always revealing to go over all the canceled checks and bank statements from personal accounts for the past few years, and post the expenditures to different columns under utilities, entertainment, loan payments, and so on. You will learn the amount of total expenditures per year, which sometimes exceeds income, and you will have a better feeling for cost of living and where budget cuts should be made. In terms of hidden assets, you may come across canceled checks for expenditures for the purchase or maintenance of property which you never knew existed. It is important to check the off canceled checks against the appropriate bank statement to make sure that you have all of the canceled checks. It is possible that certain checks were removed before they were delivered to you.

6. *Savings account passbooks*: Acquire the passbooks for any savings accounts open during the past five years or more. Look for any deposits or withdrawals that are unusual in amount, or in pattern. A monthly withdrawal or deposit of money in the same odd amount may reflect mortgage payments or income receipts from sources that you are not aware of.

7. *Securities or commodities account statements*: If one spouse has been buying and selling stocks or bonds or dealing in commodities, the broker with whom he or she trades furnishes monthly or quarterly statements indicating all transactions. A review of these statements going back a few years could reveal the existence of securities of which there was no knowledge or could raise questions as to the disposition of stock sales proceeds. Cross-checking securities transactions and bank accounts by date and amount will usually verify the source or disposition of the monies involved. If the securities are sold and the proceeds are unaccounted for, you can be sure the money's out there somewhere.

8. *Expense account abuse*: Very often, a corporate employer will allow employees a great deal of leeway in their expense-account reporting. A spouse may take advantage of this by exaggerating or even falsifying business expenditures. The employer maintains records as to expense account disbursements to the employee over the year with monthly detail. A check of these records will indicate the extent to which the employee is able to "live

off" the expense account. A cross-check between expense account disbursements and savings account or checking account deposits may indicate a pattern of expense account abuse if the deposits exceed legitimate business expenditures.

9. *Deferred salary increase, uncollected bonus, or commissions*: It is always a good idea to check directly by subpoena or otherwise with the spouse's employer to determine whether a salary increase is overdue, when it will be forthcoming, and how much it is. Employers are sometimes sympathetic to their divorcing employees and willing to bend the rules slightly to defer salary increases, bonuses, or commissions in order to suppress apparent income. Ultimately, these increases, bonuses, or commissions must be paid to keep the corporate books straight, and the employer will rarely lie when put under oath or forced to make a written statement on the subject. Sympathy goes just so far.

10. *Safe-deposit-box activity*: The bank that maintains the safe-deposit box keeps records of who enters the box and when. These records will not indicate contents of a box or what, if anything, has been removed. If the first spouse was aware of the contents at the point when the records indicate the second spouse opened the box and something is now missing, he or she has a pretty good idea of who took it.

11. *Cash transaction and in-kind compensation:* One spouse may be a physician or a shopkeeper, or in some other work where cash is paid, or he or she may receive in-kind compensation, where something of value—other than cash—is given in exchange for services. Such cash payments or noncash items are rarely reported on the income-tax return, but if you know of such income in the past and can subpoena current information, it will help in proving available income in excess of that shown on the income-tax returns. If one spouse buys things of substantial value with cash, there is probably a source of cash income somewhere. Most people don't retain cash in a noninterest-bearing form unless they're hiding its source.

12. *Children's bank accounts*: Frequently, a spouse who wishes to hide money will open a custodial account in the name of a child. Deposits and withdrawals are made without any intent that the child has use of the account except in case of the spouse's death. The interest from these accounts is not shown on income-tax returns, nor are returns filed for the children.

13. *Personal knowledge of spouse's habits:* One of the most useful discovery tools is personal knowledge of the spouse's habits with money. People who are attempting to hide money very seldom do so without making some form of written note so they can have a personal account of what they

have done. When things are going well in a marriage, the spouse may tell the other spouse about such records, but you can be sure they will disappear in case of divorce. The more secretive a person is, the more detailed such notes are likely to be. If a spouse has neglected to declare income to the IRS, the knowledge of hidden income or assets may prove to be a powerful leverage factor in reaching a satisfactory settlement.

14. *Phony income-tax returns*: When the divorce has been filed, some spouses are inclined to alter the copies of their previously filed income-tax returns to hide or adjust pertinent financial information. If you have reason to believe that furnished copies have been altered, ask for copies of jointly filed returns directly from Internal Revenue Service.

15. *Phony loans or debts*: To keep cash from being divided, a spouse may sometimes attempt to bury the money with a phony loan to a cooperative friend or relative. The loan may be tied up with a long-term note or with a claimed likelihood of un-collectibility, so as to remove this money from consideration at settlement time. The other spouse, who was never aware of the debt, of course did not sign the note because it probably came into existence *after* the divorce proceedings commenced. Sudden payment of debts to out-of-state creditors who are not available for deposition is usually a sign that the debt is a phony.

16. *"Friends" or other phonies on the payroll*: If one spouse is in a position to control the payroll of a sole proprietorship, partnership, or closely held corporation, he or she may be paying salaries to a friend or relative who is not actually providing services commensurate with the compensation. The friend on the payroll may be stashing the money away or they may be both enjoying it currently. In either case, the profit of the enterprise will be reduced accordingly and your spouse may be drawing a lesser salary. The same ploy can be used for payment to phony independent contractors.

17. *Retirement-plan abuse*: If one spouse has established a pension or profit-sharing plan in connection with a closely held corporation, the plan should be carefully checked to determine whether monies that have been contributed to the account are being invested in accordance with the plan requirements. Very often, deductions will be taken for contributions to such plans, and then the money is used for personal living expenses or taken out as loans, which are never repaid.

18. *Defined-benefit pension plans:* Defined-benefit pension plans are distinguished from defined-contribution plans by the fact that the *benefits* payable at retirement age are specified within the plan itself rather than by some contribution formula. The amount of the contributions then must be

actuarially determined, based on the age of the intended beneficiary and the point at which benefits are to be paid. A great deal of income can be buried by substantial payments into such a plan during the years preceding or during divorce litigation. The required payments can be a substantial portion of the beneficiary's income, if that is what is required to achieve the defined goal at retirement. This, of course, leaves little money available for support or division as marital property. Once the divorce is completed, the defined-benefit plan can be discarded, even though a substantial tax loss may result.

19. *Gift and inheritance tax returns*: Much useful information is available from inheritance, estate, or gift-tax returns of relatives you believe have been generous to the spouse. If these returns show that there were substantial gifts or bequests that have not been accounted for in the settlement negotiations, you are alerted that other assets could also be hidden. A tracing will have to be made from the estate's distribution to see what has happened to the assets.

NOTES

1. *The Divorce Revolution* by Lenore Weitzman, Chapter 3: "The Nature of Marital Property," The Free Press (A Division of Macmillan, Inc.), 1985.

2. The Divorce Handbook by James T. Friedman, Chapter 7, Financial Hide-and-Seek with Your Spouse, pages 49-53. Random House, 1982,1984.

CHAPTER 5

Dividing the House

In many divorces, the biggest question is who gets the house. Should the wife get it, should the husband, or should they sell it and split the profit (if there is one)? Oftentimes, the answer isn't easy or clear.

Many times, the wife has an emotional tie to the house and she wants to keep it. This is where she raised the children and decorated and entertained. Her whole life revolved around this house. Unfortunately, she does not stop to think about the value of that asset. If it is almost paid off and has a lot of equity in it, she is getting an illiquid asset that does not buy groceries for them or create any income.

THREE BASIC OPTIONS

There are three basic options to approaching the issue of who gets the house: to sell the house, to have one spouse buy out the other spouse's interest in the overall property settlement, or to have both ex-spouses continue to own the property jointly.

Sell the House

Selling the house and dividing the profits that remain after sales costs and the mortgage is paid off is the easiest and most "clean" way of dividing equity.

Concerns that will need to be addressed include: the basis and possible capital gains (addressed later in this chapter), buying another house vs. renting, and being able to qualify for a new loan.

Buy Out the Other Spouse

Buying out the other spouse's interest works if one person wants to remain in the house or wants to own the house, but there are difficulties with this option that need to be considered.

First of all, a value of the property needs to be agreed to. This is the equity in the house. Next, decide on the dollar amount of the buyout. Will the dollar amount have subtracted from it selling costs and capital gains taxes (in case the owner needs to sell it sooner than expected)?

There may be other assets that can go to the spouse who surrenders the house. If there are inadequate assets, a method of payment needs to be selected. If there is a time period to pay the other spouse, the terms need to be comfortable for both parties. The house could be refinanced to withdraw cash to pay the other spouse, or a note payable can be drawn up with terms of payment agreeable to both parties. In the case of a note, there should be reasonable interest attached to it and it should be collateralized with a deed of trust on the property. A problem with this arrangement is that it keeps the ex-spouses in an uncomfortable debtor-creditor relationship.

There is another problem with buying out the other spouse's interest. Let's say the wife gets the house and both names are on the deed. The husband can quitclaim the deed to her so that only her name is on the deed. She can sell it whenever she wants to. Although his name comes off the deed, it remains on the mortgage. He is still liable if she decided to quit making the payments. The mortgage company may not care if they are divorced or not and will probably refuse to "release" the other spouse. The only way he can get his name off the mortgage may be for her to assume the loan, refinance it or pay it off. When the husband's name is kept on the mortgage, this may impact his credit. He could be viewed as overextended unless he has proof that she is making the mortgage payments. This continues what may be an adversarial relationship.

Own the House Jointly

The other option—continuing to own the property jointly—is one used by some couples when they want the children to stay in the house until they finish school, reach a certain age or the resident ex-spouse remarries or cohabits. The couple may agree to sell the house after the children have graduated from school and split the proceeds evenly. The one who stays in the house in the meantime can pay the mortgage payment while all other costs of maintaining the house plus taxes and repairs can be split evenly. Again, this creates a tie between the ex-spouses that may create stress.

To help put all these options into perspective, here are some examples. Mark and Susan both had very good jobs when they decided to divorce in 1986. Susan wanted to stay in the house with the three children and buy out Mark's half of the house with a property settlement note. Interest rates were high. The note was drawn with her agreeing to pay him his half of the equity at 14 percent interest. Then property values began to decline. Susan's half of the equity was losing value, his half was earning 14 percent, even after the interest rates plummeted. Nobody presumed at the time they drew up this agreement that interest rates or property values were going to go down. It is always a risk when you do agreements that extend out into the future. These risks run both ways.

Lila and Keith had divided all their property with her owing him \$5,000. She kept the house and she was going to sell it in three years when their daughter was out of high school. The house had \$20,000 of equity in it at the time of divorce. They both agreed that when she sold the house in three years, she would give him his \$5,000. However, Lila's attorney knew Susan's lawyer and had heard about the case where Susan was paying 14 percent interest. Lila's attorney suggested, "Since \$5,000 represents 25 percent of the equity, why don't you agree on a percentage? That way, when you sell the house you give him 25 percent of the profits. If the house declines in value and you only get \$10,000 profit, you are not paying him half. Or if it goes up, you both win because you both get more."

If your client is talking about dividing assets beyond one year of the divorce, talk about percentages versus exact dollars. If the talk is about dividing assets prior to a year, specifying hard dollars usually works. But further in the future, it is much safer and much wiser to talk percentages.

BASIS

June and Stan are getting divorced and they have three assets: a cabin on a lake worth \$190,000, a 401(k) plan worth \$90,000 and a Certificate of Deposit worth \$140,000. Stan said, "Why don't you take the cabin and sell it?" He had borrowed \$140,000 against the cabin a year before, and put the money into a CD, which she was aware of. "If you sell it, you will get $50,000. You take the 401(k) worth $90,000, and I'll take the CD, so we each end up with $140,000."

June talked this over with her attorney and they thought that this sounded fair.

	Assets	June	Stan
Cabin	$190,000		
	-140,000		
	50,000	50,000	
401(k)	90,000	90,000	
CD	140,000		140,000
Total	$280,000	$140,000	$140,000

What Stan did not talk about—and what the attorney should have asked about was the basis in the cabin. Stan had paid $20,000 for this cabin 15 years earlier. There was a $170,000 capital gain, which created a tax of $42,500 (capital gains tax at 20% plus state tax at 5%). June received $50,000 and had to pay out $42,500, so she had only $7,500 left.

Capital gain	$170,000
Federal tax (20%)	34,000
State tax (5%)	8,500
Total capital gains tax	42,500

The after-tax value of the 401(k) plan is approximately $60,300, so June ends up with $67,800. The $140,000 that Stan borrowed from the cabin and put in the CD was his, tax-free and clear. He ends up with $140,000 and she ends up with $67,800, because the question was not asked about the basis. Do you think June's attorney had some liability here? Absolutely!

	Assets	June	Stan
Cabin	$ -6,100	7,500	
401(k)	60,300	60,300	
CD	140,000		140,000
Total		$67,800	$140,000

After being involved with over 600 divorce cases, I find that the one question most overlooked by attorneys is, What is the basis in the house (or stocks, other real estate, or other investments in the couple's portfolio)?

TAX ISSUES FOR SALE OF A RESIDENCE

The old tax law prior to Tax Relief Act 1997 (TRA '97) said,

- We could rollover our gain into a house of equal or greater value without realizing capital gains
- We could take a one time $125,000 exclusion from capital gain after age 55
- Our capital gains were taxed at 28%

Our new exclusions allowed under TRA '97 include,

- Single taxpayers can exclude $250,000 from capital gains
- Married filing jointly can exclude $500,000 from capital gains
- These exclusions are allowed for one sale every 2 years

(Change in place of employment, health or unforeseen circumstances allow an exception)

The new tax rates are,

- 20% maximum for taxpayers in upper brackets
- 10% for taxpayers in the 15% bracket

There are two special rules relating to divorce.

1. *Ownership period*

   If one spouse, pursuant to a divorce decree or separation agreement is required to grant the other spouse the right to temporary possession of the home, but retains title to the home, and the home is later sold, the non-occupying spouse will be treated as having owned the home for the period of time that the occupying spouse owned the home as principal residence.

2. *Use Period (New law)*

   In the event one spouse transfers a residence to the other pursuant to a divorce decree, the "transferring spouse" shall be able to include the "receiving spouse's" use period in computing their own use period.

Note: If one or the other remarries prior to sale of home jointly owned with the former spouse, the remarried spouse can use the new spouse's time in the home to meet residency requirements to use the "married filing jointly" exclusion amount.

Let's look at some examples.

1. John and Mary are getting divorced. John is awarded the jointly owned family home for four years. At the end of four years, John sells the home and 50% of the proceeds are sent to Mary.

   Scenario A: John sells the home for $400,000. Mary will receive $200,000 and be entitled to use her $250,000 exclusion even though she has not lived in the home for the previous four years.

   Scenario B: John sells the home for $750,000. Mary will receive $375,000. If the basis in the property was $100,000, Mary's portion of the basis is $50,000 leaving her with $325,000 gain. Even though she uses her $250,000 exclusion, she will be taxed on $75,000 of gain.

$750,000	Sales price	$750,000	Sales price
100,000	Basis	375,000	John's half
$650,000	Capital gain	375,000	Mary's half

$375,000	Mary's half of Sales Price
50,000	Mary's half of Basis
325,000	Mary's half of Capital Gain
-250,000	Mary's Exclusion
$75,000	Amount Mary will be taxed on

But, sometimes the new rule is *not* advantageous. Look at the case of Vickie and Stan.

2. Vickie and Stan are getting divorced and Vickie is taking the house worth $750,000. The basis in the house is $200,000. Vickie decides to move to another city and buy another house for $750,000. (She remembers that she needs to buy a house of equal or greater value to escape taxes, but she doesn't consult her financial planner!) Her gain on the sale is $550,000. She will be able to use her $250,000 exclusion but will still have to pay taxes on the gain of $300,000 even though she bought another house of equal value! Remember, the rollover is a thing of the past.

$750,000	Sales price
200,000	Basis
550,000	Capital gain
250,000	Exclusion
$300,000	Amount Vickie will be taxed on

One good thing that the new tax law gave us is that this is not a one-time exclusion. We can use it over again every two years. So each time we buy a house and sell it after two years, we can use the exclusion.

FROM THE CPA'S POINT OF VIEW

There are many challenges with the different variations of the theme of basis and capital gains. Gail Heinzman (a CPA in Boulder, Colorado with more than 20 years of tax experience in public accounting and in corporate settings) was asked to test our knowledge with some case studies, and had the following to say.

* * * *

In many divorces, the couple's most valuable asset is their house. Questions arise whether to keep it or sell it. If they plan to keep it, who is going to keep it? If it is going to be sold, when will it be sold? Is it going to be sold before or after the divorce? The tax implications of these questions are usually overlooked until well after the divorce. As a result, the sale of the home can create unforeseen income tax liabilities.

While the rules for home sales were radically liberalized in August 1997, most people who have been married long enough to have owned more than one home will determine their current home's basis using the old rules. Because varying rules apply depending on a couple's facts, keep in mind that relatively minor changes in facts can significantly affect the tax results of home sale transactions.

The following cases discuss the tax implication of scenarios often encountered in divorce and new-relationship situations. While these cases are not exhaustive, they illustrate some of the tax pitfalls relating to home sales often encountered while ending a marriage and other tax difficulties that may arise when entering into a new relationship. Care should be taken to thoroughly understand and document the specifics of each case to make sure you understand the rules that apply to your client.

CASE 1

Steve and Linda have been married for over twenty-five years. They purchased their first home (Home 1) years ago and sold it in 1994 when their youngest child went to college. They purchased their second house (Home 2) two days before the sale of Home 1. The information relating to these homes is summarized below.

	Home 1	Home 2
Purchase price	$45,000	$180,000
Improvements	10,000	12,000
Real estate commissions	6,000	9,000
Selling price	150,000	230,000

Question 1

What was their basis in the second house?

	Home 1	Home 2
Purchase price	$45,000	$180,000
Improvements	10,000	12,000
Gain carried over from prior residence	(89,000)	
Total basis	$55,000	$103,000
Selling price	150,000	230,000
Expenses of sale	6,000	9,000
Net selling price	$144,000	$221,000
Realized gain (loss) on sale	89,000	
Net deferred gain	$89,000	

The original house was purchased for $45,000. They completed improvements of $10,000; thus, their basis in Home 1 was $55,000. The mortgage balance is irrelevant for determining basis despite its impact on the cash that the couple will receive at sale. Home 1 was sold for $150,000, but there were commissions and closing costs of $6,000, so the net proceeds were $144,000.

Their gain was computed by subtracting their basis ($55,000) from their net proceeds ($144,000). The gain from the sale of Home 1 was $89,000. They purchased home 2 for $180,000. The old rules for home sales apply here. The purchase price of Home 2 exceeded the net proceeds from the sale of Home 1, so the entire $89,000 tax gain was deferred. Steve and Linda recognized no tax gain on the sale of Home 1 in 1994.

After the purchase of Home 2, Steve and Linda added $12,000 of improvements to the property. Therefore, they invested $192,000 in home 2 between the purchase price and improvements. However, this number is not their basis in the property under the old rules. Their basis must be adjusted downward for the deferred gain of $89,000 from Home 1. Their basis in their second house was not $192,000 but $103,000 ($192,000 minus $89,000 of deferred gain). It is against the $103,000 that the taxable gain will be computed for Home 2.

Often, when a couple has been married for an extended period of time and have owned several homes, they have no idea of what the basis is in their house. They assume, "We bought it for $180,000 and we added improvement for $12,000, so we've paid $192,000 for the house." They do not understand the income tax impact of their previous house or series of houses.

Question 2

What would the gain be on the sale of Home 2? Would there be any tax due?

The sales price was $230,000 and selling expenses of $9,000, so the net proceeds from the sale were $221,000. Steve and Linda's basis in the property was $103,000 and the tax gain on Home 2 was $118,000.

To avoid paying tax on the sale of a home, the seller(s) must meet a use test. Under the test the taxpayer must have lived in the house for at least two of the past five years before the sale, with some exceptions. Assuming that both Steve and Linda met this test, the house could be sold by Steve, Linda or the two of them together without an income tax liability. The gain of $127,000 is less than the $250,000 exclusion allowed to a single person on the sale of his/her home. Additionally, it is well below the $500,000 exclusion allowed a married couple on the sale of their joint residence. The decision when to sell the house can be made for reasons other than income taxes.

Question 3

What if Home 2 was sold for $450,000?

This sales price creates a tax gain of $338,000. Steve and Linda could sell the house together, as long as the use test was met, and exclude the entire gain.

If Steve and Linda sold Home 2 while they were still married, the $338,000 would be below the $500,000 gain allowed for a joint residence. No tax would be due. Alternatively, if Home 2 were sold after the divorce while it was jointly owned, neither would pay tax. The gain realized by each would be $169,000 ($338,000/2), which is below the $250,000 exclusion available to each.

If Linda took the house as part of her property settlement and subsequently decided to sell the house, she would have tax to pay. Her $338,000 gain would exceed her $250,000 exclusion. She would pay tax on $88,000 ($338,000 sales price - $250,000 individual exclusion). Tax would be due regardless of the cost of her next residence.

Knowing these facts is critical to deciding whether a client should keep or sell the house. The party keeping the house must understand the potential deferred tax liability he or she is assuming if keeping house is part of the divorce settlement.

Question 4

What if home 2 were sold for $102,000?

This amount is less than Steve and Linda's purchase price of the home and less than their basis. They would experience and economic loss on the sale. However, they would not receive a tax benefit for the loss because losses on sale of a personal residence are not deductible.

Question 5

Instead of selling Home 2 at a loss, assume the couple sold home 1 at a loss. How would the order of the loss affect their tax liability at divorce?

As noted above, there is not a tax deduction for selling a personal residence for a loss. The couple's basis in Home 2 would not be affected by the loss. Therefore, their basis in Home 2 would be its purchase price plus improvements, or $192,000. This circumstance would allow them to escape tax on the sale of Home two until the sales price (less selling costs) exceeded $442,000 (basis of $192,000 plus gain of $250,000.)

Question 6

Referring back to the facts of Question 1, Steve and Linda were divorced in 1994 but continued to own the house jointly while Linda was in school. Linda graduated in 1998 and sold Home 2. Linda bought a new condominium for $174,000 later that year. Steve rented an apartment and bought a sports car and a boat. Is anyone liable for tax on the gain from the sale of Home 2? If so, in what tax year is the gain recognized?

No gain is recognized.

In this case, Linda met the use test for a two-year window before the date of sale and her share of the gain was less than her $250,000 exclusion. While Steve did not meet the use test, he continues to qualify because his continued interest in the house was pursuant to a divorce decree. This liberalization of the use test will save divorcing couples significant tax dollars.

Question 7

Linda wants to keep the house, but Steve wants his share of the equity to start a new life. Steve's attorney proposes that Linda pay Steve $115,000 in cash and liquid investments to buy him out of the house. The house is paid off so there in no mortgage. What would Linda's basis in the house be when she sells the house if she accepts this proposal?

Linda's basis in the house would not be affected by the proposed payment to Steve. Her basis in the house would continue to be $103,000 even though she has given him $115,000 as part of the settlement. There is no adjustment to basis when property is split up as part of a divorce property settlement. This could raise a tax issue if Linda's sold the house for more than $353,000 because her gain would then exceed the $250,000 exclusion amount.

COMMON ISSUES IN DETERMINING BASIS

FORM 2119

Until 1998, the Internal Revenue Service required that its Form 2119, ("Sale of Your Home"), be completed and attached to an income tax return each time that an individual sold a home. This form was mandatory whether or not there was gain recognized on the sale. If available, this form should state the couple's basis in their current residence. However, if the couple prepared their own tax returns, this form was often omitted or completed incorrectly. A brief discussion with the client and/or tax preparer may be advisable.

WHAT IS AN IMPROVEMENT?

Homeowners incur many costs to maintain and improve their homes. Maintenance costs do not increase the tax basis of the home, but improvements do. If the client estimates that a substantial amount of money was spent on improvements, request a list of the improvements. Have an accountant review the list to help clarify whether the "improvements" meet the IRS definition.

For most clients, these issues are less important than they were before August 1997. However, they continue to be relevant to the wealthier clients whose homes may have appreciated more than $250,000. Care should be taken in dealing with any home with a selling price much above $250,000 to understand whether any gain is taxable.

SUMMARY OF BASIS ISSUES

When people estimate their equity in a home, they evaluate it from an economic rather that a tax perspective. The two are seldom the same under the old tax rules. Be sure to get copies of the couple's Forms 2119 from prior residences or take whatever other steps are necessary to understand the magnitude of their deferred gains if the residence is sold.

Question 8

Assume that Steve was age 57 at the time of the divorce. Would this change your planning?

No. Under old law, Steve would have been entitled to a one-time exclusion. The new rules provide that the exclusion discussed above is generally available for homes meeting the use tests. Thus, the couple can buy a house every two years and receive a full exclusion each time.

CASE 2

Jon and Margery are in their late thirties and have each been successful in their chosen careers. Each owns a home. They are planning to marry in the fall of 2000. The following table summarizes the information about their homes.

	Margery's Home	Jon's Home
Purchase price	$240,000	$280,000
Improvements	10,000	12,000
Real estate commissions	12,000	9,000
Fair market value	$400,000	$350,000

Margery purchased her house for $240,000. She finished the basement for $10,000. The house has a fair market value today of $400,000 and the mortgage has been paid off. Jon purchased his for $280,000. With improvements of $12,000, it has a fair market value of $350,000. Jon moves into Margery's house in January 2000 and purchases a half interest in her house immediately so that he can take advantage of the interest in the tax write-off.

Question 1

What are the tax implications to Margery?

Margery sold half of her principal residence for $200,000. Her economic gain will be $69,000. Her gross proceeds will be $194,000 (i.e., half of the fair market value of the house, less $6,000 for half of the real estate commission). Her basis will be $125,000 (i.e., $120,000 or one half of the purchase price plus $5,000 for half of the improvements). Her gain of $69,000 is computed by subtracting the $125,000 basis from the $194,000 in net proceeds. The presence of a mortgage would further complicate this example, depending on whether Jon became liable for a portion of the mortgage. While this issue may find further clarification in the future, current authority indicates that the gain would be recognized by Margery because it does not meet any exclusion provisions. Had they waited until after they were married, the exchange would not create a tax liability.

Question 2

What are the tax implications to Jon about his old residence?

If Jon sells his old residence so that he met the use test for it, he will have an economic gain of $44,000. This gain is well below the $250,000 exclusion and no tax would be due. However, if he does not sell his old residence until he fails the use test, then the gain would be taxable to him.

WHEN THE WIFE *SHOULD* GET THE HOUSE

There are cases when the wife should keep the house, even when doing so will create an unequal settlement. Let's look at Bill and Barbara.

Bill and Barbara are 45 and 49 respectively and have been married 18 years. They have one son, age 17. Bill earns $2,175 per month minus child support payments of $413. His living expenses are $1,400 per month, which leaves him with a surplus of $362 per month. Barbara earns $780 per month plus $413 child support. Her living expenses with the son are $1,630 per month, which creates a *negative* cash flow of $437 per month.

	Barbara	Bill
Take-home pay	$ 780	$2,175
Living expenses	-1,630	-1,400
Child support	+413	-413
Cash Flow	$ -437	$ 362

The following settlement was decided by the judge. Barbara will receive the house, which had equity of $44,100 and her IRA worth $5,000. Bill will get his IRA worth $8,900. There are no other assets. Since Barbara got the house with $44,000 worth of equity, she has to pay Bill half of that equity upon the first of the following events: if she sells the house, if she remarries, or upon the emancipation of the child, which varies from state to state. We do not know if she is going to sell the house or remarry, but we do know that the son is going to turn 19 within two years.

Barbara's house payment is $290 per month with 10 years left on the mortgage. According to this scenario, Barbara is heading for poverty from the outset. To be able to pay Bill his half of the equity in the house, she will *have* to sell the house. This will force her to rent at a much higher cost than her house payment of $290 per month. In her area, rental prices start at $400 to 450 per month.

This court order is forcing Barbara into severe poverty. In this case, it seems reasonable that Barbara should have been allowed to keep the house without paying Bill half the equity—an unequal but equitable settlement.

WHEN THE WIFE SHOULD *NOT* GET THE HOUSE

Bob and Cindy Case Study

There are cases when the wife should not keep the house. The following example of Bob and Cindy illustrates, in detail, the financial pitfalls that can arise.

Cindy is 32 years old and Bob is 33. They have been married 12 years. They have two children—ages 9 and 5—who will remain with Cindy. Bob is offering to pay $250 per month per child for Child Support.

Bob started his own business three years ago and he places a value of $200,000 on it. He argues that the business is so new that its value cannot be counted on and therefore should not be divided.

Cindy needs three more years of school to finish college. She will then be able to earn about $27,400 with net take-home of about $21,000 per year. She will not be able to earn income while finishing school. Bob is offering to help Cindy through school by paying maintenance of $2,000 per month for one year, then $1,500 per month for two additional years.

Cindy's expenses with the two children are $3,698 per month ($44,376 per year). This includes her expenses for school, which average $350 per month. Bob earns $75,000 per year and brings home $57,570 per year. His expenses are $2,050 per month ($24,600 per year).

The family home has a fair market value (FMV) of $220,000 with a mortgage of $130,000 at 7.5% interest for 15 years. Monthly payments are $1,500 per month (principal, interest, taxes, and insurance). Cindy wants to remain in the house with the children.

They have a rental house worth $90,000 with a mortgage of $50,000. Rental income is $600 per month and the mortgage payments are $600 per month.

Their IRAs total $17,000. They have credit card debt which totals $22,600.

Bob has made the following proposal called Scenario #1. Cindy will take the house, the rental, the IRAs, and the debt. Bob will keep only his business.

FIGURE 5-1

BOB'S PROPOSAL—Scenario #1
BOB AND CINDY'S ASSET LIST

Item		Value	Cindy	Bob
Home				
FMV	220,000			
Mortgage	130,000			
Equity	90,000	90,000	90,000	
Rental Property				
FMV	90,000			
Mortgage	50,000			
Selling costs	(6,300)			
Equity	33,700	33,700	33,700	
Business		200,000		200,000
IRAs		17,000		17,000
Debt		(22,600)	(22,600)	
Total		318,100	118,100	200,000

Bob feels that since his business is so new and cannot be counted on, he is making a very generous proposal if he takes his business and gives Cindy *all* the other property as well as the debt.

This couple had trouble keeping within their budget while they were married. Cindy tended to overspend and thus, increased their credit card debt. The challenge in this case will be counseling Cindy on the importance of staying within her budget.

Look at the asset table, Figure 5-1. The net equity in the home, $90,000, is in Cindy's column. The net equity in the rental, $33,700, is in Cindy's column. The business is in Bob's column. The IRAs ($17,000) and the debt ($22,600) are in Cindy's column. Let's look at the final result.

Look at Figure 5-2 which is Cindy's spreadsheet #1. The first column starts with the year 1999. The second column shows Cindy's age—she is 32 years old. The next four columns – "Take-Home Pay," "Other Income," "Child Support," and "Maintenance Support"—are income columns as indicated by the bracket above them labeled "Income."

The column labeled "Take-Home Pay" has nothing in it for the first three years while Cindy completes her degree at college. After finishing school, she expects to earn approximately $27,400 per year. The $21,000 shown in the fourth year is her *after-tax* take-home pay. The "4%" under "Take-Home Pay" indicates that it is increasing at 4% per year; the number also used for inflation in this case study. So, we are seeing that Cindy's

FIGURE 5-2

Cindy
Run No. 1

		INCOME			EXPENSE									
		Take-Home Pay	Child Support	Maint Support	Living Expenses	Real Estate Payments	Other Expense	Taxes on Maint	Annual Net Cash Flow	WORKING CAPITAL	Retirement Accounts	Fair Market Value Real Estate	Real Estate Mortgage	NET WORTH
Year	Age	4.0%	10	1	4.0%	15				5.5%	7.5%	4.0%	15 7.5%	
1998	32		10,800	24,000	44,376	1,227				33,700	17,000	220,000	130,000	
1998	32		$10,800	$24,000	$33,514	$14,727	$3,865	$6,720	($20,161)	$15,392	$18,275	$228,800	$125,023	$137,445
1999	33		$10,800	$18,000	$34,855	$14,727		$2,700	($23,482)		$7,634	$237,952	$119,672	$125,914
2000	34		$10,800	$18,000	$36,249	$14,727		$2,700	($24,876)	($19,928)		$247,470	$113,920	$113,622
2001	35	$21,000	$10,800		$33,499	$14,727	($4,200)		($16,426)	($36,354)		$257,369	$107,737	$113,278
2002	36	$21,840	$10,800		$34,839	$14,727			($16,926)	($53,280)		$267,664	$101,090	$113,294
2003	37	$22,714	$10,800		$36,232	$14,727			($17,446)	($70,726)		$278,370	$93,944	$113,700
2004	38	$23,622	$10,800		$37,681	$14,727			($17,987)	($88,712)		$289,505	$86,263	$114,530
2005	39	$24,567	$10,800		$39,189	$14,727			($18,549)	($107,261)		$301,085	$78,005	$115,819
2006	40	$25,550	$10,800		$40,756	$14,727			($19,134)	($126,395)		$313,129	$69,128	$117,605
2007	41	$26,572	$10,800		$42,387	$14,727			($19,742)	($146,137)		$325,654	$59,585	$119,931
2008	42	$27,635	$5,400		$38,682	$14,727	($5,400)		($20,375)	($166,512)		$338,680	$49,327	$122,841
2009	43	$28,740	$5,400		$40,229	$14,727			($20,817)	($187,329)		$352,227	$38,299	$126,599
2010	44	$29,890	$5,400		$41,838	$14,727			($21,276)	($208,605)		$366,316	$26,444	$131,267
2011	45	$31,085	$5,400		$43,512	$14,727			($21,754)	($230,359)		$380,969	$13,700	$136,910
2012	46	$32,329			$39,852	$14,727	($5,400)		($22,251)	($252,611)		$396,208	($0)	$143,597
2013	47	$33,622			$37,582		($3,865)		($3,960)	($256,570)		$412,056		$155,485
2014	48	$34,967			$39,085				($4,118)	($260,689)		$428,538		$167,849
2015	49	$36,365			$40,648				($4,283)	($264,972)		$445,680		$180,708
2016	50	$37,820			$42,274				($4,454)	($269,426)		$463,507		$194,081
2017	51	$39,333			$43,965				($4,633)	($274,059)		$482,047		$207,989
2018	52	$40,906			$45,724				($4,818)	($278,876)		$501,329		$222,453

income just keeps up with inflation. If inflation were 3%, we would show her income increasing at 3%.

The next column, Child Support," indicates she will receive $450 per month per child ($10,000 per year) in child support for 10 years until the 9 year-old turns age 19, and then child support will decrease to $5,400 per year until the 5 year-old turns age 19. This is based on Bob's offer.

The next column is labeled "Maintenance Support." Bob offered $2,000 per month ($24,000) for one year and then $1,500 per month ($18,000) for two additional years.

The next four columns are under the bracket labeled "Expense." The first column under expense is labeled "Living Expenses." The second one is labeled "Real Estate Payments." These two columns *together* equal Cindy's living expenses. The reason they are separated into two columns is that the Real Estate Payment column represents the principal and interest (P&I) payment *only*. It is not affected by inflation. The taxes and insurance part (T&I) of the house payment are reflected in the Living Expenses column. If the P&I were included in the Living Expenses column, that number—affected by inflation—would eventually become skewed. So, the $48,241 above the line is her total yearly living expense, which is a combination of the two numbers below the line, $33,514 plus $14,727.

The Other Expense column shows the changes in Cindy's living expenses. The first negative number—($4,200)—in the 4th year represents the fact that she has finished school and she no longer has school expenses of $350 per month ($4,200 per year). The second negative number—($5,400)—represents the year after the first child turns age 19 and leaves home. Assume that Cindy no longer has the expenses associated with that child; therefore lower her living expenses by that amount. The third negative number –($5,400)—reflects the fact that the second child has left home. The fourth negative number—($3,865)—represents the fact that she has paid off her debt.

The column labeled "Taxes on Maintenance" shows the taxes that she owes on her maintenance income.

The next column is labeled "Annual Net Cash Flow." This shows whether there is positive or negative cash flow after netting the income columns with the expense columns. We see that Cindy has a negative $20,161 in the first year; in other words, her expenses are $20,161 more than her income.

The number from the "Annual Net Cash Flow" column is automatically subtracted from (or added to if it is a positive number) the next column "Working Capital." It is shown earning an average of 5.5% after tax. Notice that Cindy's "Working Capital" column started out with $33,700, which was what remained after she sold the rental house. This asset was wiped out by the second year to help cover her negative cash flow.

The next column is labeled "Retirement Accounts." The assumption is that they will earn 7.5% before tax. When the "Working Capital" column is depleted, the "Retirement Account" column will automatically cover the negative cash flow *less taxes and penalties* if Cindy is under the age of 60. After the age of 60, taxes are taken out. Notice that this depletes her "Retirement Account" column in the second year.

The next column is labeled "Fair Market Value Real Estate" and shows the value of Cindy's home. The 4% represents the average increase in real estate in her part of her city over the past 10 years.

By age 33, Cindy's spendable assets have been depleted. She does have the house; but she can't use the house to buy groceries.

The "Real Estate Mortgage" column shows the $130,000 mortgage on Cindy's home, which has 15 years remaining at 7.5% interest.

The final column, "Net Worth," is a combination of "Working Capital" plus the "Retirement Accounts" plus "Fair Market Value Real Estate" minus "Real Estate Mortgage."

"Net Worth" is what creates the graph, Figure 5-4.

But first, let's look at Bob's spreadsheet—Figure 5-3—to see how this scenario affects him financially.

Bob's "Take-Home Pay" is $57,570 and is increasing at 4% per year, the same as Cindy's.

The next column, "Living Expenses" shows his total annual living expenses—$24,600.

The "Child Support" column shows the expense that he pays.

The "Maintenance Support" column shows what it costs him in after-tax dollars to pay maintenance.

The "Annual Net Cash Flow" column shows a positive $6,090 in the first year, which is added to the "Working Capital" column and is shown earning an average of 5.5% per year after tax.

The "Retirement Accounts" column shows that amount earning an average of 7.5% per year before tax.

The "Business" column shows the value of his business increasing at 4% per year.

Bob's "Net Worth" column is a combination of "Working Capital" plus "Business."

FIGURE 5-3

Bob

Run No. 1

		<—INCOME—>	<———EXPENSES			———>					
Year	Age	Take-Home Pay	Living Expenses	Other Expense	Child Support	Maint Support	Annual Net Cash Flow	WORKING CAPITAL	Retirement Accounts	Business	NET WORTH
		4.0%	4.0%					5.5%	7.5%	4.0%	
1998	33	57,570	24,600							200,000	
1998	33	$57,570	$24,600		$10,800	$16,080	$6,090	$6,090		$208,000	$214,090
1999	34	$59,873	$25,584		$10,800	$12,060	$11,429	$17,854		$216,320	$234,174
2000	35	$62,268	$26,607		$10,800	$12,060	$12,800	$31,636		$224,973	$256,609
2001	36	$64,758	$27,672		$10,800		$26,287	$59,663		$233,972	$293,635
2002	37	$67,349	$28,779		$10,800		$27,770	$90,714		$243,331	$334,045
2003	38	$70,043	$29,930		$10,800		$29,313	$125,017		$253,064	$378,081
2004	39	$72,844	$31,127		$10,800		$30,918	$162,810		$263,186	$425,997
2005	40	$75,758	$32,372		$10,800		$32,586	$204,351		$273,714	$478,065
2006	41	$78,789	$33,667		$10,800		$34,322	$249,912		$284,662	$534,575
2007	42	$81,940	$35,013		$10,800		$36,127	$299,784		$296,049	$595,833
2008	43	$85,218	$36,414		$5,400		$43,404	$359,676		$307,891	$667,567
2009	44	$88,626	$37,871		$5,400		$45,356	$424,814		$320,206	$745,020
2010	45	$92,171	$39,385		$5,400		$47,386	$495,564		$333,015	$828,579
2011	46	$95,858	$40,961		$5,400		$49,497	$572,318		$346,335	$918,653
2012	47	$99,693	$42,599				$57,093	$660,889		$360,189	$1,021,078
2013	48	$103,680	$44,303				$59,377	$756,615		$374,596	$1,131,211
2014	49	$107,828	$46,075				$61,752	$859,981		$389,580	$1,249,561
2015	50	$112,141	$47,918				$64,222	$971,502		$405,163	$1,376,665
2016	51	$116,626	$49,835				$66,791	$1,091,726		$421,370	$1,513,096
2017	52	$121,291	$51,828				$69,463	$1,221,234		$438,225	$1,659,458
2018	53	$126,143	$53,902				$72,241	$1,360,643		$455,754	$1,816,396

Figure 5-4 shows the graph of Bob and Cindy's Net Worth based on the previous assumptions. As you can see, the future doesn't appear too equitable.

What changes can be made in Scenario #1 to make this a more equitable settlement? The following changes represent Scenario #2, which appears in spreadsheet form in Figure 5-5.

1. Bob will assume the debt of $22,600. Note that his expenses are increased in Scenario #2 to include his making debt payments and Cindy's expenses are decreased.
2. A Property Settlement Note of $18,350 is paid to Cindy starting in the fourth year at which time the payments are $5,866 per year for five years (assuming 7% interest). This is shown in the "Other Income" column.

How does Scenario #2 affect Bob?

Look at Figure 5-6, which is Bob's revised spreadsheet. The changes are in the amount he is paying in Child Support and the Property Settlement Note shown in the column to the right of Maintenance Support. He still has positive cash flow.

The graph combining all the data of Scenario #2 is shown as Figure 5-7. Notice that Scenario #2 helps Cindy some but not enough. The problem is that she is too emotionally tied to an asset (the house) that she cannot afford. Her house payments of $1,500 per month, combined with no earned income for three years, create a disaster for her.

Let's see what happens if we come up with Scenario #3, where she sells the house in the first year after divorce, keeps the Property Settlement Note the same, and extends the $1,500 per month maintenance for an additional three years. Figure 5-8 details the changes.

Notice that her "Take-Home Pay" is still the same. She is still going to school for three years before bringing home $21,000 per year.

The "Other Income" column reflects the Property Settlement Note. The "Child Support" is according to the child support guidelines.

The "Maintenance Support" column shows maintenance of $2,000 per month ($24,000 per year) for one year and then $1,500 per month ($18,000 per year) for five years.

In Scenario #3, Cindy's "Living Expenses" and "Real Estate Payments" are the same for the first year. Then, assume the house has been sold and that Cindy rents an apartment for $780 per month. The taxes and insurance on the house ($224 per month) had been included in the "Living Expenses" column.

FIGURE 5-4

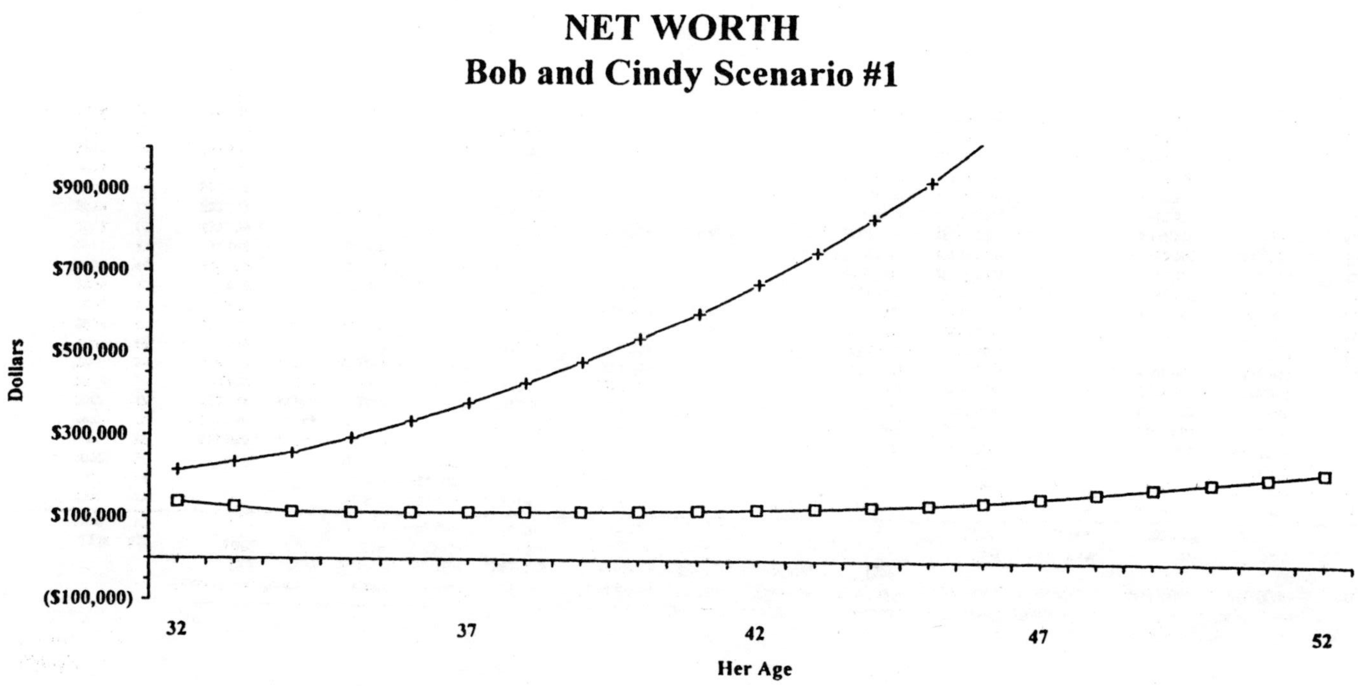
NET WORTH
Bob and Cindy Scenario #1
Dollars
$900,000
$700,000
$500,000
$300,000
$100,000
($100,000)
32
37
42
47
52
Her Age

FIGURE 5-5

Cindy

Run No. 2

		<——INCOME		——>		<——	EXPENSE		——>				Fair Market		
Year	Age	Take-Home Pay	Property Note	Child Support	Maint Support	Living Expenses	Real Estate Payments	Other Expense	Taxes on Maint	Annual Net Cash Flow	WORKING CAPITAL	Retirement Accounts	Value Real Estate	Real Estate Mortgage	NET WORTH
		4.0%		10	1	4.0%	15				5.5%	7.5%	4.0%	15 7.5%	
1998	32			10,800	24,000	44,376	1,227				33,700	17,000	220,000	130,000	
1998	32			$10,800	$24,000	$29,649	$14,727		$6,720	($16,296)	$19,257	$18,275	$228,800	$125,023	$141,310
1999	33			$10,800	$18,000	$30,835	$14,727		$2,700	($19,462)	$854	$19,646	$237,952	$119,672	$138,780
2000	34			$10,800	$18,000	$32,068	$14,727		$2,700	($20,696)	($7,060)		$247,470	$113,920	$126,490
2001	35	$21,000	$5,866	$10,800		$29,151	$14,727	($4,200)		($6,212)	($13,272)		$257,369	$107,737	$136,360
2002	36	$21,840	$5,866	$10,800		$30,317	$14,727			($6,538)	($19,811)		$267,664	$101,090	$146,763
2003	37	$22,714	$5,866	$10,800		$31,530	$14,727			($6,878)	($26,688)		$278,370	$93,944	$157,738
2004	38	$23,622	$5,866	$10,800		$32,791	$14,727			($7,230)	($33,919)		$289,505	$86,263	$169,324
2005	39	$24,567	$5,866	$10,800		$34,103	$14,727			($7,597)	($41,516)		$301,085	$78,005	$181,565
2006	40	$25,550		$10,800		$35,467	$14,727			($13,844)	($55,360)		$313,129	$69,128	$188,641
2007	41	$26,572		$10,800		$36,885	$14,727			($14,241)	($69,601)		$325,654	$59,585	$196,468
2008	42	$27,635		$5,400		$32,961	$14,727	($5,400)		($14,654)	($84,255)		$338,680	$49,327	$205,099
2009	43	$28,740		$5,400		$34,279	$14,727			($14,867)	($99,121)		$352,227	$38,299	$214,807
2010	44	$29,890		$5,400		$35,650	$14,727			($15,088)	($114,210)		$366,316	$26,444	$225,663
2011	45	$31,085		$5,400		$37,076	$14,727			($15,319)	($129,528)		$380,969	$13,700	$237,741
2012	46	$32,329				$33,160	$14,727	($5,400)		($15,558)	($145,087)		$396,208	($0)	$251,121
2013	47	$33,622				$34,486				($864)	($145,951)		$412,056		$266,105
2014	48	$34,967				$35,865				($899)	($146,850)		$428,538		$281,688
2015	49	$36,365				$37,300				($935)	($147,784)		$445,680		$297,895
2016	50	$37,820				$38,792				($972)	($148,757)		$463,507		$314,750
2017	51	$39,333				$40,344				($1,011)	($149,768)		$482,047		$332,279
2018	52	$40,906				$41,957				($1,051)	($150,819)		$501,329		$350,510

FIGURE 5-6

Bob

Run No. 2

		<—INCOME—>	<—	—EXPENSES—	—>							
		Take-Home Pay	Living Expenses	Other Expense	Child Support	Maint Support	Property Note	Annual Net Cash Flow	WORKING CAPITAL	Retirement Accounts	Business	NET WORTH
Year	Age	4.0%	4.0%						5.5%	7.5%	4.0%	
1998	33	57,570	24,600								200,000	
1998	33	$57,570	$28,465	$3,865	$10,800	$16,080		$2,225	$2,225		$208,000	$210,225
1999	34	$59,873	$29,604		$10,800	$12,060		$7,409	$9,757		$216,320	$226,077
2000	35	$62,268	$30,788		$10,800	$12,060		$8,620	$18,913		$224,973	$243,886
2001	36	$64,758	$32,019		$10,800		$5,866	$16,073	$36,027		$233,972	$269,998
2002	37	$67,349	$33,300		$10,800		$5,866	$17,383	$55,391		$243,331	$298,721
2003	38	$70,043	$34,632		$10,800		$5,866	$18,745	$77,182		$253,064	$330,246
2004	39	$72,844	$36,017		$10,800		$5,866	$20,161	$101,588		$263,186	$364,774
2005	40	$75,758	$37,458		$10,800		$5,866	$21,634	$128,810		$273,714	$402,523
2006	41	$78,789	$38,956		$10,800			$29,032	$164,926		$284,662	$449,589
2007	42	$81,940	$40,515		$10,800			$30,625	$204,623		$296,049	$500,672
2008	43	$85,218	$42,135		$5,400			$37,683	$253,559		$307,891	$561,450
2009	44	$88,626	$43,821		$5,400			$39,406	$306,911		$320,206	$627,118
2010	45	$92,171	$45,573		$5,400			$41,198	$364,989		$333,015	$698,004
2011	46	$95,858	$47,396		$5,400			$43,062	$428,126		$346,335	$774,461
2012	47	$99,693	$49,292					$50,400	$502,073		$360,189	$862,262
2013	48	$103,680	$47,399	($3,865)				$56,281	$585,968		$374,596	$960,565
2014	49	$107,828	$49,295					$58,533	$676,729		$389,580	$1,066,309
2015	50	$112,141	$51,267					$60,874	$774,824		$405,163	$1,179,987
2016	51	$116,626	$53,317					$63,309	$880,748		$421,370	$1,302,118
2017	52	$121,291	$55,450					$65,841	$995,030		$438,225	$1,433,255
2018	53	$126,143	$57,668					$68,475	$1,118,232		$455,754	$1,573,986

FIGURE 5-7

NET WORTH
Bob and Cindy Scenario #2

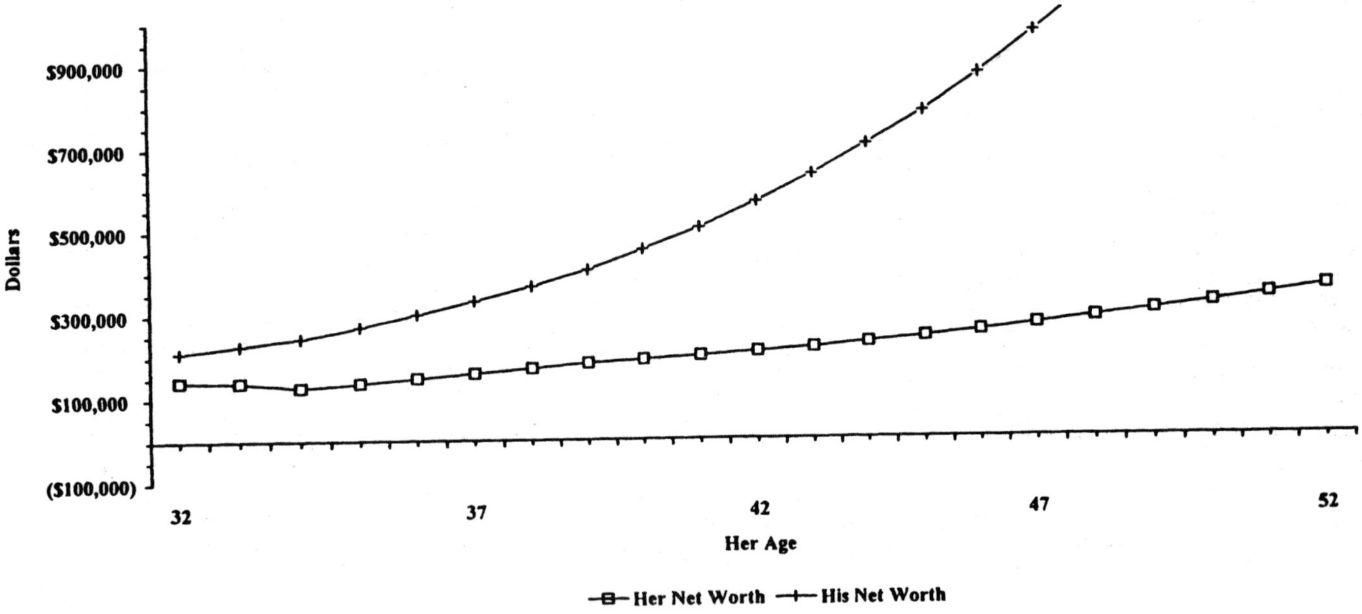

FIGURE 5-8

Cindy
Run No. 3

Year	Age	INCOME Take-Home Pay	Property Note	Child Support	Maint Support	EXPENSE Living Expenses	Real Estate Payments	Other Expense	Taxes on Maint	Annual Net Cash Flow	WORKING CAPITAL	Retirement Accounts	Fair Market Value Real Estate	Real Estate Mortgage	NET WORTH
		4.0%		10	1	4.0%	1				5.5%	7.5%	4.0%	15 7.5%	
1998	32			10,800	24,000	44,376	1,227				33,700	17,000	220,000	130,000	
1998	32			$10,800	$24,000	$29,649	$14,727		$6,720	($16,296)	$19,257	$18,275	$228,800	$125,023	$141,310
1999	33			$10,800	$18,000	$37,507		$6,672	$2,700	($11,407)	$95,597	$19,646			$115,243
2000	34			$10,800	$18,000	$39,007			$2,700	($12,907)	$87,948	$21,119			$109,067
2001	35	$21,000	$5,866	$10,800	$18,000	$36,368		($4,200)	$5,040	$14,258	$107,043	$22,703			$129,746
2002	36	$21,840	$5,866	$10,800	$18,000	$37,822			$5,040	$13,644	$126,574	$24,406			$150,980
2003	37	$22,714	$5,866	$10,800	$18,000	$39,335			$5,040	$13,004	$146,540	$26,236			$172,777
2004	38	$23,622	$5,866	$10,800		$40,909				($620)	$153,980	$28,204			$182,184
2005	39	$24,567	$5,866	$10,800		$42,545				($1,312)	$161,137	$30,319			$191,456
2006	40	$25,550		$10,800		$44,247				($7,897)	$162,102	$32,593			$194,695
2007	41	$26,572		$10,800		$46,017				($8,645)	$162,373	$35,038			$197,411
2008	42	$27,635		$5,400		$42,457		($5,400)		($9,423)	$161,881	$37,665			$199,546
2009	43	$28,740		$5,400		$44,155				($10,016)	$160,769	$40,490			$201,259
2010	44	$29,890		$5,400		$45,922				($10,632)	$158,979	$43,527			$202,506
2011	45	$31,085		$5,400		$47,759				($11,273)	$156,450	$46,792			$203,241
2012	46	$32,329				$44,269		($5,400)		($11,940)	$153,114	$50,301			$203,415
2013	47	$33,622				$46,040				($12,418)	$149,117	$54,073			$203,191
2014	48	$34,967				$47,881				($12,915)	$144,404	$58,129			$202,533
2015	49	$36,365				$49,796				($13,431)	$138,915	$62,489			$201,404
2016	50	$37,820				$51,788				($13,969)	$132,587	$67,175			$199,762
2017	51	$39,333				$53,860				($14,527)	$125,352	$72,213			$197,565
2018	52	$40,906				$56,014				($15,108)	$117,138	$77,629			$194,767

Her net increase in the "Living Expense" column is $556 per month ($6,672 per year). We show that number in the "Other Expense" column which shows the change in the "Living Expense" column.

After the first year, her "Annual Net Cash Flow" column has much lower negatives than before. In fact, she then has positive cash flow for the next three years.

When the house is sold and the selling costs and mortgage balance are deducted from the profits, the remaining balance is added to the "Working Capital" in the second year.

In Figure 5-9, we that Bob still has positive cash flow and his assets continue to increase in value. The graph combining all the data of Scenario #3 is shown on Figure 5-10.

In Scenario #4, assume that Cindy did not sell the rental house but moved into it instead, and maintenance is $2,500 per month for one year, $2,000 per month for two years, and $1,500 per month for three years. Figure 5-11 presents this data.

First of all, look at the "Fair Market Value Real Estate" column. Notice that in the second year, the value of her house is $90,000 and the "Real Estate Mortgage" is $50,000. This shows that she is now living in the rental house.

The "Real Estate Payments" column shows the reduction in the monthly payment.

Cindy no longer has the $33,700 profit from selling the rental to invest in her "Working Capital" column. But the proceeds from selling the house help her out and the "Working Capital" column shows that her proceeds will last for a much longer time if she is careful with her spending.

Figure 5-12 shows how Scenario #4 affects Bob. The higher maintenance takes essentially all his cash flow in the first year. In fact, with a negative $150 per month ($1,795 per year), the first year, it will be a very tight year for him.

When maintenance reduces in the second year, his "Annual Net Cash Flow" increases and continues to increase. The results are shown in Figure 5-13.

It doesn't make economic sense for Cindy to keep a house with a $1,500 per month house payment when she has no income and she is relying on maintenance to make that payment for her. She could rent a house in that area for $800-900 per month. Maintenance cannot be counted on. This is a case that will take a lot of counseling on cash flow and budgeting. Both parties must understand that whatever scenario is followed, it will have a major impact on their financial, emotional, parenting and relationship lives.

FIGURE 5-9

Bob

Run No. 3

		<—INCOME—>	<——EXPENSES——>					Annual	WORKING	Retirement		NET
		Take-Home Pay	Living Expenses	Other Expense	Child Support	Maint Support	Property Note	Net Cash Flow	CAPITAL	Accounts	Business	WORTH
Year	Age	4.0%	4.0%						5.5%	7.5%	4.0%	
1998	33	57,570	24,600								200,000	
1998	33	$57,570	$28,465	$3,865	$10,800	$16,080		$2,225	$2,225		$208,000	$210,225
1999	34	$59,873	$29,604		$10,800	$12,060		$7,409	$9,757		$216,320	$226,077
2000	35	$62,268	$30,788		$10,800	$12,060		$8,620	$18,913		$224,973	$243,886
2001	36	$64,758	$32,019		$10,800	$12,060	$5,866	$4,013	$23,967		$233,972	$257,938
2002	37	$67,349	$33,300		$10,800	$12,060	$5,866	$5,323	$30,607		$243,331	$273,938
2003	38	$70,043	$34,632		$10,800	$12,060	$5,866	$6,685	$38,976		$253,064	$292,039
2004	39	$72,844	$36,017		$10,800		$5,866	$20,161	$61,280		$263,186	$324,467
2005	40	$75,758	$37,458		$10,800		$5,866	$21,634	$86,285		$273,714	$359,999
2006	41	$78,789	$38,956		$10,800			$29,032	$120,063		$284,662	$404,725
2007	42	$81,940	$40,515		$10,800			$30,625	$157,292		$296,049	$453,341
2008	43	$85,218	$42,135		$5,400			$37,683	$203,625		$307,891	$511,516
2009	44	$88,626	$43,821		$5,400			$39,406	$254,230		$320,206	$574,437
2010	45	$92,171	$45,573		$5,400			$41,198	$309,411		$333,015	$642,426
2011	46	$95,858	$47,396		$5,400			$43,062	$369,491		$346,335	$715,826
2012	47	$99,693	$49,292					$50,400	$440,213		$360,189	$800,402
2013	48	$103,680	$47,399	($3,865)				$56,281	$520,706		$374,596	$895,303
2014	49	$107,828	$49,295					$58,533	$607,878		$389,580	$997,458
2015	50	$112,141	$51,267					$60,874	$702,185		$405,163	$1,107,349
2016	51	$116,626	$53,317					$63,309	$804,114		$421,370	$1,225,484
2017	52	$121,291	$55,450					$65,841	$914,182		$438,225	$1,352,407
2018	53	$126,143	$57,668					$68,475	$1,032,937		$455,754	$1,488,691

FIGURE 5-10

NET WORTH
Bob and Cindy Scenario #3

FIGURE 5-11

Cindy

Run No.

Year	Age	Take-Home Pay	Property Note	Child Support	Maint Support	Living Expenses	Real Estate Payments	Other Expense	Taxes on Maint	Annual Net Cash Flow	WORKING CAPITAL	Retirement Accounts	Fair Market Value Real Estate	Real Estate Mortgage	NET WORTH
		<—INCOME			—>	<—EXPENSE			—>						
		4.0%		10	1	4.0%	12				5.5%	7.5%	4.0%	15 7.5%	
1998	32			10,800	30,000	44,376	1,227					17,000	220,000	130,000	
1998	32			$10,800	$30,000	$29,649	$14,727		$8,400	($11,976)	($957)		$228,800	$125,023	$102,821
1999	33			$10,800	$24,000	$30,835	$7,200		$6,720	($9,955)	$74,410		$90,000	$50,000	$114,410
2000	34			$10,800	$24,000	$32,068	$7,200		$6,720	($11,188)	$67,314		$93,600	$46,550	$114,364
2001	35	$21,000	$5,866	$10,800	$18,000	$29,151	$7,200	($4,200)	$5,040	$14,275	$85,291		$97,344	$42,841	$139,794
2002	36	$21,840	$5,866	$10,800	$18,000	$30,317	$7,200		$5,040	$13,949	$103,931		$101,238	$38,854	$166,315
2003	37	$22,714	$5,866	$10,800	$18,000	$31,530	$7,200		$5,040	$13,610	$123,257		$105,287	$34,568	$193,976
2004	38	$23,622	$5,866	$10,800		$32,791	$7,200			$297	$130,333		$109,499	$29,961	$209,871
2005	39	$24,567	$5,866	$10,800		$34,103	$7,200			($70)	$137,432		$113,879	$25,008	$226,303
2006	40	$25,550		$10,800		$35,467	$7,200			($6,317)	$138,674		$118,434	$19,684	$237,424
2007	41	$26,572		$10,800		$36,885	$7,200			($6,714)	$139,587		$123,171	$13,960	$248,798
2008	42	$27,635		$5,400		$32,961	$7,200	($5,400)		($7,126)	$140,138		$128,098	$7,807	$260,429
2009	43	$28,740		$5,400		$34,279	$7,200			($7,339)	$140,506		$133,222	$1,193	$272,535
2010	44	$29,890		$5,400		$35,651				($361)	$147,873		$138,551		$286,424
2011	45	$31,085		$5,400		$37,077				($591)	$155,414		$144,093		$299,507
2012	46	$32,329				$33,160		($5,400)		($831)	$163,131		$149,857		$312,988
2013	47	$33,622				$34,486				($864)	$171,239		$155,851		$327,090
2014	48	$34,967				$35,865				($899)	$179,758		$162,085		$341,843
2015	49	$36,365				$37,300				($935)	$188,710		$168,568		$357,279
2016	50	$37,820				$38,792				($972)	$198,117		$175,311		$373,428
2017	51	$39,333				$40,344				($1,011)	$208,002		$182,323		$390,326
2018	52	$40,906				$41,957				($1,052)	$218,391		$189,616		$408,007

FIGURE 5-12

Bob

Run No. 4

Year	Age	<—INCOME—> Take-Home Pay	<——EXPENSES—— Living Expenses	Other Expense	Child Support	Maint Support	——> Property Note	Annual Net Cash Flow	WORKING CAPITAL	Retirement Accounts	Business	NET WORTH
		4.0%	4.0%						5.5%	7.5%	4.0%	
											200,000	
1998	33	57,570	24,600									
1998	33	$57,570	$28,465	$3,865	$10,800	$20,100		($1,795)	($1,795)		$208,000	$206,205
1999	34	$59,873	$29,604		$10,800	$16,080		$3,389	$1,594		$216,320	$217,914
2000	35	$62,268	$30,788		$10,800	$16,080		$4,600	$6,282		$224,973	$231,255
2001	36	$64,758	$32,019		$10,800	$12,060	$5,866	$4,013	$10,641		$233,972	$244,612
2002	37	$67,349	$33,300		$10,800	$12,060	$5,866	$5,323	$16,548		$243,331	$259,879
2003	38	$70,043	$34,632		$10,800	$12,060	$5,866	$6,685	$24,143		$253,064	$277,207
2004	39	$72,844	$36,017		$10,800		$5,866	$20,161	$45,632		$263,186	$308,819
2005	40	$75,758	$37,458		$10,800		$5,866	$21,634	$69,776		$273,714	$343,490
2006	41	$78,789	$38,956		$10,800			$29,032	$102,646		$284,662	$387,309
2007	42	$81,940	$40,515		$10,800			$30,625	$138,917		$296,049	$434,966
2008	43	$85,218	$42,135		$5,400			$37,683	$184,240		$307,891	$492,131
2009	44	$88,626	$43,821		$5,400			$39,406	$233,779		$320,206	$553,986
2010	45	$92,171	$45,573		$5,400			$41,198	$287,835		$333,015	$620,850
2011	46	$95,858	$43,531	($3,865)	$5,400			$46,927	$350,593		$346,335	$696,928
2012	47	$99,693	$45,273					$54,420	$424,296		$360,189	$784,484
2013	48	$103,680	$47,083					$56,597	$504,229		$374,596	$878,825
2014	49	$107,828	$48,967					$58,861	$590,822		$389,580	$980,402
2015	50	$112,141	$50,925					$61,215	$684,532		$405,163	$1,089,696
2016	51	$116,626	$52,963					$63,664	$785,845		$421,370	$1,207,215
2017	52	$121,291	$55,081					$66,210	$895,277		$438,225	$1,333,502
2018	53	$126,143	$57,284					$68,859	$1,013,376		$455,754	$1,469,130

FIGURE 5-13

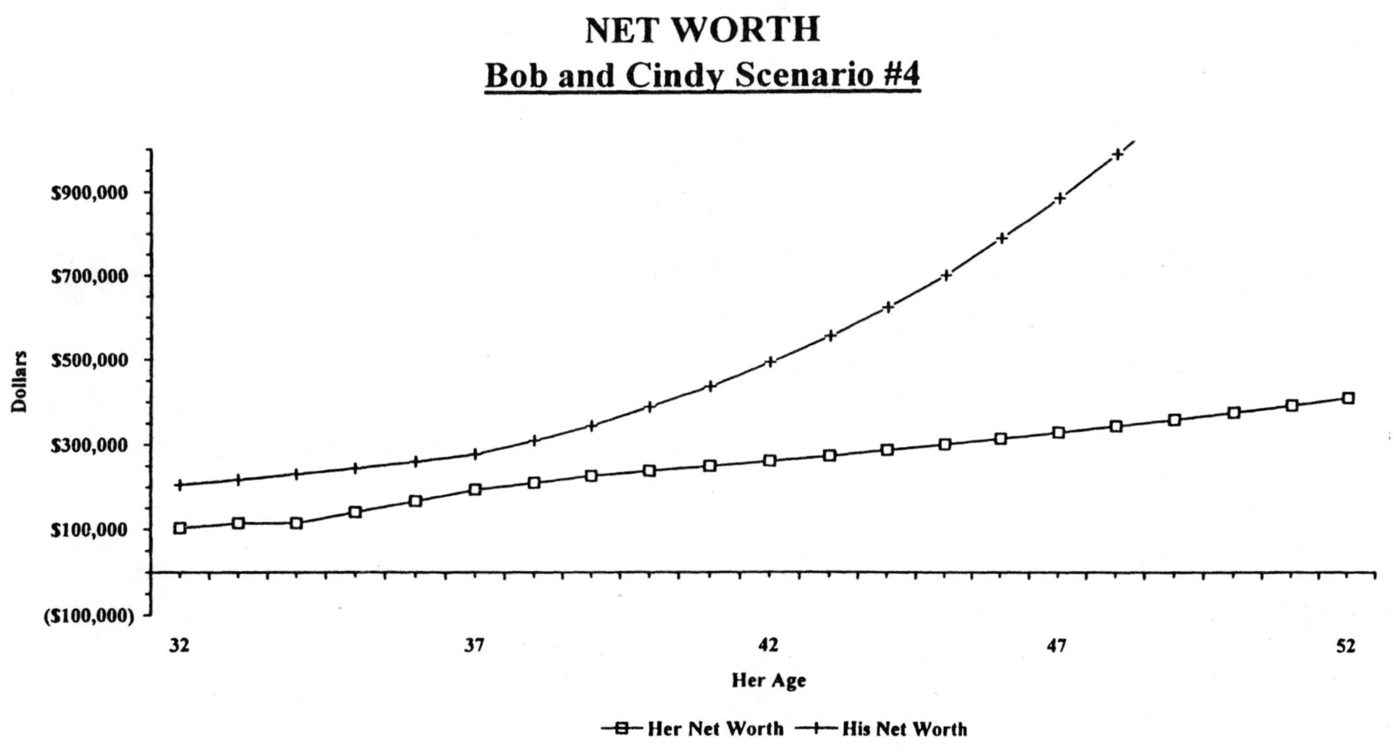
NET WORTH
Bob and Cindy Scenario #4
Dollars
$900,000
$700,000
$500,000
$300,000
$100,000
($100,000)
32
37
42
47
52
Her Age
Her Net Worth
His Net Worth

CHAPTER 6

Pensions—His, Hers . . . . . Or Theirs

This chapter on pensions is not meant to make you an expert on pensions, nor can it teach you how to evaluate pensions. There are volumes written on this subject! Rather, it is to make you aware of pensions' variations and the challenges they present to your client's fair settlement.

Pensions (also referred to as retirement plans) are recognized as property to be divided upon divorce provided that all or part is not considered to be separate property. Pension and retirement benefits that are earned during the marriage are potentially of great value. In a long marriage, they may be the couple's most valuable asset.

There is a bewildering array of basic plans, with countless diverse provisions. Anyone who has tried to explain retirement plans and pensions know that it is often very confusing.

There are two main types of retirement or pension plans: defined-contribution and defined-benefit. Here's a very basic explanation of the two types and how they work. This basic information is very important when presenting the different options to clients.

DEFINED-CONTRIBUTION PLAN

In a defined-contribution plan, there is very little problem identifying the value of the account. Monthly or quarterly statements show the dollar amount available to be divided in either the buy-out method or the future share method.

Defined contribution plans have cash value today. They issue statements that indicate an actual dollar value of the account.

They can be divided equally or un-equally by using a Qualified Domestic Relations Order (QDRO).

A portion of a defined contribution plan can be transferred to an IRA for the ex-spouse without tax consequences.

Some companies allow a plan account to be divided so that the ex-spouse also has an account with the company.

One type of defined-contribution retirement plan is the 401(k). But even in the overall group of 401(k)s, there are different types with different rules. Each company can set its own rules for its retirement plans—as long as the plan is approved by the IRS.

Three types of Defined Contribution Plans

Let's say there are three employees. Employee A is married and works for a company that has a Defined Contribution Plan. He puts all of his retirement money into the Plan and the company does not match any of his funds. He has worked there for three years and he has accumulated $1,500 in his plan. Any money that an employee puts into a 401(k) is the employee's—he or she is 100 percent vested. If he quits or is fired, he can take all of this money with him. He can use it as income, declaring such to the IRS (and most likely, receiving a penalty of 10% of the withdrawn amount) or he can roll it over to an IRA.

At the end of three years, he and his wife are in the process of getting a divorce.

	Employee A
Length of employment	3 years
Plan Value at time of divorce	$1,500
Percent vested	100%
Marital portion	$1,500

Employee B works for a company where only the employer contributes money to the Defined Contribution Plan. The employee does not put anything in. He has worked there for three years and his Plan is worth $1,500. The company uses a vesting schedule, which regulates how much money he can take with him if he quits or if he is fired. The amount depends on how long he has worked for the company. Employee B is 30% vested. Therefore, his 401(k) today is worth 30 percent of $1,500 or $450. The lower amount, $450, is assigned to the marital pot of assets.

	Employee A	Employee B
Length of employment	3 years	3 years
Value at time of divorce	$1,500	$1,500
Percent vested	100%	30%
Marital portion	$1,500	$450

Employee C, works for a company whose policy is that, for every dollar he puts into his Defined Contribution Plan, it is matched with 50 cents. He has worked there for three years and he has $1,500 in his Plan. Out of $1,500, he has put in $1,000 and the company has put in $500 with its matching program. He is 30 percent vested. However, the $1,000 that he put in was his money, so he is 100% vested in that amount and he can take that whole $1,000. He can take 30 percent of the $500—or $150. Employee C's marital portion of this Plan is worth $1,150.

	Employee A	Employee B	Employee C
Employee/Employer contribution			$1/50 cents
Length of employment	3 years	3 years	3 years
Value at time of divorce	$1,500	$1,500	$1,500
Percent vested	100%	30%	30%
Marital portion	$1,500	$450	$1,000/$500
			$1,000
			$ 150
			$1,150

The above example illustrates three different types of vesting in defined contribution plans, depending on the company's policy.

Transferring Assets from a Defined Contribution Plan

Normally, distributions made before the participant attains age 59-1/2 are called "early distributions," and are subject to a 10% penalty tax. The tax does not apply to early distributions upon death, disability, annuity payments for the life expectancy of the individual, or distributions made to an ex-spouse by a QDRO.

The tax Reg (72)(t)(2)(C) states that when you take money out of a *qualified* plan in accordance with a written divorce instrument (a QDRO), the recipient can spend any or all of it without paying the 10% penalty.

Let's take a look at what happens when the ex-spouse receives the 401(k) asset. There are some specific rules to be aware of. Here's an example.

Esther was married to an airline pilot who was nearing retirement. They were both age 55. There was $640,000 in his 401(k) and the retirement plan was prepared to transfer $320,000 to her IRA. She could transfer the money to an IRA and pay no taxes on this amount until she withdraws funds from the IRA. But Esther's attorney's fees were $60,000 and she needed another $20,000 to fix her roof. She said, "I need $80,000." She held back $80,000 of the monies before transferring the remaining amount into her IRA. She was able to spend the $80,000 without incurring a 10% penalty.

Because the 401(k) withholds 20 percent to apply toward taxes on a withdrawal, Esther should have asked for $100,000. After the 20 percent withholding, she would have $80,000 in cash and $220,000 to transfer to her IRA.

Esther does have to pay the taxes on the entire amount because she had to declare the $80,000 as income but she did not have to pay the 10% early withdrawal penalty.

After the money from a pension plan goes into an IRA, which is *not* considered a qualified plan, Esther is held to the early withdrawal rule. If she says, "Oh I forgot, I need another $5,000 to buy a car," it is too late. She will have to pay the 10% penalty *and* the taxes on that money.

Normally, distributions made before the participant attains age 59-1/2 are called *early distributions*, and are subject to a 10 percent penalty tax. The tax does not apply to early distributions upon death, disability, annuity payments for the life expectancy of the individual, or distributions made to an ex-spouse by a QDRO.

Tax Code section (72)(t)(2)(C) says that when you take money out of a *qualified* plan in accordance with a written divorce instrument (a QDRO), the recipient can spend any or all of it without paying the 10 percent penalty.

After the money from a pension plan goes into an IRA, which is not considered a qualified plan, Esther is held to the early withdrawal rule. If she says, "Oh I forgot, I need another $5,000 to buy a car," it is too late. She will have to pay the 10 percent penalty *and* the taxes on that money.

It is important to understand the difference between *rolling over* money from a qualified plan and *transferring money* from a qualified plan. The Unemployment Compensation Amendment Act (UCA), which took effect in January 1993, stated that any monies taken out of a qualified plan or tax-sheltered annuity would be subject to 20 percent withholding. This rule does not apply to IRAs or SEPs.

In other words, if money is *transferred* from a qualified plan to an IRA, the check is sent directly from the qualified plan to the IRA. In a *rollover*, the funds are paid to the person who then remits the money to an IRA. A payment to the person, whether or not there is a rollover, is subject to the 20% withholding. Only a direct transfer avoids the withholding tax.

For example, Henry was to receive his ex-wife Ginny's 401(k) of $100,000, which was invested in the ABC Mutual Fund. He asked the ABC Fund to send him the money so he could do a rollover the money into a different mutual fund of his choice. The ABC Fund sent Henry $80,000, which was the amount remaining after they withheld the 20% withholding tax.

Henry deposited the $80,000 in his new IRA mutual fund. He could have added the $20,000 which was withheld for taxes, but he didn't have $20,000 to spare even though the IRS would have refunded that amount to him after filing his taxes.

Since he could not come up with the $20,000, the next April when he filed his tax return, he paid an extra $6,600 in state and federal taxes. Of course, when he eventually takes his IRA money, $20,000 in taxes will already have been paid.

If Henry had instead *transferred* the $100,000 from the ABC Mutual Fund to his new fund, he would have $100,000 in his new fund (instead of $80,000) and would have saved $6,600 in taxes. It is important to remember the effect of having an extra $20,000 growing tax-deferred!

To *transfer funds*, Henry could have instructed the ABC Mutual Fund to send his $100,000 directly to the new IRA account he had just set up with his new mutual fund.

If a QDRO is used to order a lump sum to be paid to a former spouse from a defined-contribution plan, be sure to notify the plan administrator whether the funds are to be transferred in whole or in part to the intended recipient's separate IRA account. This will avoid the 20% income tax withholding that would otherwise be required.

IRA transfers must be made directly between trustees and not by a rollover.

In a rollover, the funds are paid to the person who then remits the money to an IRA. A payment, whether or not there is a rollover, is subject to the 20 percent withholding. Only a direct transfer avoids the withholding tax.

IRAs

An IRA is not considered to be a qualified plan and a rollover may take place without the 20 percent withholding for taxes. In a divorce situation, IRAs may be transferred in whole or in part. Since an IRA is not a qualified plan, a QDRO is not needed to transfer or divide it. The trustee may need to see the divorce decree. Check with them to see what their requirements are.

Annuitization of an IRA (substantially equal payments for the shorter of five years or the number of years to age 59½) can prevent the imposition of the 10 percent excise tax.

DEFINED-BENEFIT PLANS

Methods of Dividing a Pension

The courts are struggling with the problem of how to value and divide pensions. For some cases, they must value the interest in a retirement plan. This interest will not include any portion acquired either after the divorce or, in most states, before the marriage. To figure out how much of the pension is marital property, you need to know the specifics of the employee's retirement plan.

There are three different methods used to divide pension benefits when settling marital estates. The first is the "present value" or "cash-out" method, which awards the non-employee spouse a lump sum settlement—or a marital asset of equal value—at the time of divorce in return for the employee's keeping the pension.

The second method is the "deferred division" or "future share" method where no present value is determined. Each spouse is awarded a share of the benefits if and when they are paid.

The third method is the "reserved jurisdiction," whereby the court retains the authority to order distributions from a pension plan at some point in the future. It should be considered a last resort, as it leaves both spouses in limbo with regard to planning for their future.

A defined-benefit retirement plan promises to pay the employee a certain amount per month at retirement time. It has no cash value today.

It can be divided equally or unequally by using a QDRO. If not divided "in kind" later, it must be valued today. This value is placed in the list of marital assets to be offset by other property.

In many pensions, there are choices as to how it is to be paid out such as life, years certain, life of employee and spouse. The value of a defined-benefit plan comes from the company's guarantee to pay based on a predetermined plan formula, not from an account balance.

For instance, the amount of monthly pension could be determined by a complex calculation which could include, in addition to the employee's final average salary, an annuity factor based on the employee's age at retirement, the employee's annual average Social Security tax base, the employee's total number of years of employment and age at retirement, the method chosen by the employee to receive payment of voluntary and required contributions, and whether a pension will be paid to a survivor upon the employee's death. As you might guess, the valuation of such a plan poses a challenge and has fostered much creativity!

Transferring Assets from a Defined Benefit Plan

Here's an example of how a defined-benefit plan works with Henry and Ginny from the previous example. Assume that based on today's earnings and his length of time with the company, Henry will receive $1,200 a month at age 65 from his pension. He is now age 56, and has to wait nine more years before he can start receiving the $1,200 per month. Because of the wait, it is called a *future benefit*. You can, though, value this future stream of income and put down a present value of what it is worth today. This present value can be used in the list of assets for purposes of dividing property.

You could, for example, divide the defined-benefit plan according to a QDRO by saying that Ginny will receive $600 when Henry retires. However, when he retires, his benefit will probably be worth more than $1,200 per month because he will have worked there longer. When Henry retires, he may get $1,800 a month, but if the QDRO stated that Ginny would receive $600 per month, she won't get any more even though the value of the fund has increased.

It is important to find out whether (1) the $1,200 per month is what he will get at age 65 based on today's earnings and time with the company, or (2) the $1,200 per month assumes it is what he will get if he stays with he company until age 65 with projected earnings built in. If it is not clear on the pension statements, these questions must be asked of the plan administrator.

If the couple has less than eight years to wait until retirement, Ginny may choose to wait to get the $600 per month so she can have guaranteed income. However, if they are 9, 10, or more years away from retirement, she may wish to trade out another asset up front. This way, she'll be assured of getting some funding. The media has reported that many retirement plans have disappeared due to mismanagement of the funds or the company going out of business.

Assume that Ginny decides to wait for nine years until Henry retires to receive her benefit. They have been married for 32 years. Instead of stating in the QDRO that she will receive $600 per month, it may be more prudent to use a formula (called the Coverture Fraction) which states that she will receive a percentage or half of the following:

Coverture Fraction

$$\frac{\text{Number of years married while working}}{\text{Total number of years worked until retirement}} = \frac{32}{41}$$

If Henry's final benefit would pay him $1,800 per month:

$$\frac{32}{41} \times 1{,}800 \text{ divided by } 2 = 702$$

This may be a more equitable division of the pension based on the premise that Ginny was married to Henry during the early building-up years of the plan.

It is also important to ascertain if the plan will pay Ginny at retirement time (Henry's age 65) in the case that Henry doesn't retire. He may decide not to retire just so Ginny can't get her portion of his retirement plan! Some companies do allow the ex-spouse to start receiving benefits at retirement time even if the employee spouse has not retired. This depends on the QDRO's dividing method and the plan.

Case studies showing three different parameters of the defined benefit

Case 1 (Based on Present Value as of leaving the company today)

Richard will receive $2,600 per month at age 65 from his defined-benefit plan. (This is based on his years of service and earnings as of today.) He is now age 52. The life expectancy table shows that he has a life expectancy of an additional 26.9 years. So, his life expectancy right now is 78.9 years. He will receive $2,600 a month times 12, or $31,200 a year.

Using a Texas Instrument calculator,

31,200	=	Payment
13.9	=	*n* (number of years between age 65 and 78.9)
5.5	=	% interest (See discussion below on discount rate.)

Now calculate PV (Present Value). We find that the PV (Present Value) is $297,758. That is the amount of money needed at age 65 to be able to pay Richard $31,200 per year for 13.9 years which is his life expectancy after he retires.

Now, calculate the present value as of today:

297,758	=	FV (future value)
13	=	*n* (number of years until he is age 65)
5.5	=	% (interest rate)

We find that the PV (Present Value is $148,450. That is the present value today of his future stream of income. It represents the lump sum of money needed today invested at 5.5 percent to create a lump sum of money at age 65 that will pay Richard $31,200 per year for his life expectancy.

Not all states allow this method of valuation. Be sure to check your own state for guidelines and policies.

[These calculations have been done on a Texas Instrument (TI) calculator. Using a Hewlitt Packard (HP) calculator may produce results that vary by about 5%.]

Case 2 (Based on the same assumptions as Case 1 and that he works for the company longer than being married)

Larry and Sue have been married for 15 years and Larry has worked for his company for 20 years. Therefore, you know only 75 percent of that portion is marital property. Larry is now age 52 and his life expectancy is 78.9 years. Figure the present value exactly the same as before.

Now, when you look at the present value, you will take 15/20th or 75 percent of the present value to see what the marital portion of the pension is.

$$\frac{15}{20} \times 148{,}450 = 111{,}338$$

The Present Value of the marital portion of Larry's pension is $111,338.

Let's assume you decide to draft a QDRO for this pension so that Sue gets a portion of the monthly payment when he retires instead of looking at it as a lump-sum value. You would look at her getting 75 percent of the marital portion of the monthly payment when he retires, so you can do either a portion of the monthly payment or a portion of the present value. In this case, Sue would be getting half of 75 percent (i.e., 37 1/2 percent) of $2,600. An order could be entered that awards Sue $975 per month when Larry reaches age 65.

It might be more fair, however, to use the "coverture fraction." This is a formula that states the number of Larry's years of plan participation while married to Sue as the numerator, while the total number of years of plan participation as the denominator.

Coverture Fraction:

$$\frac{\text{Number of years married while working}}{\text{Total number of years working}} \times \text{benefit at retirement}$$

The calculated lump-sum value of a retirement plan depends on the assumptions you use for the data. There is a lot of litigation surrounding this data because it can make a substantial difference in the present value. Also, some of the discounting assumptions that you make can create a substantial difference. So, rather then fight about value, you just divide it "in kind." You do not care what the value is because of the percentage division. You could argue that the pension is worth $100,000 so he gets the pension and she gets the $100,000 house. Or, you can just divide the pension 50/50. Again, you do not care if it is worth $150,000, $100,000 or $50,000 because you are dividing it "in kind."

Case 3 (Based on the pension being protected from inflation)

Marvin is age 52 and plans to retire at age 65. His pension will pay him $2,600 per month based on today's earnings and years of service with the company. Marvin's pension benefit is protected from inflation and will have a cost of living adjustment each year.

To get the inflation-adjusted interest rate, we use the following formula:

$$\frac{1 + \text{Assumed discount rate}}{1 + \text{Inflation rate}} - 1 \times 100 = \text{Inflation-adjusted interest}$$

$$\frac{1 + 5.5\%}{1 + 4\%} - 1 \times 100$$

$$\frac{1.055}{1.04} - 1 \times 100$$

$$1.014 - 1 \times 100 = 1.44$$

After Marvin starts receiving his $2,600 per month at age 65, you figure the Present Value using the inflation-adjusted interest rate.

$31,200	=	Payment
13.9	=	Number of years between age 65 and 78.9
1.44%	=	Inflation-adjusted interest rate
$390,500	=	Present Value

Between now and Marvin's retirement, we use our regular interest rate.

$390,500	=	FV (Future Value)
13	=	Number of years until he is age 65
5.5%	=	Interest rate
$194,688	=	PV

The Present Value of Marvin's inflation protected pension is $194,688.

Qualified Domestic Relations Order (QDRO)

Legislative Background

Employee Retirement Income Security Act of 1974 (ERISA)

The enactment of ERISA in 1974 established laws relating to attachment of pension benefits, thereby putting family law courts into a quandary as to how to treat retirement plan assets that state courts clearly determined were marital property.

Uniformed Services Former Spouses' Protection Act (USFSPA)

The enactment of USFSPA in 1982 addresses military retirement benefits as marital property and asserts that a state court may divide them pursuant to state law. If the former spouse was married to the person in military service for 10 years while the spouse performed military service, then the court may order direct payment of benefits as a division of marital property but not to exceed more than on-half of the benefit.

Retirement Equity Act of 1984 (REA)

The REA of 1984 provided that all qualified plans subject to ERISA may have assets segregated for the benefit of an "alternate payee" through a court order known as a qualified domestic relations order (QDRO). Many non-ERISA plans will also honor these orders.

Tax Reform Act of 1984 (TRA)

TRA added Code Sec. 1041, which allows marital property to be shifted back and forth between spouses. The basis of the assets goes with those assets and there is no taxable event when property transfers at divorce.

The QDRO is an order from the court to the retirement plan administrator spelling out how the plan's benefits are to be assigned to each party in a divorce. It is a legal document, creating both problems and liabilities with it. QDROs must be done by professionals who know what they are doing—an attorney or someone who specializes in QDROs.

Plans divisible by a QDRO include defined-contribution plans and defined-benefit plans, 401(k)s, thrift savings plans, some profit-sharing and money-purchase plans, Keogh plans, tax sheltered annuities, Employee Stock Ownership Plan (ESOPs), and the old Payroll Based Employee Stock Ownership Plan (PAYSOPs).

Plans that are not divisible by a QDRO include some plans of small employers not covered by ERISA, and many public employee group funds such as police and fire groups, and city, state, and other governmental employees including federal employees.

The QDRO is sent to the employer's pension plan administrator. It tells how much of the money in the plan is to be sent to the spouse of the employee. This amount can be from zero to 100 percent, depending on how they have divided the other assets. It does not automatically mean 50 percent. A phrase often used by attorneys is, "We are going to QDRO that pension," and they are thinking about a 50 percent split because that is most typical. By definition, however, it does not mean 50%.

Typically, the QDRO tells not only how the money in the plan is to be divided, but what is to happen when the parties die.

Limitations in using a QDRO

You must look at the pension documents during the divorce proceedings and before the divorce is final.

There are too many horror stories where the case has gone to court, everything is settled, the judge says the divorce is final and that a QDRO should be drafted. Then, the QDRO is sent to the pension plan and the ex-spouse ends up not getting any money. Why? Because the plan (doesn't have to) and won't pay it.

From *Informational Guide on "QDROs" under the IBM Retirement Plan*:

> "How long does it take for a plan to approve a QDRO?
>
> "The answer and our experience has been that it can take several months. This is because draft orders or orders that have been entered without our

advance review often have conditions that we cannot implement or which require forms of payment which are *not allowed* under the plan. For example, we often see orders that require an immediate lump sum payment of the former spouse's total share of the benefit. Since the IBM retirement plan *does not pay* in lump sums except for accrued benefits with a present actuarial value of $3,500 or less or for PRP benefits, but pays only on a monthly basis for life, an order requiring a lump sum payment *must be rejected* and *will not be accepted* until the court has issued an order that complies with the provisions of the plan." (Emphasis added)[1]

A QDRO generally may not require that the plan provide any form of benefit not otherwise provided under the plan and may not require that the plan provide increased benefits. However, within certain limits, it is permissible for a QDRO to require that payments to the alternate payee begin on or after the participant's earliest retirement age, even though the participant has not retired at that time. One area of liability in drafting a QDRO for a pension plan is when the pension documents do not allow for the ex-spouse to receive benefits before the employee spouse has retired.

An expert from a pension department once said, "We will answer any question that you ask but we will not volunteer any information." You need to ask the questions. The client doesn't really understand how to ask questions and sometimes the attorney doesn't either. You should at least call the company's pension department and ask,

- (Do you allow a QDRO?
- (Will you pay it in a lump sum?
- (Will you separate the accounts?
- (Can the non-employee spouse receive benefits before the employee spouse retires?

Pension departments won't figure the present value for you and you cannot ask specific questions about the client's account unless you have *his or her signature that releases such information* to you.

PUBLIC EMPLOYEES PENSIONS

Another type of defined benefit plan is for public employees such as schoolteacher, principals, librarians, firemen, policemen and state troopers. This type of plan typically will not allow any division by order of a QDRO in a divorce and in some states are not assignable at all to the ex-spouse.

Each year, the employee gets a statement showing his or her contributions to this plan. This sum of money (plus interest) is what the employee can take if he quits or is fired. However, if the employee stays in the job for a minimum number of years (usually 20 or 25), he or she will receive an annuity retirement payout that is a percent of their final average pay. It is at retirement time that the employee sees the contribution of the public employer.

Janice and Frank had been married for 23 years. Frank started out as a schoolteacher and at the time of their divorce, he was the Principal of the high school in their small city. The statement of his retirement account showed that he had paid in $82,050 and that is the number that Frank used as his value of his retirement. His attorney accepted this number.

Janice's attorney encouraged her to hire a Certified Divorce Planner who determined that when Frank retires, he would get 60 percent of his final average salary, or $32,050 per year. The financial expert testified in court that the Present Value of the marital portion of that future stream of income was $373,060—a far cry from $82,050! The judge, after dividing all the other assets equally, declared that Frank still owed Janice $133,585 which should be paid to her via a property settlement note over 20 years at $957 per month. Frank's attorney looked more carefully at future clients' retirement plans!

DISCOUNT RATE OF INTEREST

In figuring the present value of a future stream of income, there is a relationship between the interest rate and the present value. The higher the interest rate, the lower the present value of the pension, and vice versa.

The Pension Benefit Guaranty Corporation (PBGC), an organization in Washington, D.C., announces monthly the interest rate for figuring pension plans for the following month. This has become the reliable national standard for computing present values of pensions in divorce cases, because it removes doubt and speculation of battling experts as to what interest rate to use. The telephone number for the Pension Benefit Guaranty Corp. is (202) 326-4000.

The rate that many companies use for figuring the present value of a future stream of defined benefit payments for the purpose of valuing a pension in a divorce is the lump sum rate according to the PBGC. It will be lower than the Annuity rate. The lump sum rate is calculated by using average annuity prices less the commission or load. The only problem with using this lower number is that it tends to inflate the value of the pension, especially for young parties.

The passage of GATT (General Agreement of Tariffs and Trades) called for the minimum interest rate being "the annual rate of interest on 30-year Treasury securities for the month before the date of distribution..." (Retirement Protection act of 1994, Sec. 767(a)(2)). Companies can use the GATT rate only if their plan is amended to allow that. However, GATT requires companies to amend their plans by the year 2000 to compute present values and lump-sum distributions using the GATT rate based on 30-year Treasuries. Within the coming five years, all affected plans will drop their reliance of PBGC rates and use GATT rates.

Another thing to remember is if you had valued a pension six months earlier, the interest rate might have been different. This would have made the value more or less, because the higher the interest rate, the less the present value. As the interest rate comes down, the value of the pension goes up.

In Colorado and many other states, the present value of a pension plan is to be figured at the earliest date of retirement that can be taken without penalty or reduction of benefit. Before this rule was established, one expert would say, "This is the value of his pension when he retires at age 65." The other expert would say, "But he is going to take early retirement at age 55 so this is the value of his pension instead." Obviously, two different values would be produced.

As a compromise, many states set a standard that the present value of the pension is to be calculated at the earliest date of retirement without reduction in benefits. If a company allows retirement at the age of 60 with full benefits, figure the present value from that point. Make sure you verify what the law in your jurisdiction is to determine which method your state courts use.

SURVIVOR BENEFITS

Keep in mind when the defined-benefit plan is divided, it is critical to work with the plan administrator in setting up survivor benefits. Your client would be unhappy if she got 50 percent of the defined-benefit plan and then the employee died and the rest of the money wasn't paid out. The QDRO needs to state it simplistically—joint and survivor annuity—which, of course, will have a reduction in ultimate benefit, or can literally take the client's portion—the 40 percent or whatever—and have it set up in a separate account. It will all be calculated and annualized at the time of payment. That way, the client gets it whether the employee dies or not, and is not choosing a joint and survivor annuity.

This is only true after the alternate payee starts receiving his or her share. Make sure that you understand the plan and that there are options available in the event of the death of the employee and that you have included them in your planning.

For example, an ex-wife can preserve her right to receive survivor's benefits if her husband should die before retirement. This means that, before he can waive such coverage, an ex-husband must obtain his ex-wife's written consent and have it notarized, *even if he has remarried and wants his new spouse to receive the benefits instead.* A divorce decree that earmarks the money for a former spouse can override the rights of a second or third spouse.

VESTING

Vesting refers to the employee's entitlement to retirement benefits. A participant is vested when he or she has an immediate, fixed right of present or future enjoyment of the accrued benefit. The percentage of vesting means what the employee is entitled to from the retirement plan when he or she retires, quits, or is fired.

When *fully vested*, an employee is entitled to all the benefits that the employer has contributed. Being *partially vested* means that if the employee quit the job, he or she would be able to take that percentage of the employer's contributions. An example would be if the employee were 30 percent vested and the employer's contributions were $1,500, the employee could take $450.

Any contributions made by the employee to the plan are immediately 100 percent vested. The employee is always entitled to take all of his contributions plus the earnings on those contributions.

An employee must be given non-forfeitable rights to his accrued benefits derived from employer contributions in accordance with *one* of the following two vesting schedules:

1. *5 year cliff vesting* An employee who has at least 5 years of service must have a nonforfeitable right to 100% of his accrued benefit. (IRC Sec. 411(a)(2)(A).
2. *3/7 vesting* An employee who has completed at least 3 years of service must have a nonforfeitable right to at least the following percentages of his accrued benefit: 20 percent after 3 years of service,

> 40 percent after 4 years of service, 60 percent after 5 years of service, 80 percent after 6 years of service, and 100 percent after 7 years of service. (IRC Sec. 411(a)(2)(B).

There is also "3 year cliff vesting" for top-heavy plans.

It is important at divorce to find out whether the state considers nonvested retirement benefits to be marital property. If so, a defined contribution plan's total value could be divided, and the employee could leave his job and never receive the nonvested amounts.

For example, Marvin worked for ABC, Inc. His 401(k) was worth $58,000, which was made up of $12,300 from his contributions and $45,700 from his employer's contributions. Marvin is 40 percent vested. If he quit his job today, he could take his own $12,300 and $18,280 of his employer's contributions for a total of $30,580. He and his ex-wife Susie agreed to value his 401(k) at the full $58,000 for purposes of dividing property. Marvin kept his 401(k) and paid Susie $29,000 for her half out of the savings account money. Six months after the divorce was final, ABC, Inc. laid off half its workforce including Marvin. He left the company with $30,580 from his retirement account. The net result was that he ended up $13,710 short in the division of marital property.

MATURE PLANS

An employee may be fully vested but may still have to wait until he or she reaches a certain age before being able to receive any benefits. For instance, some companies do not pay out benefits until the employee has reached age 60 or age 65.

And in some cases, if the employee is not vested in the plan and dies before retirement age, the benefits are lost. Nobody gets them.

DOUBLE DIPPING

Sometimes a retirement plan is divided at divorce as part of the property division. Then in some states, when the employee retires, his income from his portion of the retirement plan is considered when calculating alimony and/or child support. The end result is that the non-employee spouse is getting paid twice from the same asset. What is used as income in determining alimony depends on state law.

THE CARROT STORY

Understanding how Defined Benefit pensions really work is often confusing to even the most knowledgeable financial experts. The following excerpt from *Assigning Retirement Benefits In Divorce* by Gale S. Finley is an excellent, and delightful way to learn and comprehend the ins and out of Defined Benefit plans.[2]

* * * *

Imagine a farm in central Kentucky that raises racehorses. The owner of the farm takes his racing very seriously and comes up with a way to reward his horses for winning races for him. He calls it the "Carrot Retirement Plan." He decides that after each horse retires from racing, it will be provided an allocation of carrots each week as a supplement to its regular diet. The number of carrots a horse receives each week depends upon the number of races it wins during its racing career. Each horse will receive its weekly allotment of carrots until it goes to that big pasture in the sky.

In order to ensure an adequate supply of carrots for his retiring horses, the owner decides to plan ahead and start growing and freezing carrots. He sits down with the veterinarian and the two of them decide how many carrots he will have to grow and store each week. They look at how many horses he has, how many races each has won, when each is expected to retire, and how long each is expected to live after retirement. Based upon those initial projections, the owner comes up with a quantity of carrots that will be needed to be planted that first year. He hires an expert in carrot growing—the Keeper of the Carrots—to maintain a carrot crop that will continue to produce an adequate supply to meet future carrot obligations.

The next year the owner again sits down with his veterinarian and the Keeper of the Carrots. The owner and the veterinarian discuss factors bearing on the number of carrots that will be needed for all the retiring horses down the road, such as any new horses acquired during the year, any that have died during the year, how many races each has won, and how many will be retiring. Also, they reevaluate their projections from the previous year concerning all those same factors based upon what actually occurred during the year. The Keeper of the Carrots then reports on how well the carrot crop came in during the year and whether it will be adequate given the number of carrots the owner has projected under the Carrot Retirement Plan. They also discuss the number of carrots that will have to be planted during the next year.

Each year these three people sit down and look at the events that have occurred during the year and how those events affect future carrot obligations. The goal is always for the three of them to work together to ensure that, at retirement, each horse is given its proper weekly allotment of carrots for as long as it lives. If during a given year fewer horses than were projected are retiring, more retiring horses died than were expected to, some horses died while still active, and/or the Keeper of the Carrots brought in a bumper crop, fewer, if any, new carrots have to be planted. On the other hand, negative results as compared to the projections mean more carrots than expected must be planted.

Let's look at one of the horses covered under the Carrot Retirement Plan (the "Participant Horse"). This Participant Horse is still actively racing and occasionally winning. In addition, he has won enough races through today's date to be entitled to receive 10 carrots each week of his life beginning on the date he is permanently turned out to pasture (its "Accrued Carrot Benefit"). What can we say about this horse's rights under the Carrot Retirement Plan as of today's date? What the Participant Horse has today is a right to receive 10 carrots each week for life beginning at some future date. If he wins more races in the future, the number of weekly carrots to which he is entitled will increase. But as of today, 10 per week is the number. Remember though, it is a current right to receive carrots in the future if the Participant Horse lives long enough to receive them. The Participant Horse does not "own" any carrots. Because he is still racing, he is not currently entitled to any carrots. In fact, because he may die before he retires, he may never be entitled to receive any carrots. The owner of the horse farm owns thousands of carrots that are being stored to someday give the Participant Horse and all his co-retirees a certain number of carrots each week for their respective lives. But the Participant Horse does not own any carrots until he actually receives his first weekly allotment.

Assuming another horse—the "A-P Horse"—wants to lay claim to 50% of the Participant Horse's Accrued Carrot Benefit, what do we have to divide? We have the Participant Horse's right to receive 10 carrots per week for his life beginning when he retires. We can split that down the middle so that the A-P Horse will get 5 carrots from each 10 carrot allotment as it is distributed to the Participant Horse during his lifetime. That is the easiest way to make the division because the number of carrots to be given, the beginning date, and the ending date are already determined. No muss and no fuss.

As simple as that method may be, however, it means that the A-P Horse has absolutely no control over any aspect of the carrot distribution process.

The A-P Horse may want to start receiving her carrots sooner or later than the Participant Horse's retirement date. The A-P Horse may want the security of knowing the carrots will keep coming during *her* lifetime rather than the lifetime of the Participant Horse (rumor has it the Participant Horse's health is deteriorating). Can we simply provide that the A-P Horse will receive 5 carrots each week during *her* life, beginning when *she* chooses? We can't if our goal is to give the A-P Horse a right to only 50% of the Participant Horse's Accrued Carrot Benefit as of today's date.

To understand that, let's look at what the Participant Horse's Accrued Carrot Benefit roughly translates to. We will assume that the Participant Horse will be retired in 2 years and will start receiving 10 carrots each week beginning November 1 of that year. At that time the Participant Horse will have a life expectancy of 20 years. If these assumptions hold true, the owner will need to be prepared to provide 10,400 carrots (10 carrots x 52 weeks x 20 years) to the Participant Horse over his lifetime. If we assume a 50-50 split of the amount so that the Participant Horse receives only 5 carrots per week, the lifetime total becomes 5,200 carrots.

Now let's assume the A-P Horse, because of an age difference, has a current life expectancy of 24 years. If the A-P Horse starts to receive 5 carrots per week (based upon the 50% assignment) starting now (assuming this is the "earliest retirement age") and continuing for the assumed 24 years, she will receive an aggregate of 6,240 carrots over her lifetime. This is substantially more than the 5,200 that represent 50% of the Accrued Carrot Benefit. Moreover, when added to the 5,200 the owner expects to give to the Participant Horse, the total (11,440) is significantly higher than the 10,400 that would be given (if all assumptions are accurate) to the Participant Horse if no assignment is made. Since a predicted 10,400 is all the owner is obligated for under the Carrot Retirement Plan, something has to give.

If, in fact, the intent of the parties is to give the A-P Horse during her lifetime the *equivalent* of 5,200 carrots over the lifetime of the Participant Horse, a couple of options exist. As we mentioned earlier, the A-P Horse can receive half of the Participant Horse's weekly allotment of carrots while the Participant horse is alive. But to keep carrots coming to the A-P Horse after the Participant Horse dies, she can also require the Carrot Retirement Plan to continue to deliver to her the same weekly allotment. Of course, in order to "fund" her continuing carrot supply after the death of the Participant Horse, the Carrot Retirement Plan will need to reduce the number of weekly carrots that are given out while the Participant Horse is alive. For example, instead of giving out 10 carrots per week, 5 to the Participant Horse and 5 to the A-P Horse, who is expected to live longer than the Participant Horse, upon the death of the Participant Horse (assuming she fulfills her life expectancy). Another option is for the A-P Horse to be treated as though she has her own Accrued Carrot Benefit and to receive some smaller number per week beginning when she chooses and continuing for as long as *she* lives. In our example, the latter option would result in the A-P Horse immediately beginning to receive 4,167 (5200 divided by 24 years divided by 52 weeks) per week for her lifetime.

Either of these 2 options provides the A-P Horse the *equivalent* of 50% of the participant Horse's Accrued Carrot Benefit because it ends up, if all life expectancy assumptions for the Participant Horse and the A-P Horse hold true, to be the same aggregate number of carrots the Participant Horse will receive during his life.

PITFALLS IN DIVIDING PENSIONS IN DIVORCE

Many Qualified Domestic Relations Orders Will Trigger Malpractice Suits

Edwin C. Schilling III J.D., is in private practice in Denver, Colorado. He is among the nation's most knowledgeable divorce attorneys on the financial and legal aspects of divorce involving military retired pay and federal civil service pensions. Mr. Schilling co-authored the Air Force position paper on proposed legislation to divide military retired pay incident to divorce. He has testified before Congress concerning national divorce legislation and is a frequent nation-wide speaker on the more complex issues of divorce law. He shares with some of his expertise in this area.

* * * *

Many mistakes are being made when Qualified Domestic Relations Orders (QDROs) are drafted to divide pensions. These mistakes could result in a non-employee spouse not getting the benefits that were anticipated.

In lawyer's filing cabinets around the country, there are thousands of ticking time bombs waiting to go off. Many errors won't be discovered for years to come—when the employee retires or dies. Errors are not limited to an incorrect division of the pension; they also include the survivor benefits.

In addition, technical errors are often made that result in a pension plan rejecting the QDRO and requiring that it be resubmitted. These errors can occur on both defined-benefit and defined-contribution plans. However, the most common mistakes are with defined-benefit plans because they are more complex.

The following are the biggest mistakes to be aware of:

1. Failing to Anticipate Death

The single biggest mistake is failing to address what will happen if either party dies *before* the non-employee gets the whole share of the pension. A QDRO can either miss this issue completely or get it wrong.

What If the Employee Dies? Almost all pension plans provide for death benefits in case an employee dies *before* retirement. However, a non-employee former spouse can't share in these benefits unless the QDRO specifically provides for this. A court order must award either a dollar amount or a percentage of the death benefits, or the former spouse won't get anything when the employee dies. Frequently overlooked is the possibility that the QDRO could order the plan to treat the former spouse as a surviving spouse for the purposes of this protection.

There is a similar problem if the employee dies *after* retirement. ERISA says that a spouse is always entitled to a survivor annuity unless it is waived. But this isn't true for an *ex*-spouse. The only way to provide an ex-spouse with a survivor annuity is to spell it out specifically in the QDRO.

Another alternative to naming the ex-spouse as the recipient of the survivor annuity is to have the plan divide the account when the employee retires, and use a portion of this account to fund a lifetime annuity for the non-employee. This can be a good idea if the employee plans to remarry, since the employee will still have the option of providing a new spouse with a survivor annuity.

What If the Non-Employee Dies? If the non-employee dies before the receipt of the pension benefits, it is often assumed that the funds will pass to the non-employee's estate. This is not necessarily true. With some plans, it is not possible; with other plans, it has to be specifically provided for. If the QDRO has no language about what happens if the non-employee should die, the plan would probably take the position that it doesn't know whom to pay, and the plan would absorb the account.

2. Not Understanding Plan Provisions and Features

A big problem is drafting a QDRO without knowing what the plan provides. It's hard to negotiate what is best for your client if you don't know what is available. It is important to always obtain at least a copy of the summary plan description.

Normally, a non-employee won't start receiving benefits until the employee does, but many pension plans permit a non-employee to start receiving payments as of the employee's earliest possible retirement date. Also, many 401(k) plans permit an immediate distribution or transfer into another qualified plan or IRA at the time of divorce.

In addition, many lawyers don't understand that QDROs only apply to qualified plans under ERISA. They try to prepare a QDRO for a governmental plan that has its own set of rules. This is a common problem.

Two other common errors resulting from a failure to understand the plan:

- (Lawyers request a lump sum when it is not provided for in the plan.
- (When dealing with a defined-benefit plan, many QDROs ask for a division of the account balance as of the date of the divorce decree. But most plans still don't value their accounts on a daily basis. If the plan only values its accounts on a quarterly basis, then the pension plan cannot administer the order and it will be rejected.

3. Finalizing the Divorce Before the QDRO is Approved

The QDRO should be approved by the pension plan *before* the divorce is final. This is because the non-employee is unprotected during the period between the divorce and QDRO approval. If the employee retires, dies, or remarries in the interim, the non-employee may well end up with nothing.

These scenarios should be considered:

- *If the employee retires*, a single-life annuity could be chosen and the non-employee ex-spouse's right to a survivor annuity would be lost.
- *If the employee dies,* the non-employee ex-spouse won't get any death benefits because the non-employee is no longer a "spouse," and there is not yet a QDRO requiring the plan to make payments. As long as they are married, if the employee dies, the spouse is automatically the beneficiary under ERISA unless the option was waived.
- *If the employee remarries*, the non-employee ex-spouse may have trouble obtaining a death benefit or a survivor annuity in the

QDRO. This is because it may be unclear whether rights of the non-employee's former spouse supersede those of the new spouse. Once the marriage is terminated and there is a new spouse, it may be very difficult to get a fair order.

4. Relying only on Forms Provided by the Plan

It can be a big mistake to simply rely on a sample QDRO form provided by the plan administrator as it will often favor the plan or employee. For example, the form might state that the non-employee can't share in any retirement bonus the employee gets, or might simply not raise the bonus issue at all.

Drafters need to consider whether the language in the sample order is better for their client or better for the other party. If they don't consider this, they may not be getting the client all he or she is entitled to. It's worthwhile to obtain a model order that would be acceptable, but don't treat that as the only possibility.

5. Failing to Divide an Early Retirement Bonus

Some retirement plans offer a substantial bonus to employees who retire early. Consideration should be given to negotiating for a portion of it, or not dividing it in exchange for some concession or property.

6. Not Having the QDRO "Pre-Approved" by the Plan Administrator

Whenever possible, one should obtain a "pre-approval" of a QDRO to avoid embarrassing mistakes. Most plan administrators gladly help at this stage because it avoids problems later. Getting a QDRO pre-approved saves the embarrassment of having the order rejected and having to go back to the judge for a revision.

Ron and Nancy Case Study

Ron and Nancy have been married 20 years and have two sons, ages 8 and 5. Ron is 43 years old, has take-home pay of $51,098 per year, expenses of $25,980 per year and will retire at age 65.

Nancy is also 43 years old and works at the town library. She brings home $13,500 per year and has expenses of $35,676 per year with the two boys. Nancy wants custody of their sons.

Table 6-1 shows the proposed settlement.

TABLE 6-1

RON AND NANCY
ASSET table #1 (50/50)

Item	Value	Nancy	Ron
Home (net)	27,700		27,700
Household Goods	8,500	2,500	6,000
Automobiles	7,000	1,500	5,550
401(k)	252,700	154,475	98,225
Ron's IRA	25,300		25,300
Nancy's IRA	18,500	18,500	
Pension	32,500		32,500
Certificate of Deposit	41,750	30,000	11,750
Total	$413,950	$206,975	$206,975
Downpayment on House		($25,000)	
Working Capital Column		$5,000	$11,750
Retirement Asset Column		$172,975	$123,525

- Nancy will keep her car and take some of the furniture. She will receive custody of the sons and will get child support of $703 per month ($8,436 per year) until their oldest son is 19 years old. At this point, child support will decrease to $5,000 per year until the youngest son reaches 19 years of age. This is in accordance with the child support guidelines in their state. Nancy will receive $172,975 in retirement benefits (401(k) and IRA funds) and $30,000 from the certificate of deposit.
- Ron feels that since Nancy is getting $172,975 in retirement benefits, she does not need alimony.
- Ron will keep their house and Nancy will buy a new house with her part of the CD.
- Ron will keep his car, some furniture, and the house. He will take his pension, part of the certificate of deposit, and $123,525 in retirement benefits.

This settlement represents a 50/50 split of the marital assets as shown in Figure 6-1. Look at Table 6-1. The net equity in the home, $27,700, is in Ron's column. The household goods were split according to what each of them wanted for their homes. They each took their own car. Notice that the remain-

FIGURE 6-1

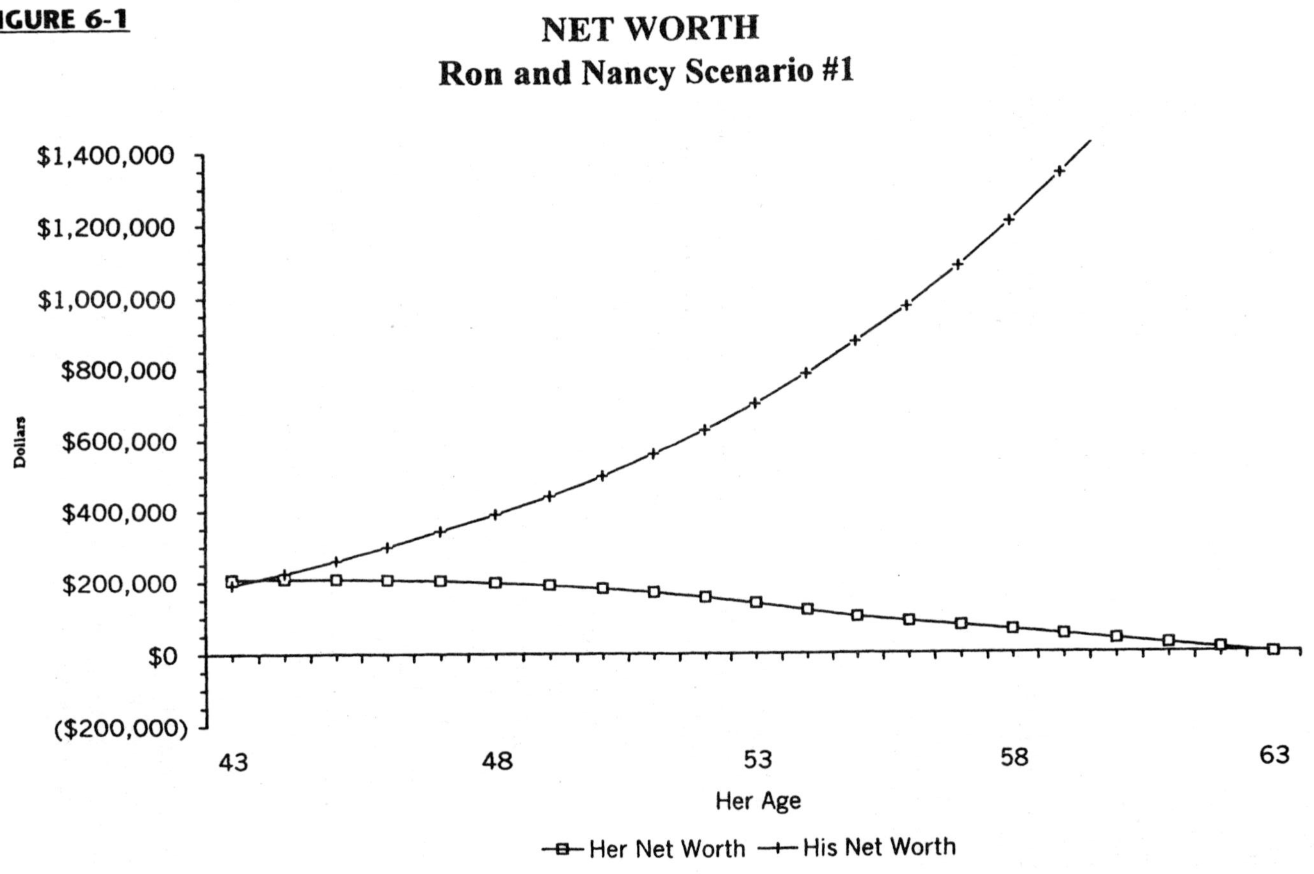
NET WORTH
Ron and Nancy Scenario #1
Dollars
$1,400,000
$1,200,000
$1,000,000
$800,000
$600,000
$400,000
$200,000
$0
($200,000)
43
48
53
58
63
Her Age
Her Net Worth
His Net Worth

der of their assets except for the CD are in retirement plans such as the 401(k), IRAs, and the pension. While each party is getting 50% of the assets, is it really an equitable settlement?

Even though they have split their assets 50/50, the majority of their assets are in retirement accounts. Let's look at the final result.

Table 6-2, is Nancy's spreadsheet for Scenario #1. The first column shows the year and it starts with 1996. The second column shows Nancy's age, 43. The next three columns are Income columns as indicated by the bracket above them labeled "Income." The "Take-Home Pay" column is her *after- tax* take-home pay. The 4% indicates that it is increasing at 4% per year. A 4% increase is factored in for inflation in this case study. Nancy's income just keeps up with inflation. If inflation were estimated at 5%, her income increase should be illustrated at 5%.

The next column is labeled "Child Support." Nancy will receive $11,600 per year in child support for 11 years until their 8-year-old son turns age 19. At that time child support will decrease to $7,500 per year until the 5-year-old is 19.

The next column is labeled "Maintenance Support" and has no dollar amounts in it. Ron does not want to pay any maintenance. Therefore, this scenario's financial result will be for both of them if no maintenance is paid.

The next four columns are under the bracket labeled "Expense." The first two columns ("Living Expenses" and "Real Estate Payments" together equal her living expenses. They are separated into two columns because the "Real Estate Payments" column represents the principal and interest (P&I) payment only. It is not affected by inflation. Taxes and insurance (T&I) are reflected in the "Living Expenses" column. If the P&I were included in the living expense column, that number, affected by inflation, would eventually become skewed. Therefore, the $35,676 above the line is her total yearly living expense which is a combination of the two numbers below the line, $29,014 plus $6,662 for 1996.

The "Other Expenses" column reflects any changes in Nancy's living expenses. It can be used to illustrate any expenses increasing or added (such as going back to school) and then decreasing (as when she finishes school.) It can be used to show debt being paid off, which will lower her living expenses. Nancy's scenario shows a negative $4,100 in the year 2007 and a negative $7,500 in the year 2010. These numbers represent the years after both sons turn age 19 and leave home. At that time, child support stops. The assumption is that Nancy no longer has the expenses associated with that child; so corresponding living expenses will be reduced by that amount.

TABLE 6-2

Nancy
Run No. 1

		<——INCOME		——>	<——	EXPENSE		——>	Annual	WORKING	Retirement	Fair Market	Real Estate	NET
		Take-Home Pay	Child Support	Maint Support	Living Expenses	Real Estate Payments	Other Expense	Taxes on Maint	Net Cash Flow	CAPITAL	Accounts	Value Real Estate	Mortgage	WORTH
													30	
Year	Age	4.0%	11	8	4.0%	30				5.0%	8.0%	4.0%	8.0%	
1999	43	13,500	11,600		35,676	555				5,000	172,975	100,000	75,000	
1999	43	$13,500	$11,600		$29,014	$6,662			($10,576)		$177,980	$104,000	$74,338	$207,642
2000	44	$14,040	$11,600		$30,175	$6,662			($11,197)		$173,651	$108,160	$73,623	$208,188
2001	45	$14,602	$11,600		$31,382	$6,662			($11,842)		$167,904	$112,486	$72,851	$207,540
2002	46	$15,186	$11,600		$32,637	$6,662			($12,513)		$160,585	$116,986	$72,017	$205,554
2003	47	$15,793	$11,600		$33,942	$6,662			($13,211)		$151,523	$121,665	$71,116	$202,072
2004	48	$16,425	$11,600		$35,300	$6,662			($13,937)		$140,531	$126,532	$70,143	$196,920
2005	49	$17,082	$11,600		$36,712	$6,662			($14,692)		$127,409	$131,593	$69,093	$189,909
2006	50	$17,765	$11,600		$38,180	$6,662			($15,477)		$111,934	$136,857	$67,958	$180,833
2007	51	$18,476	$11,600		$39,708	$6,662			($16,294)		$93,867	$142,331	$66,733	$169,466
2008	52	$19,215	$11,600		$41,296	$6,662			($17,143)		$72,946	$148,024	$65,409	$155,562
2009	53	$19,983	$11,600		$42,948	$6,662			($18,027)		$48,887	$153,945	$63,980	$138,853
2010	54	$20,783	$7,500		$40,566	$6,662	($4,100)		($18,945)		$21,380	$160,103	$62,436	$119,047
2011	55	$21,614	$7,500		$42,188	$6,662			($19,736)	($5,813)		$166,507	$60,769	$99,926
2012	56	$22,478	$7,500		$43,876	$6,662			($20,559)	($26,372)		$173,168	$58,968	$87,827
2013	57	$23,378			$38,131	$6,662	($7,500)		($21,415)	($47,788)		$180,094	$57,024	$75,283
2014	58	$24,313			$39,656	$6,662			($22,005)	($69,793)		$187,298	$54,924	$62,581
2015	59	$25,285			$41,242	$6,662			($22,619)	($92,412)		$194,790	$52,655	$49,722
2016	60	$26,297			$42,892	$6,662			($23,257)	($115,670)		$202,582	$50,206	$36,706
2017	61	$27,349			$44,608	$6,662			($23,921)	($139,591)		$210,685	$47,560	$23,533
2018	62	$28,442			$46,392	$6,662			($24,612)	($164,203)		$219,112	$44,703	$10,206
2019	63	$29,580			$48,248	$6,662			($25,330)	($189,533)		$227,877	$41,617	($3,273)

The column labeled "Taxes on Maintenance" has no dollar amounts in it. This scenario does not allow for maintenance.

The next column "Annual Net Cash Flow," shows whether there is positive or negative cash flow after netting the income columns with the expense columns. Nancy has a negative $10,576 in the first year; or her expenses exceed her income by $10,576.

The number from the "Annual Net Cash Flow" column is automatically subtracted from (or added to if it is a positive number) the next column, "Working Capital." Notice that Nancy's "Working Capital" column started out with $5,000, which was in Table 6-1's asset table. This is what remained from her CD after the down payment made on her house. This asset was depleted in the first year to help cover her negative cash flow.

The next column is labeled "Retirement Accounts" and is earning an average of 8% before tax. When the "Working Capital" column is exhausted, the "Retirement Accounts" column will automatically cover the negative cash flow *less taxes and penalties* if she is under the age of 60. After the age of 60, taxes are deducted. Notice that this depletes her "Retirement Accounts" column rather quickly.

Because she pays 28% federal tax, 5% state tax, and 10% penalty for early withdrawal, Nancy has to take out *43% more than she needs* to cover her negative cash flow. Judges and attorneys know this rule but they don't understand the real impact it has on the bottom line.

At age 54, Nancy's spendable assets have been depleted. She still owns the house, but she can't use the house to buy groceries.

The next column, "Fair Market Value Real Estate" and shows the value of the $100,000 home that Nancy just bought. The 4% represents the average increase in real estate in her part of her city over the past 10 years. The "Real Estate Mortgage" column carries the $75,000 mortgage on Nancy's home which she took out for 30 years at 8% interest.

The final column, "Net Worth," is a combination of "Working Capital" plus "Retirement Accounts" plus "Fair Market Value Real Estate" minus "Real Estate Mortgage." Figure 6-1 graphs net worth. But before discussion it, let's look at Ron's spreadsheet to see how this Scenario #1 affects him financially.

As Table 6-3 shows, Ron's take-home pay is $51,098 and is increasing at 4% per year, the same as Nancy's. The "Retire" column labeled (an income column) includes any monies he receives from his pension after he retires. Ron will start receiving $39,924 per year after retirement at age 65.

The next two columns, "Living Expenses" and "Real Estate Payments,"

TABLE 6-3

Ron

Run No. 1

Year	Age	<—INCOME—> Take-Home Pay	Retire 65	<—EXPENSES— Living Expenses	Real Estate Payments	Other Expense	Child Support	—> Maint Support	Annual Net Cash Flow	WORKING CAPITAL	Retirement Accounts	Fair Market Value Real Estate	Real Estate Mortgage 26	NET WORTH
		4.0%		4.0%	26					5.0%	8.0%	4.0%	10.3%	
1999	43	51,098	39,924	25,980	720					11,750	123,525	105,000	77,300	
1999	43	$51,098		$17,343	$8,637		$11,600		$13,518	$25,855	$133,407	$109,200	$76,625	$191,838
2000	44	$53,142		$18,037	$8,637		$11,600		$14,868	$42,016	$144,080	$113,568	$75,880	$223,784
2001	45	$55,268		$18,758	$8,637		$11,600		$16,272	$60,390	$155,606	$118,111	$75,059	$259,047
2002	46	$57,478		$19,509	$8,637		$11,600		$17,733	$81,142	$168,054	$122,835	$74,153	$297,879
2003	47	$59,777		$20,289	$8,637		$11,600		$19,252	$104,450	$181,499	$127,749	$73,153	$340,544
2004	48	$62,169		$21,100	$8,637		$11,600		$20,831	$130,504	$196,019	$132,858	$72,051	$387,330
2005	49	$64,655		$21,944	$8,637		$11,600		$22,474	$159,503	$211,700	$138,173	$70,835	$438,541
2006	50	$67,241		$22,822	$8,637		$11,600		$24,182	$191,660	$228,636	$143,700	$69,494	$494,502
2007	51	$69,931		$23,735	$8,637		$11,600		$25,959	$227,202	$246,927	$149,448	$68,015	$555,562
2008	52	$72,728		$24,684	$8,637		$11,600		$27,807	$266,369	$266,681	$155,426	$66,384	$622,092
2009	53	$75,638		$25,672	$8,637		$11,600		$29,729	$309,416	$288,016	$161,643	$64,584	$694,490
2010	54	$78,663		$26,699	$8,637		$7,500		$35,827	$360,714	$311,057	$168,108	$62,599	$777,280
2011	55	$81,810		$27,767	$8,637		$7,500		$37,906	$416,656	$335,942	$174,833	$60,410	$867,020
2012	56	$85,082		$28,877	$8,637		$7,500		$40,068	$477,556	$362,817	$181,826	$57,995	$964,204
2013	57	$88,485		$30,032	$8,637				$49,816	$551,250	$391,842	$189,099	$55,332	$1,076,859
2014	58	$92,025		$31,234	$8,637				$52,154	$630,966	$423,190	$196,663	$52,394	$1,198,425
2015	59	$95,706		$32,483	$8,637				$54,585	$717,100	$457,045	$204,530	$49,153	$1,329,521
2016	60	$99,534		$33,782	$8,637				$57,114	$810,069	$493,608	$212,711	$45,579	$1,470,809
2017	61	$103,515		$35,134	$8,637				$59,744	$910,317	$533,097	$221,219	$41,637	$1,622,996
2018	62	$107,656		$36,539	$8,637				$62,480	$1,018,312	$575,745	$230,068	$37,288	$1,786,837
2019	63	$111,962		$38,001	$8,637				$65,324	$1,134,552	$621,804	$239,271	$32,492	$1,963,135

include his total living expenses: $17,343 plus $8,637 equal $25,980. The "Child Support" column is the amount that he pays. The "Annual Net Cash Flow" column is a positive $13,518 in the first year. This is added to the "Working Capital" column and is shown earning an average of 5% per year after taxes.

The "Retirement Accounts" column shows $123,525 that he received (as shown in Table 6-1) earning an average of 8% per year before tax. The "Fair Market Value Real Estate" reflects the value of his $105,000 home increasing at 4% per year. The "Real Estate Mortgage" column shows that he has 26 years left to pay on his $77,300 mortgage at 10.3% interest. Ron's "Net Worth" column is a combination of "Working Capital" plus "Retirement Accounts" plus "Fair Market Value Real Estate" minus "Real Estate Mortgage."

Figure 6-1 graphs Ron and Nancy's Net Worth based on the previous assumptions. Why is the result of this divorce settlement so uneven when we divided the assets equally? The answer, again, comes down to the disparity in earning potential. In the early years of their marriage, they made the decision that Nancy would raise the children and not go back to work until the children were in school. Because of this, Nancy was out of the work force for several years. Her career didn't develop as Ron's did.

Let's go on to Scenario #1-A in Figure 6-2. It shows what many judges and attorneys think will happen. Again, they are aware of the rule about paying taxes and penalties when withdrawing retirement money before the age of 59-1/2, but they don't understand the full impact. They think that it will look like the chart represented in Figure 6-2.

Notice that the "Retirement Accounts" column earns at the rate of 8% and covers the negative cash flow. It is not reduced for taxes and penalties. The amount of money reflected in the retirement account lasts until she is about 65 years of age instead of being depleted at age 54. But this scenario is not accurate! The taxes and penalties must be taken into account.

What change can be made in Scenario #1 to make this a more equitable settlement? Look at the spreadsheet for Scenario #2 shown in Table 6-5. It shows the result of Nancy's receiving maintenance. In the "Maintenance Support" column, $1,250 per month ($15,000 per year) is included for five years. It is then reduced to $1,000 per month ($12,000 per year) for the last 5 years. The "Taxes on Maintenance" column reflects the taxes that she pays on this additional income. With the adjustment in maintenance payments, she has positive cash flow for five years which enables her "Working Capital" to grow slightly before she exhausts it at age 51. At that time, she can withdraw

TABLE 6-4

Nancy
Run No. 1-A

Year	Age	INCOME: Take-Home Pay	INCOME: Child Support	INCOME: Maint Support	EXPENSE: Living Expenses	EXPENSE: Real Estate Payments	EXPENSE: Other Expense	EXPENSE: Taxes on Maint	Annual Net Cash Flow	WORKING CAPITAL	Retirement Accounts	Fair Market Value Real Estate	Real Estate Mortgage	NET WORTH
		4.0%	11	8	4.0%	30				5.0%	8.0%	4.0%	30 8.0%	
1999	43	13,500	11,600		35,676	555				5,000	172,975	100,000	75,000	
1999	43	$13,500	$11,600		$29,014	$6,662			($10,576)		$181,237	$104,000	$74,338	$210,899
2000	44	$14,040	$11,600		$30,175	$6,662			($11,197)		$184,539	$108,160	$73,623	$219,076
2001	45	$14,602	$11,600		$31,382	$6,662			($11,842)		$187,460	$112,486	$72,851	$227,096
2002	46	$15,186	$11,600		$32,637	$6,662			($12,513)		$189,944	$116,986	$72,017	$234,913
2003	47	$15,793	$11,600		$33,942	$6,662			($13,211)		$191,929	$121,665	$71,116	$242,478
2004	48	$16,425	$11,600		$35,300	$6,662			($13,937)		$193,346	$126,532	$70,143	$249,735
2005	49	$17,082	$11,600		$36,712	$6,662			($14,692)		$194,122	$131,593	$69,093	$256,623
2006	50	$17,765	$11,600		$38,180	$6,662			($15,477)		$194,175	$136,857	$67,958	$263,074
2007	51	$18,476	$11,600		$39,708	$6,662			($16,294)		$193,415	$142,331	$66,733	$269,014
2008	52	$19,215	$11,600		$41,296	$6,662			($17,143)		$191,745	$148,024	$65,409	$274,360
2009	53	$19,983	$11,600		$42,948	$6,662			($18,027)		$189,058	$153,945	$63,980	$279,024
2010	54	$20,783	$7,500		$40,566	$6,662	($4,100)		($18,945)		$185,238	$160,103	$62,436	$282,905
2011	55	$21,614	$7,500		$42,188	$6,662			($19,736)		$180,321	$166,507	$60,769	$286,059
2012	56	$22,478	$7,500		$43,876	$6,662			($20,559)		$174,188	$173,168	$58,968	$288,387
2013	57	$23,378			$38,131	$6,662	($7,500)		($21,415)		$166,708	$180,094	$57,024	$289,779
2014	58	$24,313			$39,656	$6,662			($22,005)		$158,040	$187,298	$54,924	$290,415
2015	59	$25,285			$41,242	$6,662			($22,619)		$148,064	$194,790	$52,655	$290,199
2016	60	$26,297			$42,892	$6,662			($23,257)		$137,652	$202,582	$50,206	$290,028
2017	61	$27,349			$44,608	$6,662			($23,921)		$124,742	$210,685	$47,560	$287,867
2018	62	$28,442			$46,392	$6,662			($24,612)		$100,130	$219,112	$44,703	$274,539
2019	63	$29,580			$48,248	$6,662			($25,330)		$74,800	$227,877	$41,617	$261,060

FIGURE 6-2

NET WORTH
Ron and Nancy Scenario #1-A

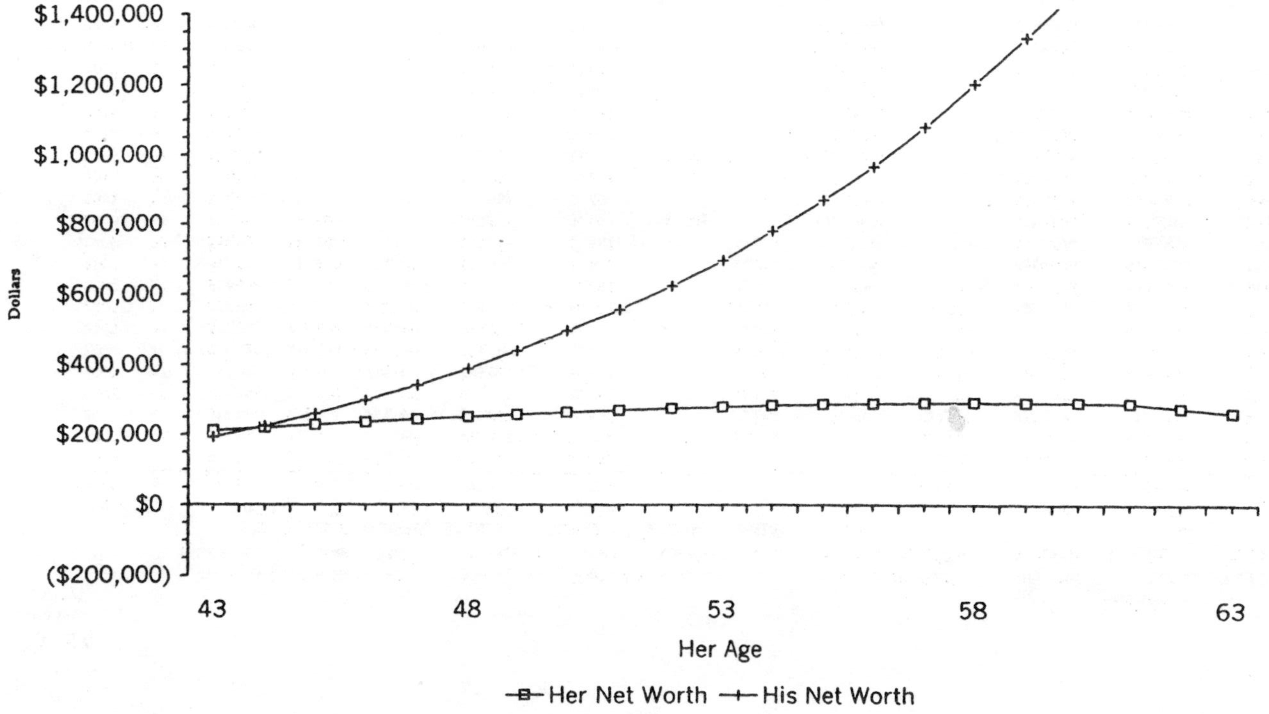

TABLE 6-5

Nancy
Run No. 2

		<——INCOME		——>	<——	EXPENSE		——>	Annual	WORKING	Retirement	Fair Market	Real Estate	NET
		Take-Home Pay	Child Support	Maint Support	Living Expenses	Real Estate Payments	Other Expense	Taxes on Maint	Net Cash Flow	CAPITAL	Accounts	Value Real Estate	Mortgage	WORTH
Year	Age	4.0%	11	5	4.0%	30				5.0%	8.0%	4.0%	30 8.0%	
1999	43	13,500	11,600	15,000	35,676	555				5,000	172,975	100,000	75,000	
1999	43	$13,500	$11,600	$15,000	$29,014	$6,662		$1,645	$2,779	$8,029	$186,813	$104,000	$74,338	$224,504
2000	44	$14,040	$11,600	$15,000	$30,175	$6,662		$1,645	$2,158	$10,589	$201,758	$108,160	$73,623	$246,884
2001	45	$14,602	$11,600	$15,000	$31,382	$6,662		$1,645	$1,513	$12,631	$217,899	$112,486	$72,851	$270,166
2002	46	$15,186	$11,600	$15,000	$32,637	$6,662		$1,645	$842	$14,105	$235,331	$116,986	$72,017	$294,404
2003	47	$15,793	$11,600	$15,000	$33,942	$6,662		$1,645	$144	$14,954	$254,157	$121,665	$71,116	$319,660
2004	48	$16,425	$11,600	$12,000	$35,300	$6,662		$1,045	($2,982)	$12,719	$274,490	$126,532	$70,143	$343,597
2005	49	$17,082	$11,600	$12,000	$36,712	$6,662		$1,045	($3,737)	$9,618	$296,449	$131,593	$69,093	$368,567
2006	50	$17,765	$11,600	$12,000	$38,180	$6,662		$1,045	($4,522)	$5,576	$320,165	$136,857	$67,958	$394,640
2007	51	$18,476	$11,600	$12,000	$39,708	$6,662		$1,045	($5,339)	$516	$345,778	$142,331	$66,733	$421,892
2008	52	$19,215	$11,600	$12,000	$41,296	$6,662		$1,045	($6,188)		$364,076	$148,024	$65,409	$446,691
2009	53	$19,983	$11,600		$42,948	$6,662		$1,045	($19,072)		$361,574	$153,945	$63,980	$451,540
2010	54	$20,783	$7,500		$40,566	$6,662	($4,100)		($18,945)		$359,082	$160,103	$62,436	$456,749
2011	55	$21,614	$7,500		$42,188	$6,662			($19,736)		$355,078	$166,507	$60,769	$460,817
2012	56	$22,478	$7,500		$43,876	$6,662			($20,559)		$349,389	$173,168	$58,968	$463,588
2013	57	$23,378			$38,131	$6,662	($7,500)		($21,415)		$341,826	$180,094	$57,024	$464,896
2014	58	$24,313			$39,656	$6,662			($22,005)		$332,678	$187,298	$54,924	$465,053
2015	59	$25,285			$41,242	$6,662			($22,619)		$321,781	$194,790	$52,655	$463,916
2016	60	$26,297			$42,892	$6,662			($23,257)		$312,811	$202,582	$50,206	$465,187
2017	61	$27,349			$44,608	$6,662			($23,921)		$302,133	$210,685	$47,560	$465,257
2018	62	$28,442			$46,392	$6,662			($24,612)		$289,570	$219,112	$44,703	$463,979
2019	63	$29,580			$48,248	$6,662			($25,330)		$274,930	$227,877	$41,617	$461,189

TABLE 6-6

Ron

Run No. 2

		<—INCOME—>		<———EXPENSES				———>				Fair Market		
		Take-Home	Retire	Living	Real Estate	Other	Child	Maint	Annual Net Cash	WORKING	Retirement	Value	Real Estate	NET
Year	Age	Pay	65	Expenses	Payments	Expense	Support	Support	Flow	CAPITAL	Accounts	Real Estate	Mortgage	WORTH
		4.0%		4.0%	26					5.0%	8.0%	4.0%	26 10.3%	
1999	43	51,098	39,924	25,980	720					11,750	123,525	105,000	77,300	
1999	43	$51,098		$17,343	$8,637		$11,600	$10,050	$3,468	$15,805	$133,407	$109,200	$76,625	$181,788
2000	44	$53,142		$18,037	$8,637		$11,600	$10,050	$4,818	$21,414	$144,080	$113,568	$75,880	$203,181
2001	45	$55,268		$18,758	$8,637		$11,600	$10,050	$6,222	$28,707	$155,606	$118,111	$75,059	$227,365
2002	46	$57,478		$19,509	$8,637		$11,600	$10,050	$7,683	$37,825	$168,054	$122,835	$74,153	$254,562
2003	47	$59,777		$20,289	$8,637		$11,600	$10,050	$9,202	$48,918	$181,499	$127,749	$73,153	$285,012
2004	48	$62,169		$21,100	$8,637		$11,600	$8,040	$12,791	$64,155	$196,019	$132,858	$72,051	$320,981
2005	49	$64,655		$21,944	$8,637		$11,600	$8,040	$14,434	$81,796	$211,700	$138,173	$70,835	$360,834
2006	50	$67,241		$22,822	$8,637		$11,600	$8,040	$16,142	$102,028	$228,636	$143,700	$69,494	$404,870
2007	51	$69,931		$23,735	$8,637		$11,600	$8,040	$17,919	$125,049	$246,927	$149,448	$68,015	$453,408
2008	52	$72,728		$24,684	$8,637		$11,600	$8,040	$19,767	$151,068	$266,681	$155,426	$66,384	$506,791
2009	53	$75,638		$25,672	$8,637		$11,600		$29,729	$188,350	$288,016	$161,643	$64,584	$573,424
2010	54	$78,663		$26,699	$8,637		$7,500		$35,827	$233,595	$311,057	$168,108	$62,599	$650,161
2011	55	$81,810		$27,767	$8,637		$7,500		$37,906	$283,180	$335,942	$174,833	$60,410	$733,544
2012	56	$85,082		$28,877	$8,637		$7,500		$40,068	$337,407	$362,817	$181,826	$57,995	$824,054
2013	57	$88,485		$30,032	$8,637				$49,816	$404,093	$391,842	$189,099	$55,332	$929,702
2014	58	$92,025		$31,234	$8,637				$52,154	$476,451	$423,190	$196,663	$52,394	$1,043,910
2015	59	$95,706		$32,483	$8,637				$54,585	$554,859	$457,045	$204,530	$49,153	$1,167,280
2016	60	$99,534		$33,782	$8,637				$57,114	$639,716	$493,608	$212,711	$45,579	$1,300,456
2017	61	$103,515		$35,134	$8,637				$59,744	$731,447	$533,097	$221,219	$41,637	$1,444,126
2018	62	$107,656		$36,539	$8,637				$62,480	$830,499	$575,745	$230,068	$37,288	$1,599,023
2019	63	$111,962		$38,001	$8,637				$65,324	$937,348	$621,804	$239,271	$32,492	$1,765,931

money from her "Retirement Account" column, but it has a higher value than before and is able to support her for a much longer time.

How does paying this maintenance affect Ron? Turn to Table 6-6, which is Ron's spreadsheet. Look at his "Maintenance Support" column. Since maintenance is deductible from Ron's taxable income, the numbers in this column reflect the *after-tax* cost to him of paying Nancy maintenance. Figure 6-3 graphs Scenario #2.

Paying maintenance to Nancy enables her to conserve retirement assets until she is nearly 70 years of age instead of depleting them by age 54. Ron's annual net cash flow isn't quite as large as when he paid no maintenance, but he is still able to increase his net worth at a healthy rate. The result shown in Scenario #2 is much more equitable than that shown in Scenario #1.

NOTES

1. Informational Guide on "QDROs" Under the IBM Retirement Plan, Prepared for Counsel in Domestic Relations Matters. June 1, 1991.

2. *Assigning Retirement Benefits in Divorce, A Practical Guide to Negotiating and Drafting QDROs*, by Gale S. Finley, pages 17-21, American Bar Association, 1995.

FIGURE 6-3

NET WORTH
Ron and Nancy Scenario #2

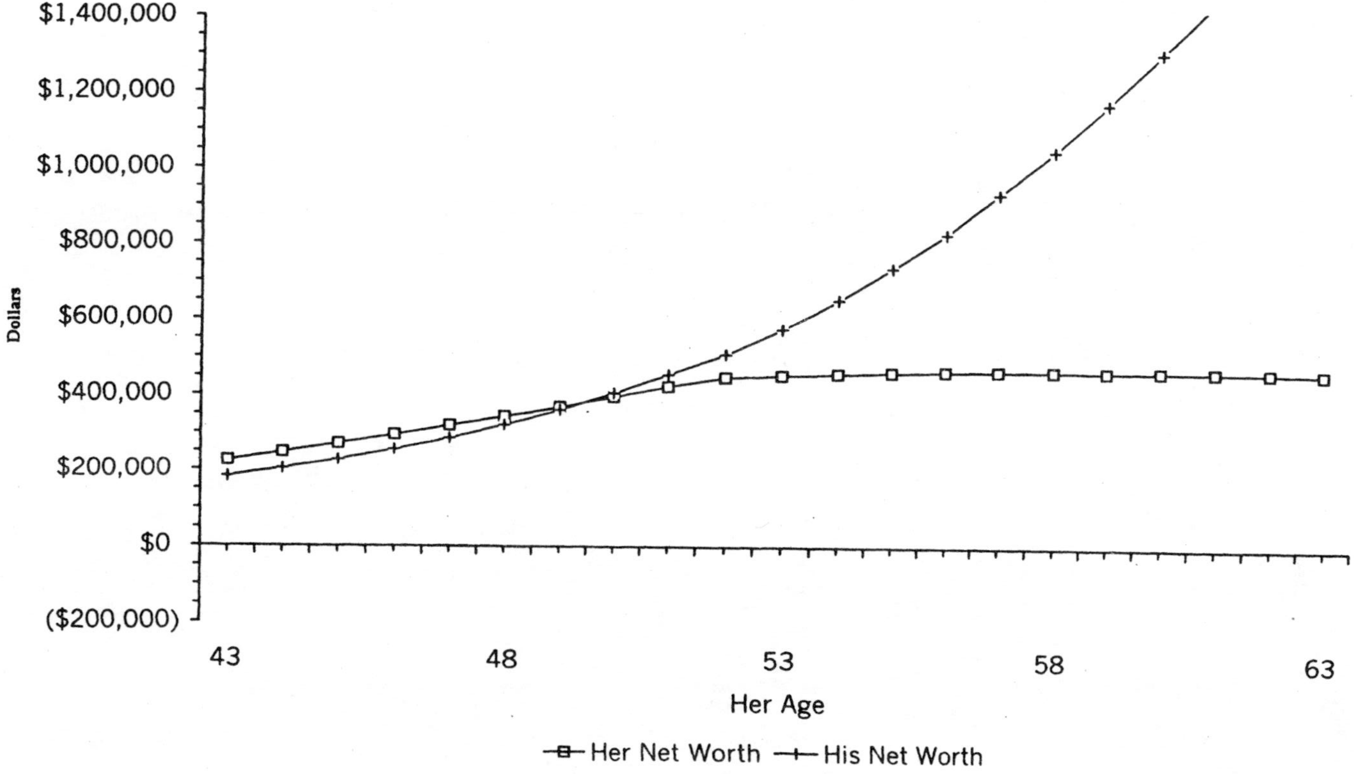

CHAPTER 7

The Financial Affidavit

THE IMPORTANCE OF THE FINANCIAL AFFIDAVIT

The Financial Affidavit is the backbone of each divorce case. It becomes part of the recorded documents that are filed with the court. It is a sworn statement and is notarized.

Included in the Affidavit are the following:

- All income and deductions from income
- All living expenses
- All debt
- All property

Almost every state has some kind of form that collects this information even though it may be called by another name. And even though they are sworn to be true, it is amazing how often they change. The client may keep re-working their expenses as they recall quarterly or yearly payments. Or they may change their mind about how much they will be spending on vacations, clothes, hobbies, and so on. And the changes always seem to entail an increase in expenses.

Gloria was getting divorced from a very highly paid executive. She had not filled out an affidavit when she came to my office for her first appointment. I asked how much she spent each month and she replied that she had no idea—she just wrote checks. I asked where the money came from. She said that her husband put the money into the checking account and she just wrote the checks. I then asked how much he put into the checking account and Gloria replied, "I don't know. I don't even know how much he earns. I just know that it's a lot. All I know is that I write checks for whatever I want and there is always enough in the account to cover it."

In Gloria's case, we went back through months of check registers and credit card statements to produce a spreadsheet of expenses. It was very time-consuming but necessary. You will come across hundreds of Gloria's in your practice. This chapter will guide you through the areas I have identified as essential in the reporting income and expenses by both husband and wife.

How to Find Errors

After having seen hundreds of these affidavits, I have come to some conclusions as to average spending habits and where the errors are most commonly made.

For an example of this, let's look at Sara and Bob's financial affidavits. We will be looking at a standard affidavit used in the state of Colorado. Sara and Bob have been married 12 years and they have one child. Figures 7-1 and 7-2 represent Sara's income and expense pages.

Sara's Income

There are numerous errors and adjustments on Sara's forms. On the Income page, note:

1. On line 3, Sara is paid $440 every other week. She thinks that by doubling each number, she will reflect monthly totals. In fact, she needs to multiply each number by 26, and divide by 12 to get her monthly figures. (Another way to do this is to multiply 880 by 13 and divide by 12.)
2. Line 4: her correct gross is **$953**, not $880.
3. Line 5: Again, Sara has doubled the $65 deduction on her paycheck. Multiply 65 by 13 and divide by 12. Her correct federal income tax should be **$70**.
4. Her correct Social Security is **$59**.

5. Her correct state income tax is **$23**.
6. Her correct Medicare is **$14.**
7. Her corrected Total Deductions are **$166**.
8. Line 6: Her corrected Net Income is **$787**.
9. Line 7: "Other sources of income" includes other jobs, retirement income, dividend income that is actually paid out, bonuses, etc.
10. Line 8: Deductions would include taxes from items in Line 7.

Sara's Expenses

Sara's expenses also needed adjustments. Included are:

11. Line 14 C: Groceries—Sometimes this amount may seem out of line with their standard of living so check these numbers carefully. Entertaining will push the average up, especially if liquor is served. Teenagers also keep the grocery bill on the high side. Women usually have higher grocery bills than men.
12. Line 14 C: Restaurant Meals—Businessmen tend to spend more than homemakers on eating out because of business lunches, etc.
13. Line 14 D: Medical and dental—If medical costs are reimbursed by the insurance company, most tend to forget how much is received. These categories are for unreimbursed expenses only!
14. Line 14 D(4): "Other" in 90% of the cases is for therapy. It seems that everyone going through divorce is in therapy!
15. Line 14 E: Under Health Insurance, a lot of mistakes are made. Typically, the wife puts zero, because she is not paying an insurance payment. Or she will say, "Well, I am going to get COBRA, but I do not know how much it is." You or she can call the benefits department of the husband's company and ask how much the COBRA payment is. If Sara decides to be insured by COBRA instead of obtaining her health insurance on her own, she will need to make this payment, so it should be added to her Financial Affidavit. She must not skip a payment or COBRA can drop her and they do not need to re-instate her.
16. Line 14 F: Transportation. What if her car is paid for and she shows no payment? Talk to the attorney on the case and think about entering an estimated payment for a future car. (This is especially applicable when the car is 10 or more years old.)

Maintenance includes tires, license plates, oil changes, repairs, etc. There is always discussion about whether the expenses should be reduced when the car is paid off in a few years. We think that people typically buy a new car when the old one is paid off, so it makes sense to keep the car payment in the expenses.

17. Line 14 G: Clothing. Her Clothing costs are on the low side for herself and her teenage son.
18. Line 14 L: Miscellaneous. Some large expenses fall in Miscellaneous. They include:

    - gifts (Ask what they spend per year on Christmas, birthdays, weddings and divide that by 12)
    - donations
    - magazines, books, newspapers
    - cable TV
    - pets
    - hobbies
    - personal care such as haircuts, manicures, lawn service
    - miscellaneous

19. Line 15: Debts. Under Debts, do not put the house mortgage or car loan here. They have already been included in the Housing (A) and Transportation (F) sections. This section is used for credit cards, other bank loans, lines of credit, or anything that they owe anybody else. Be sure to check for doubled up expenses in this area.

Bob's Income

Now turn to Bob's income page. He earned a gross income of $7,667 per month.

1. Line 5: Monthly payroll deductions. His Social Security deduction of $475 is an obvious error because he is in a high tax bracket. His Social Security is taken out at the front of the year so he is putting down that whole payment and he is not averaging it over the year. The average deduction would be **$375**. This is his

FICA at 6.2% of the tax base of $72,600. It has been corrected, increasing his cash flow by $100 per month.

2. Line 5: It might be good idea to recalculate his income taxes. He has $2,062 for federal tax when it should be **$1,760** and he has $392 for state tax when it should be **$354**. Another $340 has been found. We sometimes see federal taxes increase on a husband's affidavit when he knows he will be divorced by the next April. By that time, a refund is claimed.
3. Line 5: Credit Union. Always ask the question, "What is this for?" In this case, Bob was saving $200 per month in his credit union. His car payment was $250, he had obtained the loan through the credit union. But if you check Figure 7-4 under F—Transportation, you will notice the same $250 under Vehicle Payment. Bob is double entering his car payment. The entire $450 payment comes back into additional cash flow.
4. Line 5: 401(k). Same with the 401(k). The court allows you to put voluntary contributions to retirement plans back into cash flow. The reasoning is that the family needs the money before the savings account does.
5. Line 5: Total deductions from this employment. Corrected total deductions are $2,600.
6. Line 6, Net Monthly Take Home Pay from primary employer. Corrected net take-home pay is $5,067.

Bob's Expenses

7. Line 14 A: Housing. In this case, Bob has moved out and is renting a room from a friend at a low rate. This is not likely to continue and this expense can be expected to go up.
8. Line 14 C: Food. His expense for food is lower than eating out which is typical for a husband. If you find his grocery expense at $400 to $500 per month for one person, ask if he cooks a lot or entertains a lot. If the answer is "no," he is probably padding his expenses.
9. Line 14 K: Recreation. Bob's recreation is higher because he is dating again, which is expensive.
10. Line 15 Debts: Notice that Bob has the same Citibank Visa debt as Sara. This is common because at this point, they don't know which of them will take the debt. It will either be divided or it

FIGURE 7-1

FINANCIAL AFFIDAVIT

Name *Sara Anderson*

1. Occupation ______

2. Primary Employer's name ______
   Hours worked per week ______

3. I am paid ☐ weekly ☐ (every other week ☐ twice each month ☐ (monthly
   Amount of each check (gross) 440

4. Month gross income ~~880~~ 953

5. Monthly payroll deductions
   (Number of exemptions being claimed: ____)
   Federal Income Tax ~~65~~ 70
   Social Security ~~55~~ 59
   Colorado tax ~~21~~ 23
   Medicare ~~13~~ 14
   State Income Tax ______
   Health Insurance Premium ______
   Life Insurance Premium ______
   Dental Insurance Premium ______
   401(k) ______
   Total deductions from this employment ~~154~~ 166

6. Net Monthly Take Home Pay from primary employer ~~726~~ 787

7. Other Sources and Amounts of Income

SOURCE	AMOUNT
______	______
______	______

8. Deductions from Other Income Sources Listed in Part 7

DEDUCTIONS	AMOUNT
______	______
______	______

9. Net Monthly Income from Other Sources ______

10. NET MONTHLY INCOME from ALL sources ______

11. Net Monthly Income of Children ______

12. Income Reported on Last Federal Return ______

13. Monthly Gross Income of Other Party ______
    Monthly Net Income of Other Party ______

14. MONTHLY EXPENSES for 1 adult and 1 children:

A. HOUSING

Rent/first mortgage	360	
Second Mortgage		
Homeowners Fee		
TOTAL HOUSING		360

B. UTILITIES

Gas and Electric	100	
Telephone	50	
Water and Sewer		
Trash Collection		
TOTAL UTILITIES		150

C. FOOD

Grocery Store Items	400	
Restaurant Meals	75	
TOTAL FOOD		475

D. MEDICAL (after insurance)

Doctor	25	
Dentist	30	
Prescriptions	20	
Other		
TOTAL MEDICAL		75

E. INSURANCE

Life Insurance	50	
Health Insurance	175	
Homeowners	25	
TOTAL INSURANCE		250

F. TRANSPORTATION

Payment	200	
Fuel	50	
Repair & Maintenance	65	
Insurance	50	
Parking		
TOTAL TRANSPORTATION		365

G. CLOTHING — TOTAL CLOTHING 150

H. LAUNDRY — TOTAL LAUNDRY ______

I. CHILD CARE (and related)

Child care		
Allowance		
TOTAL CHILD CARE		

J. EDUCATION (and related)

For children

School costs ______

Lunches ______

For spouse

Tuition, books and fees ______

TOTAL EDUCATION ______

K RECREATION

TOTAL RECREATION 250

L. MISCELLANEOUS

TOTAL MISCELLANEOUS 325

M. TOTAL REQUIRED MONTHLY EXPENSES 2,400

15. DEBTS

	Creditor	Unpaid Balance	Monthly Payment
A.	*Citibank Visa*	$ 2,650	$ 80
B.		$	$
C.		$	$
D.		$	$
E.		$	$
G.	TOTAL MONTHY DEBT PAYMENT(S)		$

I. TOTAL MONTHLY EXPENSES PLUS DEBTS $ 2,480

FIGURE 7-2

FINANCIAL AFFIDAVIT

Name *Bob Anderson* ________________________________

1. Occupation ________________________________
2. Primary Employer's name ________________________________
   Hours worked per week ________________________________
3. I am paid ☐ weekly ☐ (every other week ☐ twice each month ☐ (monthly
   Amount of each check (gross) ________________________________
4. Month gross income ________________________________ $7,667
5. Monthly payroll deductions
   (Number of exemptions being claimed: ____)
   Federal Income Tax ________ ~~$2,062~~ 1760
   Social Security ________ ~~475~~ 375
   Colorado tax ________ ~~392~~ 354
   Medicare ________ 111
   State Income Tax ________
   Health Insurance Premium ________
   Life Insurance Premium ________
   Credit Union ________ ~~450~~ 0
   401(k) ________ ~~400~~ 0
   Total deductions from this employment ________ ~~3991~~ 2600
6. Net Monthly Take Home Pay from primary employer ________ ~~3676~~ 5067
7. Other Sources and Amounts of Income

SOURCE	AMOUNT
________	________
________	________

8. Deductions from Other Income Sources Listed in Part 7

DEDUCTIONS	AMOUNT
________	________
________	________

9. Net Monthly Income from Other Sources ________________________________
10. NET MONTHLY INCOME from ALL sources ________________________________
11. Net Monthly Income of Children ________________________________
12. Income Reported on Last Federal Return ________________________________
13. Monthly Gross Income of Other Party ________________________________
    Monthly Net Income of Other Party ________________________________

14. MONTHLY EXPENSES for __1__ adult and __0__ children:

A. HOUSING

Rent/first mortgage __500__
Second Mortgage ______
Homeowners Fee ______
TOTAL HOUSING __500__

B. UTILITIES

Gas and Electric __100__
Telephone __50__
Water and Sewer ______
Trash Collection ______
TOTAL UTILITIES __150__

C. FOOD

Grocery Store Items __175__
Restaurant Meals __220__
TOTAL FOOD __395__

D. MEDICAL (after insurance)

Doctor ______
Dentist __30__
Prescriptions ______
Other ______
TOTAL MEDICAL __30__

E. INSURANCE

Life Insurance __80__
Health Insurance ______
Homeowners __25__
TOTAL INSURANCE __105__

F. TRANSPORTATION

Payment __250__
Fuel __75__
Repair & Maintenance __100__
Insurance __80__
Parking ______
TOTAL TRANSPORTATION __505__

G. CLOTHING TOTAL CLOTHING __75__

H. LAUNDRY TOTAL LAUNDRY ______

I. CHILD CARE (and related)

Child care______
Allowance______
TOTAL CHILD CARE ______

J. EDUCATION (and related)

For children

School costs ____________

Lunches ____________

For spouse

Tuition, books and fees ______

TOTAL EDUCATION ____

K RECREATION

TOTAL RECREATION 370

L. MISCELLANEOUS

TOTAL MISCELLANEOUS 300

M. TOTAL REQUIRED MONTHLY EXPENSES 2,430

15. DEBTS

	Creditor	Unpaid Balance	Monthly Payment
A.	*Citibank Visa*	$ 2,650	$ 80
B.		$	$
C.		$	$
D.		$	$
E.		$	$
G.	TOTAL MONTHY DEBT PAYMENT(S)		$

I. TOTAL MONTHLY EXPENSES PLUS DEBTS $ 2,510

will be given to one of them to pay off, in which case it would be deducted from the other's expenses.

In this case, both of their affidavits are correct even though they each list the debt. They are correctly stating the debt that is asked for on the financial affidavit. The CDP, however, will probably assign the debt to one or the other so it is not being doubled in the final analysis.

As you saw by reviewing Sara and Bob's affidavits, it is important to know exactly how much the clients are spending and what their spending patterns are. Otherwise it is impossible to determine what their needs are and how to best meet those needs.

WORKING WITH THE CLIENT

Working with the client is sometimes necessary to produce an accurate Financial Affidavit and eliminate many of the errors you saw in the Financial Affidavits for Bob and Sara. In the case of an uninvolved, uninformed spouse such as Gloria, you may have to look at checking account records and charge account statements for at least three months and create a spreadsheet of actual expenses. This can be tedious but it may also be necessary.

Case Study of Kim and Ted

Kim and Ted had been married for 18 years and had four children. Ted was a corporate executive who earned $561,860 per year with take-home pay of $301,800. Kim had never worked outside the home. She raised the children and made sure they had the best of everything, including lessons in many skills. She also did a lot of volunteer work, and, she took care of the family home.

Their assets were as follows:

Home (free and clear)	$1,400,900
Retirement funds	528,340
Cash assets	448,000
Interest in 27 companies	1,625,340
TOTAL	$4,002,580

Kim wants half the assets, or $2,000,000, which would include the house, which is paid off. It is a huge mansion with hidden staircases and other hideaways, which makes it a wonderful place for children to live and entertain their friends. Other than the house, Kim wants the remainder ($600,000) in cash to invest for income.

Kim was accustomed to a life style that showed they spent more than $250,000 per year. Her Financial Affidavit showed her monthly expenses were $17,140 per month or $205,700 per year. She didn't work and was asking for $18,000 per month alimony to cover her expenses and some of the taxes on her alimony.

Her husband was livid and insisted she could live very nicely on $5,000 per month plus child support of $2,400 per month and that was all he was willing to offer. "After all," he said, "that's way above what the average American lives on and she'll do just fine. And with investing her cash wisely, she'll have more than enough to live on." He said her Financial Affidavit was grossly inflated.

Part of Ted's concern was the fact that he was giving Kim all the current cash assets and then borrowing from his 401k to give her the $600,000 cash she is requesting. Many of his companies were start-up companies and their future was very precarious. He did not have the assurance that they would continue to do well for him. He was ending up with no cash assets, a reduced 401k, and illiquid assets. This position made him very nervous and even though he was very concerned about his children, he felt he was making all the concessions in the financial arena.

In Kim's case, because you can show previous life style and his high earning ability, she very well may be entitled to receive high maintenance. But let's look at her expenses and the "reasonableness" of them.

Kim's Expenses (see Figure 7-3)

1. Line A 3: The Maintenance Fee is actually the taxes and insurance on the house.
2. Line C 1: Food for Kim and four children seems very high. She says the children constantly have friends over who stay for meals and overnights.
3. Line D 1: The doctor bills are high. Kim takes the kids to the doctor excessively.
4. Line F 1: The cars are paid off.
5. Line G: Kim buys the children all the latest fashions.
6. Line I: Even though Kim doesn't work, she needs child care while she is at the country club, or doing volunteer work, and she even hires extra help with the children while she is home.

7. Line L: The children take lessons of many varieties.
8. Line M: The miscellaneous is more than the average family spends in a month. Always find out what is included in miscellaneous. It is necessary to know what it is spent on to be able to do effective budget counseling. (See an attached listing for Recreation and Miscellaneous following Kim's Financial Affidavit.)

RECREATION SCHEDULE (LINE L)

Outings	$290
Country clubs	185
Brownies	18
Video rentals	92
Swim lessons	45
Karate lessons	28
Piano lessons	145
Tennis lessons	58
Skiing	162
Camp	362
TOTAL	1,385

MISCELLANEOUS SCHEDULE (LINE M)

Handyman/yardwork/snow removal/landscaping	$ 910
Home repairs/carpet cleaning	690
Security system	95
Travel	1,200
Gifts/entertaining	415
Subscriptions/books	128
Haircuts	100
Children's allowances	145
Charities/donations	155
Pets	165
Home/decorating/furniture	720
TOTAL	$4,723

As time went on, it became apparent that Ted was not going to budge. His position was that the investment of her part of the marital property would earn about $4,000 per month. And cutting her expenses would show a need for no more than an additional $5,000 per month, which is what he was offering for alimony.

In an effort to help this couple reach a settlement and to also help Kim look at life a little more reasonably, our first suggestion was that she sell the house. This would reduce the high upkeep expenses. There was a house on

FIGURE 7-3

FINANCIAL AFFIDAVIT

14. MONTHLY EXPENSES for 1 adult and 4 children:

A. HOUSING

Rent/first mortgage		
Second Mortgage		
Homeowners Fee		
	TOTAL HOUSING	938

B. UTILITIES

Gas and Electric	480	
Telephone	280	
Water and Sewer	140	
Trash Collection	35	
	TOTAL UTILITIES	935

C. FOOD

Grocery Store Items	2360	
Restaurant Meals	400	
	TOTAL FOOD	2760

D. MEDICAL (after insurance)

Doctor	1065	
Dentist	160	
Prescriptions	40	
Other		
	TOTAL MEDICAL	1265

E. INSURANCE

Life Insurance	50	
Health Insurance	250	
Homeowners	320	
	TOTAL INSURANCE	620

F. TRANSPORTATION

Payment		
Fuel	145	
Repair & Maintenance	285	
Insurance	176	
Parking		
	TOTAL TRANSPORTATION	606

G. CLOTHING	TOTAL CLOTHING	1155
H. LAUNDRY	TOTAL LAUNDRY	50

I. CHILD CARE (and related)

Child care__________

Allowance__________

TOTAL CHILD CARE ____2190____

J. EDUCATION (and related)

For children

School costs ____80____

Lunches __________

For spouse

Tuition, books and fees ______

TOTAL EDUCATION ____80

K RECREATION (See attached list)

TOTAL RECREATION ____1385

L. MISCELLANEOUS (See attached list)

TOTAL MISCELLANEOUS ____4723

M. TOTAL REQUIRED MONTHLY EXPENSES 16,707

15. DEBTS

	Creditor	Unpaid Balance	Monthly Payment
A.	__________	$__________	$______
B.	__________	$__________	$______
C.	__________	$__________	$______
D.	__________	$__________	$______
E.	__________	$__________	$______
G.	TOTAL MONTHY DEBT PAYMENT(S)		$______

I. TOTAL MONTHLY EXPENSES PLUS DEBTS $______

the market for $480,000 that seemed to meet her needs. Her first reaction was, "Oh, I couldn't *do* that to my children!" But later, she saw the sense in the decision.

We also looked at cutting her expenses in several other ways and actually got her monthly expenses (with a new house) down to $9,940. With $5,000 alimony, $2,400 child support, and $4,000 investment income, we were getting close to settlement. And hopefully, with good financial counseling after the divorce is over, she would not need all the investment income to spend, but rather could allow it to reinvest and grow for her future retirement.

Case Study of Cathy and Michael

Tax Calculations

Cathy has hired you to look at the financial issues in her divorce. She has been separated from her husband, Michael for 2½ years. Michael, has shared his Financial Affidavit which shows the following information:

Michael earns $180,000 per year or $15,000 per month

His July 1999 Financial Affidavit shows the following:

Monthly gross income	15,000
Deductions	
Federal tax	4,162
Colorado tax	712
FICA	930
Medicare	218
401(k)	2,250
Total deductions	8,272
Net take home pay	6,728
	x 12
Yearly net pay	80,736

It's important to check for accuracy. Start by looking at the 1999 tax return for deductions from his taxable income.

Michael owns a house with a monthly payment of $2,200 per month (PITI).

We look at *Schedule A – Itemized Deductions*, 1999 tax return to see his itemized deductions which shows:

$ 7,600	State and local taxes
$ 4,200	Real estate taxes
$21,600	Interest paid on home mortgage
$ 6,000	Gifts to charity
$39,400	Total itemized deductions

We subtract the Total itemized deductions from his Gross pay to get his Taxable Income:

180,000	Gross pay
-39,400	Total itemized deductions
140,600	Taxable income

Remember that the Social Security FICA tax of 6.2% is only taxed on the first $72,600 earned in the year 1999. Michael's pay stub was correct, but as soon as he reached $72,600 in earnings, the FICA withholding stops. Therefore, we need to average the FICA withholding over the whole year. The Medicare deduction of 1.45% has no limit and his entire earnings are taxed at that rate.

We now apply the 1999 tax table for a Single person:

38,882	federal tax	3,240	per month
7,030	Colorado tax	586	per month
4,501	FICA	375	per month
2,610	Medicare	218	per month
53,023	Total deductions	4,419	per month

180,000	15,000
-53,023	-4,419
126,977 per year take home	**10,581 per month**

You will notice we did not allow Michael's contribution to his 401(k) as a deduction. The courts allow us to pull that back into cash flow. Their reasoning is that the needs of the family come before contributions to retirement.

There is another problem with Michael's contribution to his 401(k). The maximum amount that he can contribute is $10,000 per year no matter how much he earns. His employer can contribute more but Michael's portion is limited to $833 per month or $10,000 per year. He may have put the higher amount on his Financial Affidavit because he was investing the remainder of the $2,250 in his own investments. You may not see this very often but you should be aware of the limitations.

Chapter 15 (Forms and Information Needed) has a more complete sample of a financial affidavit which will be helpful to you in gathering information.

CHAPTER 8

Maintenance (Alimony)

After dividing property, we then look at maintenance. We need to look at the division of property first because, as you will see later in this section, the amount of property awarded will impact the need for and the amount of maintenance.

For all practical purposes, alimony and maintenance mean the same thing. Both words are used interchangeably. Simply put, alimony is a series of payments from one spouse to the other, or to a third party on behalf of the receiving spouse. In most cases, the wife is the recipient; in some the husband receives it. Alimony is taxable income to the person who receives it and, it is tax-deductible by the person who pays it.

Alimony can be very important for the non-working spouse. Sometimes in a long-term marriage (in some states, more than 10 years), either the wife has not worked outside the home or she has stayed home with the children until they are in school or left home. Both of these positions limit her ability to build a career. She and her husband may have decided as a couple that she would be responsible for running the household and/or caring for the children.

In most cases, if she did hold a job, her income was usually less than her husband's—sometimes, substantially lower. If a transfer or move were indicated, the decision would be based on his job and career. If they moved, she would usually have to quit her job and start over somewhere else.

Career decisions and divorce can negatively affect the husband, as well. If the wife's career is more lucrative, the husband may have refused a job transfer so that his wife could pursue her career. He is stuck in a dead-end position that he can't leave without jeopardizing his pension.

When you are "fired" from the job of husband or wife, no one offers you an unemployment check. Is it any wonder, then, that alimony often becomes a major battleground in divorce?

Deciding whether a spouse should receive alimony (and, if so, how much) is based on certain criteria. Some state statutes give detailed criteria. In addition, the spouse might be awarded rehabilitative maintenance, or the terms might state the payments be modifiable or non-modifiable. Of course, as with any source of income, there are tax laws you need to be aware of, including front loading of maintenance options, life insurance treatments, and exceptions to recapture rules.

CRITERIA FOR RECEIVING MAINTENANCE

It used to be that "fault" determined alimony. Today while fault may still be a factor in some states, alimony is based on many criteria. Among the most typical are:

- need
- ability to pay
- length of marriage
- previous lifestyle
- age and health of both parties.

1. Need

The criterion of need asks the basic question, "Does the recipient have enough money to live on?" This would include income from earning ability, earnings from property received in the property division, and earnings from separate property. Alimony may be necessary to prevent the wife (and sometimes the husband) from becoming dependent upon welfare.

Minor children are also considered when evaluating need. Although child support is a separate issue, the mother (if she is the custodial parent) must be able to care adequately for the children. That means a roof over the kid's head, utilities to heat, light and provide water in their home.

Even though a spouse may think an alimony award is needed, the court sometimes finds otherwise. Take this example. Sophia wanted maintenance from her husband. However, she had a trust set aside that was separate property, and in that trust was over $1 million dollars. The court deemed that she did not need maintenance because she had property that would provide income to her.

After you have established need, how do you determine the amount? That's not so easy. A case study was given to judges at a conference to see what variability there would be in their opinions. The case involved a short-term marriage between two lawyers and the situation where the wife had developed multiple sclerosis and was in serious condition. The judge's opinions ranged from "No maintenance as it was a short term marriage" to "Lifetime maintenance because of her health situation" and all points in between.

If we look at the following simplistic formula, we will see that there can be many problems.

Husband's income	Wife's expenses
<u>-expenses</u>	<u>- income</u>
Ability to pay	Need

It is easy to say that somewhere in between his ability to pay and her need is the amount of maintenance to be paid, but questions arise about their true incomes and expenses. It's not as easy as it seems.

2. Ability to pay

The criterion of ability to pay takes into account whether the payor can afford to pay what is needed and still have enough to live on or to support a lifestyle roughly equivalent to his or her previous lifestyle.

An angry wife may say, "I want $6,000 a month," which is his entire salary. The wife is acting out of anger, which is not unusual. It is your responsibility to get her to be more reasonable and realistic.

And what about all the cases where we see his commissions and bonuses dry up when it is time to get divorced? We know that divorce causes an extreme amount of stress. And after the divorce is final, his income goes back up. In this situation income may be imputed to the husband when calculating the amount of maintenance.

For instance, there was the famous Boulder, CO case where the high earner husband decided to quit his job and go into the mountains to grow mushrooms. (We don't have the details on what kind of mushrooms!) The husband claimed he no longer had the income to pay high maintenance. The judge ruled that the husband had the income producing capacity and therefore the husband could grow mushrooms if he wished, but he would have to figure out how to pay the maintenance that the court awarded the wife.

3. Length of marriage

A two-year marriage may not qualify for permanent alimony but a 25-year marriage probably would. However, this depends on all the economic factors in the divorce and the property division.

Duration of maintenance or the length of time it should be paid is always a consideration. Alimony can be of limited duration (for a certain number of years) or open-ended (continues until it is modified or terminated). A 20-year marriage which began when she was 18 and ended when she was 38 may not indicate long-term maintenance. But a 20 year marriage that started at age 40 and she is now age 60 may well indicate long-term maintenance. A rule of thumb that is often used is that alimony may be awarded for half the number of years married. However this rule of thumb can be far from the right answer depending on other factors.

- Some rules to remember about duration:
- Maintenance stops upon the death of either party
- Maintenance usually ends upon the remarriage of the recipient
- Maintenance continues until it is modified (unless the amount and/or duration is non-modifiable)

4. Previous lifestyle

Previous lifestyle is a criterion that takes into account how the spouses are accustomed to living. In a 23-year marriage where the husband earns over $500,000 per year, he probably won't be able to justify that his wife only needs $50,000 per year in alimony. In contrast, neither member of a young couple who didn't earn much money should not expect to become wealthy as a result of the divorce.

5. Age and health of both parties

The age and health of both parties is the final criteria when deciding maintenance.

- Is he or she disabled?
- Is he already retired? If so, does he have guaranteed permanent income?
- If she is 50 years old and has never worked, it will be very difficult for her to find employment. She may need open-ended maintenance.
- If she is in poor mental and/or physical health, she may not be able to find adequate employment.

REHABILITATIVE MAINTENANCE

In the 70s, courts began to recognize the need for a transition period. It was unrealistic to expect or assume that the wife (or husband when the wife was the breadwinner) could instantly earn what her husband did, if ever. With that awakening, rehabilitative maintenance was born.

If the wife, for example, needs three years of school to finish her degree or time to update old skills, she may get *rehabilitative maintenance*. This will give her the temporary financial help in the interim that she needs until she is able to earn an amount sufficient enough to support herself.

In discussing rehabilitative maintenance, it's important to be realistic on you and your client's parts. Why? Sometimes a normal three-year degree becomes impossible while caring for three kids. Realistically, five years may be more in line. It shouldn't be viewed as an entitlement—to be stretched until every drop is taken. Rather, a bridge from one "career" to the next.

Finally, depending on all other factors, particularly her age and the duration of the marriage, paying alimony just for a rehabilitative period may not be the right result.

MODIFICATION OF MAINTENANCE

The one constant in life is change. Given that, it doesn't make much sense to assume that the final alimony settlement decided in court will apply to all future scenarios. Property is almost always final. Alimony is usually modifiable. For example, one spouse may become unemployed; the other may become ill. Change can be positive too. One of the spouses may land a job that creates lucrative stock options and incentives; one could inherit a substantial sum of money, win a lawsuit or even win the lottery. This type of windfall could lead to a decrease in maintenance.

To allow some flexibility to accommodate these potential changes, the court where the divorce is granted often maintains "jurisdiction" over the case. This allows any order of support to be modified when a change of circumstances makes it reasonable to do so.

These changes in circumstances include increases or decreases in the income or expenses of either or both spouses, especially when such changes were outside the control of the individual.

What if the ex-wife gets a roommate who pays all the expenses? The husband's attorney could use this as a fact to reduce his current alimony payment. Some states presume that when a spouse who receives maintenance moves in with another person, he or she needs less monetary support.

After the divorce is final and a modifiable order of support is entered, either spouse can go back into court and ask for a modification, either up or down. However, you and your client need to be aware that the judge may deny the request for modification, either up or down (unless it was stipulated to be non-modifiable).

However, you need to be aware that the judge may deny the request for modification. Not only that, but he or she may even rule in the opposite direction! So, before you go back to court to ask for a modification, be sure to examine the position and the soundness of the evidence.

Non-modifiable maintenance is not used very often because it is a challenge to both sides but there are certain advantages to it in some cases. Let's say that the divorce decree says that he is going to pay six years of maintenance non-modifiable. This means that even if she gets married in two years (provided that the order says the obligation survives remarriage), she still gets four more years of maintenance. While this appears to be a great deal for the recipient, it can work against her. What if she becomes disabled or otherwise needs more income? She cannot get more. At six years, all payments stop. Legally, she has no way to continue the maintenance income.

Many times, after maintenance is set up, the husband retires early. He won't want to pay maintenance anymore. To change the original orders, he'll have to go back to court and have them changed by a new court order. This means money is spent—both parties will have to hire attorneys to get it changed. Even if they both agree, they have to draw up a new agreement. They each should be represented by an attorney.

Sometimes the parties can't settle and the case will end up in court. Rarely does the wife want to reduce the maintenance amount. Or perhaps he wants to drop it totally, while she is receptive to some decrease, but not a decrease to zero. If they cannot agree on what number should be used, they end up in front of a judge.

For the above reasons, many payers of maintenance prefer the term to be non-modifiable. They know there will be a predetermined end to the stream of payments. It makes it easier for them to accept than to worry about the uncertainty of when closure will take place. However, depending on the facts of the case and the law, the recipient may only agree to this if there is a disproportionate division of property.

TAX ISSUES OF MAINTENANCE

To be considered maintenance, the payments must meet all of the following requirements:

1. All payments must be made in cash, check or money order
2. There must be a written court order or separation agreement
3. The couple may not agree that the payments are not to receive alimony tax treatment
4. They may not be residing in the same household
5. The payments must terminate upon the payor's death
6. They may not file a joint tax return
7. No portion may be considered child support.

Let's look at each requirement in more detail:

1. In order to qualify as alimony, payments made from one spouse to the other must be made in cash or the equivalent of cash. Transfers of services or property do not qualify as alimony.

a. It is possible for payments made to a third party on behalf of his or her spouse to qualify as alimony.

Under the terms of their divorce decree, Stanley is required to pay his ex-wife, Marilyn, $5,000 per year for the next five years. Six months after the decree is entered, Marilyn decides to return to school to qualify for a better paying job. She calls Stanley and asks him to pay her $5,000 tuition instead of sending her the monthly alimony checks. Stanley agrees and on September 4, 1994, pays $2,500 for Marilyn's first semester tuition. For Stanley to deduct this payment as alimony, he must obtain a written statement from Marilyn indicating that they agreed that his payment of the tuition was alimony. This written statement must be received before Stanley files his original (not an amended) income tax return for 1994.

As tax return time approaches, Stanley is eager to get his tax refund. On February 14, he files his 1994 return without waiting for the written statement from Marilyn. On March 1, he receives the statement from Marilyn. He may not deduct the payments as alimony because he failed to get the required written statement before the return was filed.

Here's another example. Under the terms of their separation agreement, Robert must pay the mortgage, real estate taxes, and insurance premiums on a home owned solely by his ex-wife, Julia. Robert may deduct these payments as alimony. Julia must include the payments in her income, but she is entitled to claim deductions for the amount of the real estate taxes and mortgage interest if she itemizes her deductions.

- If the payor pays rent on the ex-spouse's apartment, the rent may be considered alimony. This must be stated in the divorce decree.
- If the payor pays the mortgage on the house owned by the ex-spouse, the payment may be considered to be alimony. This must be stated in the divorce decree.
- If the payor pays the mortgage on the house owned by the payor, the payment is not considered to be alimony.
- If the payee spouse owns the life insurance policy on the life of the payor, the payments made by the payor will qualify as alimony if so stated in the divorce decree.

The bottom line is, if the payor is making payments on something owned by the payor for the benefit of the ex-spouse, the payments do not qualify as alimony. If the payor makes payments on something owned by the ex-spouse, the payments do qualify as alimony if stated in the divorce decree.

b. Payments made to maintain property owned by the payor-spouse may not qualify as alimony.

Assume the same facts from above, except that Robert and Julia own the residence as joint tenants. Since he has a 50% ownership interest in the home, Robert may deduct only one-half of the payments as alimony. However, he is entitled to claim deductions for interest with respect to his own half of the mortgage payments. Similarly, Julia must report one-half of the payments and income and can only claim one-half of the deductible interest.

c. Transfer of services do not qualify as alimony.

Assume that Jake offered to mow his ex-wife's lawn all summer. He figured that would be worth $550 and it could be considered alimony. Sorry, Jake, it won't qualify.

2. There must be a written separation agreement or court order in order for the payments to qualify as alimony.

As an example, Craig and Sally are separated. Craig sends Sally a letter offering to pay her $400 a month alimony for three years. Sally feels this is a slap in the face since she raised his kids and kept his house clean for 18 years. She does not respond. Craig starts sending the $400 per month. Sally cashes the checks. Since there is no written agreement, he may not deduct the payments as alimony.

Here's another example. According to their divorce decree, Allen is to send Marian $750 per month alimony for 10 years. Two years after their divorce, Marian loses her job and prevails on Allen's good nature to increase her alimony for six months until she gets started in a new job. He starts sending her an extra $200 per month. This was an oral agreement, not written. No post-decree modification was made and he may not deduct the additional amounts.

3. The divorcing couple must not opt out of alimony treatment for federal income tax purposes.

Maintenance is taxable to the person who receives it and tax-deductible by the person who pays it (unless agreed upon otherwise. See Taxable vs. non-taxable).

4. The divorcing couple may not be members of the same household at the time payment is made after the final decree.

Sometimes a couple gets divorced but neither can afford to move. They reach an agreement: she lives upstairs and he lives downstairs. He pays her maintenance—as specified in the decree—but he cannot deduct it on his tax return. Since they live in the same house, it is not considered maintenance. However, for temporary alimony, the parties may be members of the same household.

5. The obligation to make payments must terminate upon the recipient's death.

The obligation ceases upon the death of the payor or the payee.

6. The ex-spouses may not file a joint tax return.

Many couples file for the year they got divorced. This is an error. The filing status is the status they have on December 31st of the year they are filing. If they are divorced during the year of 1999, on December 31, 1999 they are not married and may not file a joint return.

7. If any portion of the payment is considered to be child support, then that portion cannot be treated as alimony.

If alimony is reduced six-months either side of the date upon which a child reaches the age of 18, 21, or the age of majority in their state, the amount of reduction is considered to be child support and not alimony. This can trigger a re-capture of taxes on alimony. (See a more complete discussion in Chapter 5.)

TAXABLE VS. NON-TAXABLE

During the temporary separation period and until the divorce is final, the couple can decide whether the alimony payments should be considered taxable or nontaxable. Many times, any money that is paid to the spouse up to the time of permanent orders is not considered maintenance. On the other hand, sometimes the temporary orders can consider it to be maintenance so it is taxable. Written agreements and good communication are essential here. Nothing should ever be assumed by either party or attorney.

FRONT-LOADING OF MAINTENANCE

The IRS has a rule that says that if the payor of alimony wants to deduct everything over $15,000 per year, payments must last for at least three years.

The recapture rules were designed to prevent non-deductible property settlement payments from being deducted as alimony. The rules come into effect to the extent that alimony payments decrease annually in excess of $15,000 during the first three calendar years.

To the extent that the payor spouse has paid "excess alimony", the excess alimony is to be recaptured in the payor spouse's taxable income beginning in the third year after divorce. The payee spouse is entitled to deduct the recaptured amount from gross income in the third year after divorce.

For example, Trish tells her husband Robert that after the divorce, she plans to go back to school for two years and finish her degree. Then she will be able to get a certain job that, after a year, will pay her $30,000 a year and she will no longer need alimony. She asks Robert if he will support her for those two years. He agrees. Her expenses for those two years, including school costs, are $60,000 the first year and $30,000 the second year.

A friend tells Robert about an IRS rule that says if he wants to deduct everything over $15,000, alimony must go for at least three years, but the rule doesn't stipulate as to the amount he must pay. Robert wants to deduct the whole amount so he offers to pay Trish $1,000 the 3rd year to satisfy the IRS ruling. Here's what it looks like.

1st year	$60,000
2nd year	$30,000
3rd year	$ 1,000

However, the friend didn't tell Robert about the 2nd part of the IRS rule. Some friend! The IRS says that if the payments drop by more than $15,000 from one year to the next, there is tax recapture on the amount over $15,000. In Robert's case, the alimony dropped by $30,000 from Year 1 to Year 2, and by $29,000 from Year 2 to Year 3. Robert will have to pay tax recapture. Let's see how it works.

The formulas for figuring Front-loading of Alimony (sometimes called Recapture of Excess Alimony) include these steps.

1. Determine the 2nd year recapture amount.

Recapture amount = alimony paid in 2nd yr - alimony paid in 3rd yr - $15,000

2nd year recapture amount = **$30,000 - $1,000 - $15,000 = $14,000**

2. Adjust 2nd year alimony for Recapture Calculation.

Adjusted 2nd year = 2nd year actual Payment - 2nd year recapture calculation

Adjusted 2nd year = **\$30,000 - \$14,000 = \$16,000**

3. Determine 3rd year recapture amount.

$$\text{Recapture Amount} = \frac{\text{Adjusted alimony in 2nd yr} + \text{alimony paid in 3rd yr}}{2}$$

Average alimony (years 2 and 3) = **$\frac{\$16{,}000 + \$1{,}000}{2}$ = \$8,500**

3rd year recapture amt = 1st year - avg of 1st year and 2nd year - **\$15,000**

3rd year recapture amt = **\$60,000 - \$8,500 - \$15,000 = \$36,500**

4. Determine total recapture in 3rd year for tax return.

Total recapture = 2nd year recapture + 3rd year recapture

Total recapture = **\$14,000 + \$36,500 = \$50,500**

RESULT: Robert will add \$50,500 to gross income in 3rd year and Trish will subtract \$50,500 from gross income.

EXCEPTIONS TO RECAPTURE RULE [71(f)(5)]

The recapture rules do not apply if:

1. *either spouse dies before the end of the third post-separation year or the spouse entitled to receive the payments remarries before the end of the third post-separation year.* [71(f)(1)]
2. *the amount of payments fluctuates for reasons not in control of the payor spouse*. For example, the payments might be a fixed percentage of income from a business or property, or from compensation for employment or self-employment.

Example A: Bert agrees to pay Maggie 25% of the net income from his farm each year for a period of three years. In the first year, the net income from the farm was $120,000 and Bert sent Maggie a check for $30,000. During the second year, the area was hit by severe weather and most of his crops were wiped out. That year, the farm's net income was only $32,000 so Bert sent Maggie a check for $8,000. In the third year, the farming business suffered a loss of $10,000 and Bert did not make a payment to Maggie that year. In this case, no recapture is required.

Example B: Tim, a successful attorney, was ordered to pay his ex-wife 25% of his income from his practice annually for the next four years. Six months after the final decree, Tim walked away from his law practice and moved to the mountains to grow mushrooms. Tim will not be able to avoid recapture because the fluctuation *was* within his control.

3. *the payments are temporary support payments*

4. *the alimony payments decline for $15,000 or less over the three-year period.*

Example: The divorce decree says that Tom pays Helen as alimony the sum of $315,000. This sum if payable as follows: $60,000 in 1999, $55,000 in 2000, and $50,000 in 2001, 2002, 2003, and 2004. The recapture provisions do not apply since the alimony payments over the three-year period do not decrease by more than $15,000.

DECLINING MAINTENANCE

Keeping in mind the front-loading of maintenance rules, there are some advantages to structuring maintenance that decreases from year to year. For example, Lucy and Brian structured their divorce settlement so that Lucy would receive payments over a six-year period. She would receive $2,000 per month for 2 years, while she was finishing her physical therapist degree. After completing her degree, she would get $1,500 per month for 2 years, while she was getting her business set up. During the final two years, she would get $1,000 per month. At the completion of six years, all payments would stop.

Lucy liked this arrangement because the gradual decline gave her a chance to get used to it and prepare to adjust her standard of living. In addition, she could tell how much she would need to work to replace the lost income.

Brian liked this arrangement because he could see and feel the decline of maintenance. And, he knew it wasn't going to go on forever. This is an important factor for the majority of individuals who are required to pay maintenance. There is a light at the end of the tunnel.

GUARANTEEING MAINTENANCE

Even though the divorce decree stipulates one spouse is to pay the other a certain amount of maintenance for a certain period of time, it doesn't mean it will happen. There are several ways an ex-spouse can get out of making the payments. Fortunately, there are several ways to guard against this and guarantee the payments will be made. These include life insurance, disability insurance, and annuities.

Life Insurance

Alimony payments stop upon the death of the payor. Therefore, it should be stipulated in the divorce decree that life insurance will be carried on the life of the payor to replace alimony in the event of the payor's death.

If a new policy is to be purchased, it should be done before the divorce is final.

For example, Alex agreed to buy a life insurance policy to insure his alimony payments to Sarah. After the divorce was final, he applied for the insurance and took his health exam. He was found to be un-insurable. If Sarah had known this before the divorce, her attorney would have asked for a different settlement. It was now too late.

The recipient spouse should either own the life insurance or be an irrevocable beneficiary for two reasons:

1. To insure payment of premiums. For example, Bernie was ordered by the court to carry a $50,000 life insurance policy on his life payable to Betty in the event of his death. A few years later, Bernie got tired of making the insurance payments and canceled the life insurance policy. No one was aware that he did this. When Bernie died, there was no insurance to cover Betty's alimony.

2. *Tax treatment.* If the beneficiary spouse either owns the policy or is an irrevocable beneficiary, and the premium payments are made under a legal obligation imposed by the divorce decree, the premiums are considered to be alimony (tax deductible by the payor and taxable to the recipient).

Disability Insurance

A second way to guarantee the stream of maintenance income is to have disability insurance on the payor's ability to earn income. Assume, for example, that a husband is to pay his ex-wife $1,200 per month based on his salary of $6,000 per month. Then he becomes disabled. If he had disability insurance, he might then receive $4,000 per month tax-free and could continue making maintenance payments. If he had no insurance and no income, he would probably go back to court and ask to have maintenance modified.

The ex-wife cannot own the disability policy but she may make the payments on it so that she knows it stays in force. She will also, in that case, be notified of any changes made in the policy.

Annuity

A third way to guarantee maintenance is to have the payor buy an annuity that pays an amount per month that equals the maintenance payment.

Assume that Ted buys a $200,000 annuity that will pay out $850 per month (the agreed-upon maintenance payment) in interest only. If the payment represents interest-only payments, they are taxable to him as income, but deductible by him as alimony. His wife, Judy, will pay taxes on the payments. This way, the payment is always made on time, the payor does not need to worry about it, the recipient does not have to worry about it, and the principal can still belong to the payor. At the end of the agreed upon term of maintenance, Ted can stop the interest-only payments.

If the agreed-upon maintenance is $1,000 per month and Ted chooses to annuitize the annuity and receive $1,000 per month, part of the payment will be taxable to him, say $850, but he will be able to deduct the whole $1,000 as alimony payments. At the end of the term of maintenance, he will continue to receive the $1,000 per month.

CHAPTER 9

Child Support

Every parent is obligated to support his or her children, regardless of divorce. In a divorce situation, the non-custodial parent is usually ordered to pay some child support to the custodial parent from which the custodial parent pays the child's expenses.

The federal government passed laws that the states wouldn't get certain Federal financial assistance unless the states implemented child support guidelines. All states now have child support guidelines that help the courts decide the amount of child support to be paid. Check in your own state for your guidelines. And you will most likely be able to get software to automatically calculate your state guidelines.

The courts in each state have the power to deviate from the child support guidelines (award a different amount). The state statutes tell what constitutes acceptable deviations. The parents can also agree to a different amount provided that the court approves the agreement.

States have upper income limits for application of the child support guidelines. If the income of the parents exceeds certain limits of their state, the parents are not bound by the child support guidelines.

Some child support guideline formulas are based on the ratio of each parent's income, the percentage of time the child spends with each parent, and consider the amount of alimony paid to the custodial parent.

Here's an example of the application of an income ratio child support guidelines formula:

Paul's gross income is $4,300 a month and Becky's gross income is $900 a month; together they earn $5,200.

Paul	$4,300	83%
Becky	900	17%
	$5,200	

Paul is earning 83 percent of the total and Becky is earning 17 percent. They have two children. The Child Support Guidelines for two children is $983. Using the Guidelines, take 83 percent of the suggested monthly payment of $983 and you will determine that Paul owes Becky $813 in monthly child support if he pays no maintenance.

But let's assume that he is going to pay her maintenance of $1,000 a month. At this point, you would then subtract the $1,000 from his income and add it to hers.

Paul	$4,300	-	$1,000 =	$3,300	63%
Becky	900	+	$1,000 =	$1,900	37%
	$5,200			$5,200	

The totals stay the same but the percentages change. Now, his percentage is 63 percent. Using the same Guidelines formula, multiply $983 by 63 percent, and you determine that Paul will pay $624 per month instead of $813.

The rule of thumb in this type of a formula is, as maintenance increases, child support decreases

Unfortunately, the amount of child support paid is often less than the actual amount required to meet the needs of growing children. And secondly, many times the child support is not paid at all.

Many times there is suspicion or anger from the husband. He thinks, "I am not sure that my ex-wife will spend the money on the children . . . she probably will spend it on herself!" Child support is often based on income so, obviously, it is based on some kind of lifestyle that was already established.

The husband thinks, "If I want my children to live in this kind of a house, I have to pay enough child support that will make that kind of house payment. That means my ex-wife is going to be there, too." So, many times, the husband will get angry because his ex-wife is getting maintenance on top of child support. Or, if she is not getting maintenance, he feels that she is living off the child support. However, there are many fathers who understand that for the children to live in the kind of house they're accustomed to, the wife has to be there with them.

Paul and Becky present a very simplistic example. There are other factors that enter in, such as whether he is paying for childcare, health insurance, and/or education or school expenses. These factors would make adjustments necessary to the child support amount. Also, if there are four children and three will live with the mother and one with the father, that would impact the financial picture. Another factor that affects the outcome is the percentage of time the children live with the father under the parenting schedule.

MODIFYING CHILD SUPPORT

What happens when circumstances change after the divorce is final? Say, the husband loses his job, the wife loses her job, one person becomes disabled, a settlement or judgment is awarded that was started when still married, or one of them wins the lottery.

Child support is always modifiable.

The courts really try to protect the children. Therefore, even though couples with young children can agree on almost any settlement issue, they cannot generally enter a binding agreement to waive the amount or duration of child support.

The property settlement is final and you usually cannot change anything about the property settlement unless you can prove fraud or other state statutory factors. However, the child support and maintenance can be modified unless there was agreement to the contrary. They are usually modified for a substantial change of circumstances. How much of a change constitutes a "substantial" change in circumstance? If the income changes, in some states that might change the child support according to the Child Support Guidelines if the amount changes by some minimum presumptive amount like 10-15%.

There is an interesting issue. Assume there are two children and child support is agreed upon. At some point, the older child decides to go live with Dad, in the summertime. Since he's paying the full cost of supporting this child at his house (at least for several months), Dad says, "Now I only have to pay half the child support," and he sends a check for half the amount. Because it was not changed by a court order, in most states he still owes the whole amount and the ex-wife could force him to pay that back child support he did not pay.

Or, suppose that both kids go to live with Dad during the summer. Dad says, "I do not have to pay any child support during the summer since both kids are living with me," but the court order says that he must pay so much every month. It does not say "nine months out of the year." Unless it is in the court order, he is liable for those payments, and his ex-wife could sue him for that money. It is important to have written agreements as circumstances change.

INCOME TAX CONSIDERATIONS

Child support payments cannot be deducted by the payor and are not includable in the income of the recipient.

If the divorcing parents have only one child, that child can be counted as an exemption by only one parent in a given year. Unless otherwise specified, the exemption usually goes to the parent who has physical custody of the child for the greater portion of the calendar year.

The exemption can be traded back and forth year to year between the parents with a written waiver or IRS Form 8332. Once the custodial parent has executed the waiver, the noncustodial parent must attach the form to his or her income tax return. If the waiver is for more than one year, a copy of the form must be attached to the noncustodial parent's return for each year.

If the family has more than one child, the parents may divide up the exemptions. The children's Social Security numbers must be listed on each parent's tax return.

IMPORTANT: If both parents claim the same child or children on their tax return, they are inviting an IRS audit.

For either parent to claim the exemption, the child must be in custody of at least one parent for more than one-half of the calendar year. If the child lives with a grandparent or someone other than a parent for more than one-half of the calendar year, neither parent can claim the exemption.

CHILD CONTINGENCY RULE

If any amount of alimony specified in the divorce decree is reduced (a) upon the happening of any contingency related to the child or (b) at a time that can be clearly associated with a contingency related to the child, then the amount of the reduction will be treated as child support, rather than alimony, from the start. Code Sec. 71(c)(2). Reg. (1.71-1T(c) (Q&A) 18.

In order to prevent re-characterization of the payments, it is necessary to avoid a reduction of alimony at a time associated with the occurrence of a child-related contingency. Sidestepping this trap is made easier by the fact that there are only two situations in which payments that would otherwise qualify as alimony will be presumed to be reduced at a time clearly associated with the occurrence of a contingency related to the child.

1. Six-month rule

The first situation occurs when the payments are to be reduced not more than six months before or after the date on which the child reaches age 18, 21 or the age of majority in their state.

Example: Michael is to pay Susan $2,000 per month in alimony. The amount of alimony is to be reduced to $1,000 beginning with the January 2002 payment. Their child, Todd, was born April 5, 1984 and will reach the age of majority (19) on April 5, 2002. The date six months before April 5, 2002 is October 5, 2001, and the date six months after is October 5, 2002. Thus, if there is any reduction in payments during the period from October 5, 2001 through October 5, 2002, it may be presumed that the amount of the reduction constitutes child support and not alimony.

October 5, 2001

less than 6 months

April 5, 2002

less than 6 months

October 5, 2002

Thus, only $1,000 per month will qualify as alimony because the reduction in the payment falls within six months of a time associated with the occurrence of a child-related contingency.

2. Multiple reduction rule

The second situation is when there is more than one child. In this instance, if the payments are to be reduced on two or more occasions which occur not more than one year before or after each child reaches a certain age, then it is presumed that the amount of the reduction is child support. The age at which the reduction occurs must be between 18 and 24, inclusive, and must be the same for each of the children.

Example: Ralph is to pay Theresa $2,000 per month in alimony. Theresa has custody of their two children, Heidi and Thor. However, the payments are to be reduced to $1,500 per month on May 1, 2002 and to $1,000 per month on May 1, 2006. When the first reduction occurs, Heidi will be 20 years and 3 months old. On the date of the second reduction, Thor will be 21 years and 8 months old.

February 1, 2002	
	less than 1 year
May 1, 2002	
August 1, 2005	
	less than 1 year
May 1, 2006	

Under these facts, it is presumed that $1,000 of the payments constitutes child support, rather than alimony. Both reductions in payments occur not more than one year before or after each child reaches the age of 21 years.

Discussion: Many attorneys say "Johnnie is graduating from high school in 5 years, so let's give Mom alimony for 5 years." Or they will say, "Since Johnnie is graduating in 5 years, let's give Mom alimony of $2,000 a month for 5 years and then reduce it to $1,500 a month for an extra 3 years."

This is creating a serious tax problem for Dad. If the IRS considers the reduction of $500 a month to be child support, they will make it retroactive from the beginning or 5 years (60 months) times $500 is $30,000 that he will have to pay tax recapture on!

CHILD CARE CREDIT

A custodial parent who pays child care expenses so that he or she can be gainfully employed may be eligible for a tax credit. To claim this credit, the parent must maintain a household that is the home of at least one child, and the day care expenses must be paid to someone who is not claimed as a dependent.

Only the custodial parent is entitled to claim both the child and the dependent care credit. This is true even if the custodial parent does not claim the dependency exemption for the child. A noncustodial parent may not claim a childcare credit for expenses incurred even if that parent is entitled to claim the exemption for the child.

Here's an example. Carl and Mandy's son Bret, age 4, lives with Mandy four days a week and with Carl three days a week. Both Carl and Mandy work outside the home and each pays one-half of the $5,000 per year that it costs to have Bret in daycare during the workweek. Mandy is entitled to claim a childcare credit for her share of the daycare expenses. Although Carl and Mandy each have custody of Bret for a significant portion of the week,

Mandy is considered the custodial parent because Bret spends a greater percentage of time with her than he does with Carl.

HEAD OF HOUSEHOLD

A head-of-household filing status is available for those who are divorced (single), who provide more than one-half the cost of maintaining the household, and whose household is the principal home of at least one qualifying person for more than one-half of the year. A qualifying person is their child or any other person who qualifies as their dependent.

In determining whether the home is the principal home of the child for more than one-half of the year, do not count absences for vacation, sickness, school, or military service as time spent away from home if it was reasonable to assume that the child would return to the home.

CHAPTER 10

Insurance

Earlier, you read about career assets that need to be considered as dividable property. There are two more that you need to know about: health insurance and life insurance.

HEALTH INSURANCE AND COBRA

In the traditional marriage where the husband is the main wage earner, one concern is maintaining health insurance for the ex-wife after divorce.

It is not uncommon for women over 40 years of age to develop severe health problems. Some become almost uninsurable, at least at a reasonable cost. This is a real concern where, all of a sudden, they are on their own and responsible for acquiring health insurance.

The Older Women's League (OWL) worked hard to get the Consolidated Omnibus Budget Reconcilation Act (COBRA) law passed in 1986. It allows women to continue to get health insurance from their ex-husband's company (if it has at least 20 employees), for three years after the divorce. The normal COBRA provision states that, if an employee is fired or leaves a job, he or she can get health insurance from that company for 18 months. However, in a divorce, it is extended to three years or 36 months.

Assume that Sara from Chapter 7 ("Financial Affidavit") decides to continue health insurance under COBRA. Sara must pay the premium as agreed. If she misses a premium payment, the health insurance company can drop her and they do not need to reinstate her. So, she must pay that premium on time. Typically, Sara will not get the discounted group rate but will be charged the full rate. It is important to shop for health insurance, even though the COBRA provision may supply a quick solution to health care coverage, it may not be the best. It may be purchased at a lesser cost somewhere else.

Talk to your female clients about health insurance. A client (healthy or not) could say, "I am going to be covered by COBRA from Bob's work." Tell her about clients who develop health problems.

Encourage clients over age 40 to explore other options. Tell them, "I would advise that you shop for health insurance because if you can match the rate from Bob's company or get a lower premium with another company, you should buy your own. Then if something happens, as long as you pay your premiums, you are covered. Otherwise, at the end of three years, COBRA drops you, and then you have to start shopping for your own insurance. By that time, you might be uninsurable and not able to find insurance."

Most states have insurance for those who are uninsurable and cannot get health insurance any other way. As may be expected, this insurance is very costly. It is better to look ahead and get individual health insurance for a lower premium while you are still healthy than to gamble that you will still be healthy three years later.

Is health insurance a marital asset? Some companies provide health benefits for employees after they retire. Some lawyers are starting to consider this an asset since the Financial Accounting Standards Board in 1993 began requiring employers to calculate the present value of the future benefits and show a liability for that value in their financial reports.

If the benefits are a liability to the employer, there's a good argument they should also be an asset to the employee.

LIFE INSURANCE

Since maintenance usually stops upon the death of the payor, the stream of payments can be covered by life insurance on the life of the payor if there is no other adequate source of security for the future stream of income. This should be part of the final divorce settlement.

Always recommend that the wife own the life insurance policy and make the premium payments. This prevents any changes in the policy without her knowledge.

Here's an example. Joan was receiving $400 per month in alimony from her ex-husband Jerry. The court had ordered Jerry to carry life insurance on his life payable to Joan as long as alimony was being paid. After three years, Jerry was tired of making the insurance payments so he stopped and the insurance was canceled. Nobody knew about it until one year later. Jerry was in a car accident and died two weeks later of complications from his injuries. Alimony came to an abrupt halt and there was no life insurance! Yes, Jerry was in contempt of court but it didn't make any difference now, because his estate was insufficient to pay the claim of the wife.

Also recommend that, if the wife can afford it, the life insurance build cash value. Then, the cash account within the policy is hers to do with whatever she wishes. She may even use it for retirement. She can borrow from it at any time, or cancel the policy and use the cash.

Another option would be to purchase level term insurance for the life of maintenance if the wife can't afford the whole life premium payments. She could "buy term and invest the difference" in a mutual fund that she can watch and manage.

A third recommendation is to make sure that, if new insurance is needed, it be applied for before the divorce is final. Then, if he cannot pass the physical and cannot get new insurance, there is still time to modify the final settlement to make up for this possibility.

If the court orders the husband to purchase insurance to cover maintenance and/or child support, those premium payments are treated like alimony for tax purposes and he can deduct them from his taxable income. Likewise, the wife will need to declare them as taxable income, unless the parties agree in their separation agreement to exempt the payment from the alimony tax treatment.

Is term insurance ever considered a marital asset? Yes, in some states it is if the insured has since become uninsurable, it could be considered an asset. It is something to be aware of.

CHAPTER 11

Social Security

For all the examples in this chapter, we will assume that the wife was the lower-earning spouse. In real life, the husband could be the lower-earning spouse, in which case all rules would apply to him.

You probably know that if a couple has been married for 10 years or longer and they get divorced, the wife is entitled to half the husband's Social Security provided certain provisions are met:

1. The husband is entitled to receive Social Security benefits,
2. They had been married for 10 years before the divorce became final,
3. The wife is not married,
4. The wife is age 62 or over, and
5. The wife is not entitled to a retirement benefit which equals or exceeds one-half the husband's benefit.

Since this rule does not diminish the amount the husband receives at retirement, he usually doesn't worry about this.

A wife who is age 62 or over and who has been divorced for at least two years will be able to receive benefits based on the earnings of a former husband regardless of whether the former husband has retired or applied for benefits.

If the wife of a retired or disabled worker is caring for the worker's under-age-16 or disabled child, the monthly benefit equals one-half of the worker's benefit regardless of his age. If the wife is not caring for a child, monthly benefits equal one-half of the husband's, but if the wife chooses to start receiving benefits at age 62, the benefit that she would receive at age 65 is reduced by 20%. If the wife chooses to receive the reduced benefit at age 62, she is not entitled to the full benefit upon reaching age 65.

Assume the husband will get $750 a month when he retires. If they have been married 10 years or longer, she would be able to get $375 (half of the husband's benefit) at age 65.

Husband	$750
Wife	$375

What if he gets remarried? If he is married to his second wife for 10 years and they get divorced, wife 2 gets $375, wife 1 gets $375, and he still gets $750. The limit is four marriages! As long as he is married to each one for 10 years or longer, they each get half of his Social Security benefit.

Husband	$750
Wife 1	$375
Wife 2	$375

One of the reasons why Social Security is in so much financial trouble is that the fund is covering and paying for items that it was not originally designed to do.

What if the wife gets remarried? If she is married at retirement time, she looks to her current husband for her benefit. But if she has been married to husband 2 for 10 years and they get divorced, she is entitled to half of husband 1's benefits or half of husband 2 benefits. She has a choice.

Husband 1	$750	Husband 2	$600
Wife	$375	Wife	$300

If husband 2 is entitled to $600 at retirement, she obviously will choose the benefits from husband 1. They are more.

Assume she begins working after the kids are raised and that by the time she retires, she is going to be able to earn $450 from her own Social Security account. Now she has the choice at retirement time of taking $450 from her own account, $300 from husband 2's account, or $375 from husband 1's account. She can only have one—hers, his or his. Obviously, she would take her own account, which would pay her $450 per month.

What if they get divorced and he dies? The wife is entitled to full widow's benefits (100 percent of the deceased husband's benefits) if:

1. The deceased husband was entitled to Social Security benefits,
2. They had been married for 10 years before the divorce became final,
3. The widow is age 60 or over, or is between ages 50 and 60 and disabled,
4. The widow is not married, and
5. The widow is not entitled to a retirement benefit that is equal to or greater than the deceased husband's benefit.

Wife 2 also gets full widow's benefits if she meets the above five requirements.

A widow's remarriage after age 60 will not prevent her from being entitled to widow's benefits on her prior deceased husband's earnings.

A widow's remarriage before age 60 will prevent entitlement to widow's benefits unless the subsequent marriage ends, whether by death, divorce, or annulment. If the subsequent marriage ends, the widow may become entitled or reentitled to benefits on the prior deceased spouse's earnings beginning with the month the subsequent marriage ends.

As an example, assume that Maude's first husband died. At age 58, she met a wonderful widower and wanted to get remarried but she realized that she would lose her entitlement to all of the deceased spouse's Social Security benefits when she turned age 60. This may explain why many senior citizens are living together unmarried.

Social Security benefits payable to the ex-wife are reduced by governmental retirement payments to the husband. These payments are based on his own earnings in employment not covered by Social Security on the last day of such employment. The reduction is two-thirds of the pension. Thus, the wife's benefit is reduced $2 for every $3 of the government pension.

CHAPTER 12

Debt, Credit, and Bankruptcy

DEBT

As you read earlier, property is classified as marital and separate. The same classifications apply to debt. In general, in many states both parties are responsible for any debts incurred during the marriage—it does not matter who really spent the money. When the property is divided up during the divorce, the person who gets the asset usually also gets the responsibility for any loans against that asset.

It's in your client's best interests to pay off as many debts as possible before or at the time of the final decree. To do so, clients could use liquid assets such as bank accounts, stocks, or bonds. It may make sense to sell assets to accumulate some extra cash. The best assets to sell include extra cars, vacation homes, and excess furniture.

If your clients can't pay off the debts, then the decree must state who will pay which debt and within what period of time. However, the parties are still personally liable to the third party creditor regardless of what the court order says.

There are generally four types of debt to consider: secured debt, unsecured debt, tax debt, and divorce expense debt.

Secured debt

Secured debt includes the mortgage on the home or other real estate, and loans on cars, trucks, and other vehicles. It should be made very clear in the separation agreement who will pay which debt. If one spouse fails to make a payment on a debt that is secured by an asset, the creditor can pursue the other spouse.

Unsecured debt

Unsecured debt includes credit cards, personal bank loans, lines of credit, and loans from parents and friends. These debts may be divided equitably. The court also considers who is better able to pay the debt, in the context of the full financial settlement.

For unsecured debt, the separation agreement needs to include a hold harmless clause. In most cases, this will indemnify the non-paying spouse, which means that the paying spouse gives the non-paying spouse the right to collect all missed payments, and in some cases, also damages, interest, and attorneys fees if payments were not made.

Financial advisors, lawyers and clients all need to be aware that even though something is agreed to and included in the divorce decree, it doesn't mean that it will happen as planned. Often, the legal decision and the financial outcome are very different things.

Here's an example: Tracy and Paul were married for 8 years, during which time Tracy ran her credit cards to the limit with her compulsive spending. The court held Tracy solely responsible for paying the $12,000 in credit card debt. After the divorce, however, Tracy didn't change her ways and was unable to pay off her debt. The credit card companies came after Paul, who ended up paying them off. One solution would have been to pay off the credit cards with assets at the time of divorce or for Paul to have received more property to offset this possibility.

Tax Debt

Just because the divorce settlement is final doesn't mean the parties are exempt from possible future tax debt. For three years after the divorce, the IRS can perform a random audit of the divorced parties' joint tax return. In addition, the IRS can question a joint return—if it has good cause to do so—

for seven years. It can also audit a return whenever it feels fraud is involved. To avoid potential tax costs, the divorce agreement should have provisions that spell out what happens if any additional interest, penalties, or taxes are found, as well as where the money comes from to pay for an audit. However, if a joint tax return was filed, each party is individually responsible to the IRS unless a spouse qualifies under the innocent spouse regulations.

Divorce Expense Debt

At times, one or the other party may have paid some divorce expenses before the divorce process was officially started.

Your clients will accrue costs during the divorce process, including court filing fees, appraisals, mediation, and attorneys. Other less obvious expenses are accounting, financial planning, and counseling. The separation agreement needs language that states who is responsible for these expenses.

There are also divorce expenses that may accrue after the decree, such as attorney fees for doing QDROs and title transfers. Other such post-decree expenses are tax preparation for the final joint tax return, mediation fees, and long-term divorce counseling for the parents or the children. Who pays? The attorney should spell it out clearly so there are no disputes at a later date.

CREDIT

A creditor cannot close an account just because the account holder's marital status has changed. An exception would be if there is a proven inability or unwillingness to pay. However, the creditor can require a new application if the original application was based on only the other spouse's financial statement. The creditor must allow use of the account while the new application is being reviewed.

If the spouses hold charge accounts jointly, they will both have the same credit history. If one spouse merely used the accounts as a signee, it may be necessary to confirm the fact that he or she was equally responsible for the payments. This can be done with proof of canceled checks and a financial statement that shows that spouse's ability to pay.

If your client has a good credit history and the necessary income, he or she should have little or no problem opening new accounts in his or her name only. If, however, the client was unemployed during the marriage and never had a credit card in his or her name, he or she may need a cosigner.

Your client may still be responsible for joint accounts even after the divorce is final. You should see to it that prior to the final decree, all joint accounts are paid off and closed, and that new accounts are started in the individual's names.

Also warn your clients about running up charge account bills as part of divorce planning or retaliation. If it can later be proven that these expenditures were not agreed upon jointly (or they were not for necessities such as food, housing, clothing, or health care) they may not be considered joint debt depending on the state law and the case.

Note: Creditors don't care how the separation agreement divides responsibility for debt. Each person is liable for the full amount of debt on joint cards until the bill is paid.

BANKRUPTCY

The word *bankruptcy* strikes fear in the hearts of many people—especially those going through divorce. Many wives who are trying to decide whether it is better to ask for alimony or a property settlement note are caught in indecision. Perhaps the husband has threatened to either leave the country if he has to pay alimony or to file bankruptcy if he has to pay a property settlement note. Let's look at some of the rules of bankruptcy as they apply in divorce situations.

There are two types of bankruptcy available: Chapter 13 (which allows you to develop a pay-off plan over a three-year period) or Chapter 7 (which allows you to liquidate all of your assets and use the proceeds to pay off debts, erasing the debts which cannot be paid in full).

Chapter 7 bankruptcy forgives all unsecured debts, and requires the forfeiture of all assets over certain minimum protected amounts. Creditors have the right to repossess their fair share of the assets. The net proceeds from the sale of assets are divided pro rata among the creditors.

Chapter 13 bankruptcy may preserve the assets and allow the debtor to pay off all the secured debt, as well as a portion of the unsecured debt, and discharge the rest of the unsecured debt. The debtor needs to make payments under a plan.

Here are some things to remember:

- (If a spouse files bankruptcy before, during, or after divorce, the creditors will seek out the other spouse for payment—no matter what was agreed to in the separation agreement.

- (While the couple is still married, they can file for bankruptcy jointly. This will eliminate all separate debts of the husband, separate debts of the wife, and all jointly incurred marital debts.

Certain debts cannot be discharged in bankruptcy. These include child support, maintenance, some student loans, and recent taxes.

Promissory notes or property settlement notes, especially unsecured notes, are almost always wiped out in bankruptcy. Some secured notes, depending on the property that secures them, can also be discharged.

As an example, say Sam and Trudy divided all their assets. However, to achieve a 50/50 division, Sam still owed Trudy $82,000. Sam signed a property settlement note to pay Trudy the $82,000 over a 10-year period at 7 percent interest. After the divorce, Sam filed for bankruptcy and listed the property settlement note as one of his debts. Trudy never received a penny of the money that was due her.

CHAPTER 13

Mediation

Care needs to be taken that couples who want to work out a settlement with a minimum of stress don't get caught up in the knock-off of *The War of the Roses* starring Michael Douglas, Kathleen Turner and Danny DeVito. Unfortunately, once the flames have been flamed, the only person who will ever win is the attorney and/or his or her attorney whose motivation in the divorce is to fight. But, most clients don't' want to use their financial resources for a court battle. The war of Justin and Stacy illustrates just that.

THE WAR OF JUSTIN AND STACY

Justin and Stacy Smith had decided to call it quits after six years of marriage. They had no children. Justin had a new girlfriend and was feeling very guilty. He was a highly paid executive and offered to give Stacy almost everything—the house valued at $375,000, the $87,000 brokerage account, half his 401(k) which would give her $92,000, and $3,000 per month for three years. He also offered to pay the expenses for her to finish her master's degree in nursing. Before the breakup of the marriage, when they were on amiable terms, she estimated that she would earn $40,000 - $50,000 per year with her master's degree in nursing.

Initially, Stacy was worried and upset about his offering her everything. What was she missing? What was he hiding? Her friends kept telling her this was too good to be true. Instead of talking to Justin about a settlement, she hired the most expensive attorney she could find and paid him a large retainer to answer her questions. The attorney immediately filed a petition for divorce and initiated motions for protective orders and temporary maintenance.

Before Stacy had hired an attorney, the two of them had been communicating without legal counsel. When Justin called Stacy, she told him, "Have your attorney call my attorney." Since Justin did not have an attorney, he called Stacy's attorney and put forth his settlement offer again. The attorney stalled. He said he needed to do discovery and depositions. Because he felt he was being put off, Justin again called Stacy and tried to settle but she ignored him.

As time went by, he started feeling less guilty and more irritated. Justin hired his own attorney and paid another large retainer. Further negotiations for any type of settlement failed and they came to a standstill. What shouldn't have happened, happened. They prepared to for a court trial.

Stacy's attorney asked for it all. He asked the court to give her the house, the entire brokerage account, her half of the 401(k), $4,000 per month for four years and $37,000 to pay her attorney's fees.

Justin's attorney knew that originally, Justin offered to give Stacy the house, the brokerage account, half his 401(k), $3,000 per month maintenance for three years plus the amount needed for her to finish college. Things have been difficult for him financially. He has had to spend an exorbitant amount of money in legal fees and expert witness fees. His business has actually declined due to the attention he had to pay to attacks made by Stacy and her attorney. As a result, Justin's attorney took a position in court much less generous than Justin's initial offer.

After hearing all the arguments, the judge was irritated. He gave Stacy $50,000 in cash, $500 per month maintenance for two years, and nothing extra for her attorney's fees. He gave Justin the house and his 401(k). The remainder of the brokerage account was long gone to pay attorney's fees.

* * * *

It is important for the clients to get involved to bring sanity to highly volatile and emotional environment. This is why mediation can work.

WHAT IS MEDIATION?

This chapter is not meant to train the reader to be a mediator. Rather, it is to educate the reader about the process of mediation, what is involved, and some of the skills necessary to conduct successful mediation sessions with clients. Mediation is a relatively new process that is gaining recognition world wide for its successful accomplishments. In our quest for divorce settlements instead of court trials in divorce, mediation is an important concept for us to be aware of.

This chapter would not be complete without mentioning the pioneer and forefather of divorce mediation, Gary J. Friedman, J.D. He realized in 1976 that there was a better way to resolve the issues surrounding divorce. Friedman shifted his focus "from doing battle, to helping people work together to make decisions regarding their lives rather than making one party a winner and the other a loser." He founded and directs the Center for Mediation in Law in Mill Valley, California. He is an internationally recognized authority on mediation and has been training mediators and teaching mediation at Stanford Law School. His book, *A Guide to Divorce Mediation* is considered essential reading for anyone interested in mediation.

Christine Coates, J. D. has been mediating divorce cases in Colorado since 1984. As a nationally known trainer and speaker on mediation, gives the insider's view of what the process involves.

Christine:
What is mediation? Mediation is a process where a neutral person works with the divorcing parties to devise solutions that work for both of them. The mediator is a neutral, impartial person who doesn't take sides, has no interest in the outcome of the mediation, does not give or make decisions for the parties, and does not give legal advice. This is an important point. Even if an attorney is working as a mediator, it would be unethical for him or her—as the mediator—to give legal advice. However, the mediator can give legal *information*.

In the mediation process, the goal is to work with the parties and help them identify the issues. Together they uncover what each party really needs in order to have a fair settlement. To do that, all the facts are presented that are necessary to making an informed decision, and the mediator helps both parties resolve the issues to their satisfaction in a way that's fair to them.

Mediation is generally a voluntary process. The courts may order people to enter mediation, but the courts cannot order people to settle. Across the country, the courts are favoring mediation and ordering people to participate to make sure that they've had a chance to talk together before they end up in court.

The mediator's job is to be a facilitator and to help the couple work together. The mediator has no authority to force a decision upon them. Mediation is not therapy even though some divorce mediators are therapists. It is not meant to work out what went wrong in their marriage, nor is it arbitration (where one person makes a decision for the couple). It is a very different method of resolving disputes.

Mediation is generally confidential depending on the state law. If confidential, the mediator cannot be called into court to testify against either of the parties or to tell the court or the judge what has occurred in the mediation session. However, each state has its own rules on this issue. Mediation should be a safe forum where the couple can talk about proposed solutions with each other, resolve their disputes, and perhaps come up with a settlement.

The goal of mediation is to get past the positions that people come in with and work toward what they really need in order to be satisfied with an agreement and to walk out with a fair and satisfying agreement.

How does mediation work? There is a fairly predictable process although mediators have different styles and approaches. First of all, when two people visit the mediator, he or she gets to know them and spends some time telling them about mediation and how it works. The mediator asks them to sign telling them what is expected from them and what they can expect from the mediator, and how the fees are charged.

Before beginning the mediation session in earnest, it is good to set ground rules. Two basic rules are: (1) each person has the right to speak without being interrupted by the other, and (2) neither spouse should put down the other or resort to name-calling.

The parties are told that the goal of mediation is to resolve their disputes, but the mediator is not going to do that for them. It is going to be their job and they are going to have to make their own decisions. The mediator will help them with what they need to know, what data they need to gather, and what information they need to bring to the table. He or she will help them figure out what to do and what agreements they need to reach. But the mediator is not going to reach decisions for them.

After meeting with them initially, some mediators meet with each person separately to get a sense of what each of them is feeling, what their fears are, and what's been going on with them that they may not feel comfortable talking about in front of the other. The mediator finds out what it is that they really need to have happen to feel that they have had a fair agreement. However, some mediators never meet with the parties alone. This depends on the style of the mediator.

After meeting with each alone, the three get back together to set the agenda. The mediator will have helped each of them to sort out the issues so they can decide which topics to talk about, such as property division, child support, maintenance, and so on. Then they select an issue on which to begin working.

Sometimes, the mediator may decide with which issue to start with. He or she may choose the issue that seems the easiest especially if there is an issue on which they agree even though they may not have told each other. Choosing that issue will help them get a quick agreement right off the bat so they can reinforce their ability to continue to work together to make future agreements. However, sometimes they come in with issues that demand immediate attention. If they don't deal with them that first day, mediation may go nowhere. In those cases, the process may start with a tough issue.

After agreeing to the ground rules, they start the negotiating process. However, the couple often can't simply jump in and resolve issues. Many times, they first need to gather the information that is needed to make a decision. They need to know what their financial situation is, how much they spend, what the IRAs are worth, and so on. They will begin by filling out the standard financial affidavit form that is used in their state in compiling such information. Next, they will list all the property. As a CDP, you can help them gather all this information.

Once all the information is on the table, the mediator can start generating options for settlement.

THE NEGOTIATING PROCESS

After the ground rules are set and the couple has all their financial data in order, it is time to start the negotiating process. Michael Caplan, J.D. has been training mediators in Colorado since 1988 and is a mediator himself. He explains how a mediator typically approaches it.

There are basically two ways of negotiating or bargaining. The first method is *positional bargaining*. Positional bargaining starts with the solution. One party proposes a solution and the other makes an offer. There are counteroffers until, somewhere along the line, they hit on something that is successful and that works for both of them.

While this process sounds very calm and fair, there often is an undercurrent of selfishness. One client goes in with a low-ball offer and the other comes in with their high-ball offer. Somewhere in the middle, hopefully they will find a place where they are going to meet and where they think they are okay. Both people are also working from the notion that the "pie" is limited. They think, "There is only so much here and I have to get as much as I can. I am looking to win and for me to win, you have to lose. That is my goal. I want to win as much as possible. For me to do that, you have to lose as much as possible."

Secondly, there is *interest-based bargaining*. It starts with parties educating each other about their interests. So instead of saying, "I must have this," they say, "I need this because this is what it will do for me."

It is based instead on "the pie is not limited, there is enough there for what we both want and need." Now, that may not always be true but that is the assumption that they start with. It is based on the premise that all our needs may not be met 100% in the way we most would like them to be, but they will be met in a way we can live with.

For example, when the wife says, "I need to have the house," the mediator shouldn't say, "You can't have the house if you can't afford it." What the mediator could say is, "Tell me more about why that is important to you." Then she might tell you that, "Well, the house is the only asset in which I have any money and it's the only asset I can get some money out of." This response gives valuable information

When the parties come in with their information, we often start getting information disagreements. I might say, "It looks like we need to determine the value of the house. What process do you want to use to determine what the value of that real estate is?" If they don't have a clear idea of what this means, I will suggest they get some help, such as from their own financial planner or other expert.

* * * *

Christine Coates agrees with the importance of interest-based bargaining.

Christine:
How do people negotiate? It means they turn from a position-based style to an interest-based style. A position is the specific proposal or solution that a party adopts to meet his or her interests or needs. It is the party's solution to what they would really like to see happen. They want the other party to say yes or no.

This differs from the interest-based style, which is the concern or what the party wants to accomplish through his or her position. In almost every mediation, people come in with a position—they are very strong in what they want. But when the mediator starts probing, he or she finds that there is more than just that position. There is a need underneath it.

When anyone is stuck in a position, there is not a lot of room to negotiate.

If a the wife says, "I must have $2,000 per month maintenance and that's final." Or the husband says, "I'll pay $2,000 per month for five years. That's it. No more." Neither party can go very far with that. But when they start talking about what is underneath all that—is it for school, is it to meet reasonable needs, is it to support the household until the children are out of school—there emerges room to negotiate.

THE ROLE OF LISTENING IN MEDIATION

True, active listening is a big part of the mediator's job. According to Michael Caplan, "Effective listening is the other part of what we are doing." Here are some of his additional thoughts on listening.

Michael:

Effective listening is the other part of what we are doing. How many times do we think we already know what the other person is trying to say? It takes energy to listen and you need to focus on the speaker. If I have my own talk going on in my head, I am going to have a hard time being able to hear. We need to check out what we think we heard to find out if we have it right and then we need to let the other party know that we really heard them.

So many times, women in the more traditional marriages have not really been heard. They really have not been listened to by their mate. The anger is there and sometimes it gets suppressed, so when it does come out it spills out more like a volcano and involves issues that really may not be important.

Listening is different from problem-solving or giving advice. How many times have you gone to a friend and started talking to them and they said, "Yeah, I had that problem once and this is what I did" or "You know, if you would only do this that would do it."

What I want to do when I am active listening is to feedback the feeling and content. "So you are really upset and a bit anxious about the fact that I came in late and you were worried about whether I was going to show up."

Look for what the feeling is and give back the feeling first and try to match intensity.

* * * *

Christine Coates agrees.

Christine:
The mediator can never assume that he or she heard what the clients mean. For example, when women listen, many nod their head and say "Uh-huh, uh-huh." Men just sit and listen, rarely showing any facial expression, much less head movement. When men hear women saying, "Uh-huh, uh-huh," they think the woman is agreeing with them when the woman is actually only indicating that she is listening. When men sit and listen but don't say anything, women think the man is not listening. This gender difference in listening styles leads to miscommunication.

Listening involves asking questions to make things more clear, but it is not interviewing. People want to know that they are being heard and then will get the facts afterward. *Listening is not problem-solving.* It is not hearing what someone has to say and then jumping in with, "Here's what you need to do. I know exactly how you can fix this problem."

Common Mistakes in Active Listening

- (Trying to solve the problem instead of focusing on what the other person is trying to say. Each person has the inherent ability to solve his or her own problems.
- (Telling the other person that we understand.
- (Continuing to ask closed-end questions instead of open-ended questions.

WHERE TO FIND A MEDIATOR

When your client needs a mediator, who do you send them to? Being an attorney or therapist does not necessarily mean they would make a good mediator. Unfortunately, few states have certification or a minimum amount of training necessary to become a mediator.

Mediators need different sets of skills, especially in handling conflict. Before hiring a mediator, check out his or her qualifications. It's important to know who has had training and experience. Ask. The minimum amount of training acceptable is 40 hours.

There are mediation organizations in each state. Check the telephone book under "mediation," or call the Academy of Family Mediators, (617) 674-2663, in Lexington, Massachusetts that can provide a list of mediators in your area.

WHEN MEDIATION MAY NOT WORK

Some people feel that they are not candidates for mediation because they can't talk to each other, they can't communicate, or they're in high conflict. Well, almost everyone going through divorce is in that situation. People in divorce are often confused. It is known as the "crazy time." They know how to push each other's buttons. It is the rare couple that can really communicate even when they're going through divorce. The mediator is trained to deal with conflict.

Even so, there are some people who should not mediate. Often people going through divorce where there has been domestic violence should not be in mediation because there has been power imbalance in that relationship.

In situations where there is mental illness or substance abuse, mediation will probably not work. If there is some type of substance abuse going on, the person should not be in mediation. The substance abuse is an indication that one of the parties does not have the power to do what they need to do. If they are addicted to a substance, the likelihood is that they also are unable to follow through on agree-upon solutions.

Another area in which mediation should not be used is when one or both of the parties are ignoring the children's best interests.

In addition, if the clients want the mediator to make the decisions, or if one party seems to be giving in on all matters and you sense this was the norm in their relationship, these may not be good parties for mediation. Here's an example.

Norm and Donna came in to see the mediator. The one item that raised a red flag was the fact that Norm had done a lot of work in forming a software company. Because of his work and some contracts that he had put together, he had signed agreements that promised him bonuses for the next five years. Depending on profits, these agreements could give him up to $1 million per year for five years. Donna said that she had no right to those because they would come in after the divorce. She constantly looked at him for approval of what she was saying. The mediator asked Norm if he felt those were marital property and he guessed they were. The mediator then asked Donna again if she agreed that they were marital property. She looked timid and repeated that she wouldn't want to take those away from Norm. Finally, the mediator had to advise Donna to see an attorney before they could proceed further. She needed to know her legal rights.

ARBITRATION

What is the difference between mediation and arbitration? In mediation, two parties share the decision. In arbitration, the power to decide is solely with the arbitrator. The two parties meet with the arbitrator; present each of their positions (much like mediation), and then the arbitrator makes the decision for them, which is binding (in most states).

Some couples want to arbitrate because they disagree and can't seem to move past their deadlock. They feel that the only possible solution is to hand over the power of deciding to a third party. If the parties agree ahead of time that the arbitration will be binding, they are guaranteed a resolution of their dispute. It can be both efficient and informal, and thus a good alternative to going to court. Its effectiveness depends on the arbitrator's ability to gain a clear enough understanding of the issues to make a wise decision.

Arbitration is especially tempting for people who think they are right, because they are sure that their position will be vindicated by the arbitrator. And because people who feel they are right often see the other person as wrong, it is easy for them to see the process as one that will end in victory for themselves and defeat of the other. The fact that they agree to turn over their decision-making power tends to encourage the parties to skew the information they present to the arbitrator, painting their own views with righteousness and trying to invalidate the other's position. Defending one's position is a natural human tendency that is enhanced when one does not have the power to decide.

HOW CAN CERTIFIED DIVORCE PLANNERS HELP PREPARE THEIR CLIENTS FOR MEDIATION OR ARBITRATION?

The CDP can play a valuable role in the mediation process. They can educate the lawyer as to the need for a professional planner. With information from the client and the lawyer, the CDP will examine all assets and liabilities.

Before the mediation statement is written, the CDP may suggest alternative solutions to the attorney and the client. After the mediation statement is written, the CDP might even review it. If appropriate, the CDP could attend the mediation session or at least be available by phone and fax.

COLLABORATIVE DIVORCE

Collaborative Divorce is a new and highly effective divorce method that utilizes Collaborative Law. Teams of professionals trained in the Collaborative Divorce interdisciplinary method are springing up all over the United States. Trainings are given by the founders of Collaborative Divorce together with Collaborative Law attorneys in 2-day training sessions. For information, call 925-253-0700.

1. What is Collaborative Divorce?

Collaborative Divorce is a team approach to divorce that includes gender-balanced divorce coaches, neutral financial specialists, Collaborative Law attorneys and when needed, child specialists. Divorcing families obtain professional help from specialists in the psychotherapy, financial and legal fields to help them settle their case. Each team member assists the family in his/her area of expertise, and then works integratively with other team members and with the collaborative law attorneys who help families reach viable divorce settlements. The team teaches communication skills so that parents can communicate better with each other and in the future around their children's needs. Finances are addressed, budgets are created, and financial skills taught where needed. Although more professionals are involved in collaborative divorce cases, the cost is lower for the family overall because the family receives specific and focused divorce assistance which allows for more productive work when meeting with their attorneys to reach settlement. Collaborative Law attorneys are the legal professionals on a Collaborative Divorce team.

2. What is Collaborative Law?

Collaborative Law is a new dispute resolution model in which both parties to the dispute retain separate, specially trained lawyers whose only job is to help them settle the dispute. All participants agree to work together respectfully, honestly, and in good faith to try to find "win-win" solutions to the legitimate needs of both parties. No one may go to court, or even threaten to do so, and if that should occur, the Collaborative Law process terminates and both lawyers are disqualified from any further involvement in the case.

3. What is the difference between Collaborative Law and mediation?

In mediation, there is one "neutral" who helps the disputing parties try to settle their case. The mediator cannot give either party legal advice, and cannot help either side advocate its position. If one side or the other becomes unreasonable or stubborn, or lacks negotiating skill, or is emotionally distraught, the mediation can become unbalanced, and if the mediator tries to deal with the problem, the mediator is often seen by one side or the other as biased, whether or not that is so. If the mediator does not find a way to deal with the problem, the mediation can break down, or the agreement that results can be unfair. If there are attorneys for the parties at all, they may not be present at the negotiation and their advice may come too late to be helpful.

Collaborative Law was designed to deal more effectively with all these problems, while maintaining the same absolute commitment to settlement as the sole agenda. Each side has quality legal advice and advocacy built in at all times during the process. It is the job of the lawyers to work with their own clients if the clients are being unreasonable to make sure that the process stays positive and productive.

4. What kind of information and documents are available in the Collaborative Law negotiations?

Both sides sign a binding agreement to disclose all documents and information that relate to the issues, early and fully and voluntarily. "Hide the ball" and stonewalling are not permitted. All information is shared openly. Attorneys and clients work together to create win-win solutions for all members of the family.

5. Why is Collaborative Law such an effective settlement process?

The Collaborative Law attorneys have a completely different state of mind about what their job is than traditional lawyers generally bring to their work. We call it a "paradigm shift." Instead of being dedicated to getting the largest possible piece of the pie for their own client, no matter the human or financial cost, collaborative lawyers are dedicated to helping their clients achieve their highest intentions for themselves in their post-divorce restructured families.

Collaborative lawyers do not act as a hired gun. Nor do they take advantage of mistakes inadvertently made by the other side. They expect and encourage the highest good-faith problem-solving behavior from their own clients and themselves.

Collaborative lawyers trust one another. They still owe a primary allegiance and duty to their own clients but they know that the only way they can serve the true best interests of their clients is to behave with, and demand, the highest integrity from themselves, their clients, and the other participants in the process.

Collaborative Law and Collaborative Divorce offer a greater potential for creative problem-solving than does either mediation or litigation, in that only Collaborative Law puts two lawyers in the same room pulling in the same direction to solve the same list of problems. No matter how good a lawyer they are for their client, they cannot succeed as a Collaborative Lawyer unless they also can find solutions to the other party's problems that their client finds satisfactory. This is the special characteristic of Collaborative Law that is found in no other dispute resolution process.

HIRING AN ATTORNEY

Some couples think they can hire one attorney and save costs. But the fact is, if they can't reach a settlement and have to go to court, each spouse will need their own attorney. One-lawyer divorces are ill advised and prohibited in many states as unethical.

Issues may arise that neither party thought about but which must be resolved. It will be almost impossible for one attorney to help the couple resolve these issues if the solution is advantageous to one party and adverse to the other. In such a case, one of the spouses will have to hire another lawyer.

WAYS TO RESOLVE DIVORCES

Reconcile

Some couples realize, after much soul-searching and perhaps some counseling that they still want to be married to each other. Many make an effort to make changes in their situation to save their marriage.

Death

If one party dies while in the midst of divorce proceedings, all legal activity will cease. The surviving party will probably end up with everything, depending on a will and/or prenuptial provisions.

Negotiate

The parties may negotiate, with or without attorneys, their property settlement, child custody issues, family support, and so on. This gives each of them a feeling of controlling their own decision and therefore, they are more likely to adhere to the agreements made.

Mediate

The couple meets with an impartial third party who helps them reach a solution that they both agree to. The mediator does not give advice or tell them how they should resolve their situation.

Arbitrate

The couple meets with an arbitrator who, after hearing all the issues, makes the decision for the couple.

Mediate – Arbitrate

Also called "med/arb," this way of resolving conflict is to start with mediation and when all issues are on the table through the mediation process, a decision is made by the facilitator.

Court conference

A meeting with the couple and their attorneys, with or without a judge present, to try to come to resolution.

Trial

When all else fails, the couple's situation is presented to a judge in a formal court hearing and the judge hands down a binding decision.

LEGAL SEPARATION

An option for some couples is a legal separation instead of a divorce. Under a legal separation, they divide their property and there may be child support and maintenance, but they are still legally married. A couple may choose this route for several reasons:

1. *Religious reasons.* Some religions frown on divorce. Many people are uncomfortable going against the teachings of their religion.
2. *Health insurance.* Even though COBRA allows the ex-spouse to retain health insurance for three years after the divorce is final, if the ex-spouse is uninsurable, this can be a great concern. A legal separation allows the ex-spouse to remain on the working spouse's health insurance plan.
3. *Not wishing a divorce.* Many couples can't stand living together but they also hate the thought of being divorced. A legal separation allows them to live their separate lives. And some spouses hold the secret thought that the marriage could be put back together. If the marriage turns out to be impossible to salvage, then a divorce can be filed and is easily accomplished as all the details, such as dividing the property have already been done.

(Special thanks for contributions to this chapter go to Christine Coates, J.D., nationally known trainer and speaker on mediation from Boulder, CO; Michael Caplan, J.D., a mediator trainer in Boulder, CO; Gary J. Friedman, J.D., of the Center for Mediation and Law, Mill Valley, CA; and Pauline Tesler, J.D., of the American Institute of Collaborative Professionals, Santa Rosa, CA.)

CHAPTER 14

If You Have to Go to Court

We all hope for the best of all worlds: that we can settle our cases with both spouses feeling that they got a fair shake.

Obviously, however, some cases aren't settled and they have to be decided in court. If there is even just one thing that cannot be agreed upon, the case will go to court for the judge to rule on that item only. Here are some examples. As you'll see, sometimes it isn't worth your client's time and money to go through the process.

> Bill and Connie had agreed on child support. They agreed on alimony. They had even divided all their property—except for one thing. They both wanted the set of fine crystal they had bought on their honeymoon in England. Neither would give in. After spending thousands of dollars on attorneys trying to work this out, they finally ended up in court. There, they spent thousands of dollars more before the judge finally handed down his decision. In the end, they spent many times the value of the crystal!

> Ed and Sue had divided all their assets but one. Ed didn't want Sue to have any part of his "poker savings account" a $19,000 savings account representing his winnings from poker over a 12-year period. Sue insisted that half of it was hers so Ed hired an expensive attorney and went to court rather than give in. He ended up spending $22,000 in fees—but he kept Sue from getting his savings account!

If a case you are working on does not settle, you could be called upon to appear as an expert witness in court on behalf of your client. If this happens, you want to be knowledgeable and prepared.

Helen Stone (a partner in Stone, Sheehy, Rosen & Byrne, P.C., in Boulder, Colorado) specializes in family law and bankruptcy. She lectures frequently on these topics. She has this to say about being an expert witness:

> Going to court does not make you an expert witness. What makes you an expert is your training as a CFP, the experience you have had analyzing what people's incomes are, and doing calculations and predicting—that is what your expertise is and that has nothing to do with you going to court. It is your expertise that is helpful in this case and helpful to this person who is now going to court.

ACTING AS AN EXPERT WITNESS

What is an expert witness? A book that advises federal court juries gives the following definition.

> The rules of evidence ordinarily do not permit witnesses to testify as to opinions or conclusions. An exception to this rule exists as to those whom we call "expert witnesses." Witnesses who, by education and experience, have become expert in some art, science, profession, or calling, may state an opinion as to relevant and material matter, in which they profess to be expert, and may also state their reasons for the opinion.[1]

Helen Stone explains this further.

The reason expert testimony is presented to a judge is to assist the trier of fact in determining and understanding specific evidence. The rules of evidence for lawyers provide for the use of expert testimony to do that. You are presented to the judge as an expert because you have specialized knowledge that will assist the judge in determining what the evidence is and how to sort through it. The rule says that if there is scientific, technical, or other specialized knowledge that will assist the trier of fact in understanding the evidence, then the lawyer can call an expert witness who has the requisite knowledge, skill or experience, training, and education to testify. That is the basis on which financial planners, certified public accountants, or lawyers are used as expert witnesses.

As a financial planner, you have some specialized knowledge that the judge lacks. Although the judge is going to be a person who has had legal training and has experienced a wide variety of cases, he or she is not likely to be a financial expert.

The judge may not have any background in the financial arena, or the judge may know some financial concepts but need a refresher in the subject area. You are valuable to the court because you have that expertise.

The one thing that should give you some comfort when you first take the witness stand is that you know more about your subject matter than anybody in the courtroom. Even if you make a mistake, even if you are uncomfortable, and even if it is your first time in court, nobody there knows more about financial planning—especially what you have investigated and researched with respect to this case. Keeping that in mind will give you some comfort and some self-confidence because it is absolutely true. Your purpose in court is to communicate the information that you know to the judge.

* * * *

Before actually presenting your report to the court and being questioned about it, some other things happen first. Your qualifications (or curriculum vitae) will be presented, you will be "qualified" as an expert witness, and there may be *voir dire*.

Your Curriculum Vitae

When you start working with an attorney, one of the first things that attorney is going to ask for is your curriculum vitae or resume. He or she wants to see your credentials to determine if you can be an expert witness in court. The attorney cannot act as his or her own expert witness. The attorney has to hire outside experts. You are the expert who produced the financial charts and graphs for your client. Now, you are the one who has to answer the questions about them. Therefore, the attorney wants to know that you are going to qualify as an expert witness in court.

To be an expert witness, your curriculum vitae will list your qualifications that show you are qualified as an expert in the area of the financial issues in divorce. Start with your educational background and all the things that qualify you to be a financial planner. Your curriculum vitae should show:

- current position
- education and training

- work history relating to financial planning
- details of continuing education
- publications including books and articles
- workshop presentations, lectures, and teaching
- honors and recognitions
- expert witness experience
- anything else related to being an expert in financial issues in divorce.

Getting Qualified as an Expert Witness in Court

In court, you are sworn in by the judge or an assistant to the judge. After you repeat the oath, you sit in the chair for the expert witnesses. Then, your client's attorney starts questioning you as to your qualifications unless there is an agreement between the attorneys that you are an expert. The attorney has not offered you as an expert yet. First, the attorney must show that you are qualified and will question the information from your vitae. The whole purpose of this is to show that you are an expert in this area. Finally, you will be offered to the court as an expert in financial planning.

Voir Dire

After your client's attorney has offered you as an expert witness, the other attorney has a chance to do what is called *voir dire*. This means you will be asked questions designed to disqualify you by showing that you are not an expert or to show the judge why less weight should be placed on your testimony. The goal of voir dire is to show that you are not qualified to give an expert opinion.

Barbara Stark is an attorney in private practice in New Haven Connecticut. A fellow of the American Academy of Matrimonial Lawyers, she co-authored *Divorce Practice Handbook: Skills and Strategies for the Family Lawyer.* According to Ms. Stark, this is what to expect from voir dire.

When an expert witness takes the stand and testifies to all of his or her qualifications, the other lawyer can get up and challenge you as an expert. This is known as voir dire. You'll be asked questions about your qualifications and experience, and those questions are designed to convince the court that you are not an expert.

> Witnesses who have training and experience above that of the normal layperson may be admitted as an expert witness. The reason that people go into your qualifications so much both in the direct examination and the voir dire is so the judge can have in his or her mind the weight that should be given to your testimony.

After voir dire is complete and you have been qualified as an expert witness, you will go on to the next steps of the court process: direct examination and cross-examination.

DIRECT EXAMINATION

There are four things you'll need to do on the witness stand.

1. Your first step is to explain the nature and the scope of your assignment. Every expert witness has an assignment. For instance, in this case, say your assignment was to take certain property division, alimony, and child support scenarios and project the future economic consequences.
2. The second step is to explain how divorce planners use scenarios to show financial results of any given settlement. This mainly entails explaining methodology.
3. Next, summarize your work in the case—who you talked to, what information was assembled, what assumptions were made, and so on.
4. Last, admit your exhibits and explain your reports. Of course, before the trial, you will have coordinated with the attorney as to when the reports should be admitted.

As Barbara Stark says,

> Direct examination is where your lawyer puts you on the stand. During direct examination, you are telling a story. Although your lawyer is asking you questions, he or she might as well not be there. You are the one on display. During direct examination, you are asked open-ended questions by your client's attorney. These are questions that cannot be answered "yes" or "no," but rather need more complete responses. This gives you a chance to tell your story.
>
> In direct testimony, you must be understandable and interesting. Your presentation style and content must persuade the judge that your conclusions are fair and reasonable.

Barbara Stark, who has done countless cross-examinations, gives this example of direct examination. (You probably won't be asked about your breakfast in a real trial, but this dialogue gives you an idea of what to expect.)

Attorney: (A) What is your name?
You: (Y) Carol Ann Wilson.
A: Where are you staying here in Los Angeles?
Y: I am staying at the Sheraton.
A: Did you have breakfast there this morning?
Y: Yes, they have a wonderful breakfast buffet.
A: What did you have?
Y: I had fruit and toast and eggs with coffee.
A: Did you have any bacon with that?
Y: No, they didn't have any bacon on the buffet so I had one piece of sausage.
A: How much did you pay for your breakfast?
Y: The breakfast was included with the price of my room so I didn't pay anything this morning.

* * * *

Helen Stone gives this advice about the direct examination process.

During your direct examination, probably the most common objection that the other lawyer will raise is that what you are testifying to is hearsay. Remember that you are allowed to rely on hearsay. A vocational expert is the kind of expert you have not talked to, but you are relying on the conclusions in the report, and that is permissible.

Be on the lookout for questions that ask you to give legal advice. It is okay for the lawyer to ask the question, "Is there enough money in this household to meet the necessary expenses?" That is an acceptable question because it asks only for a simple cash flow analysis, which you do frequently in your business. On the other hand, asking the question, "Having looked at your chart and considered the expenses, is your client entitled to maintenance?" is calling for a legal conclusion. The lawyer will object and be sustained.

In direct examination, one of the areas that comes up fairly regularly is the objection made by the other side that you are speculating, and speculation is not permitted. You are not there to speculate. You are there to talk about the logical inferences and conclusions with respect to various alternatives. Your training is about that, and you are there as an expert to look at consequences and alternatives.

Practical Pointers for Direct Examination

1. The aim of testimony is to be listened to, to be believed, and to be convincing.
2. You need adequate preparation. Although even CPAs from top firms have had errors in their testimony, that doesn't mean you should have errors. You want to go through your report very carefully. The best way to find errors is to explain that report to somebody else in great detail.
3. Answer questions deliberately. Do not hurry and do not lecture.
4. Be concise; do not ramble. Good preparation will result in well-organized, crisp testimony.
5. Avoid jargon. Remember that the judge may not know what you mean when talking about financial terminology, concepts, and so on. While these things are just common sense to us, try to say things in ways that everybody can understand.
6. Do not nod or gesture in lieu of an answer. The court reporter can only write down words that have been spoken.
7. Know the weak spots in your report and discuss them with your attorney. It may be better to deal with them under direct examination than to wait for the cross examiner to hammer on them.
8. An expert witness is not an advocate. The lawyer is the advocate. You are not a hired gun, producing reports slanted toward your client. You must be consistent with your financial opinions. Use the same assumptions from case to case. This is the mark of a true professional

CROSS EXAMINATION

In cross-examination, you are asked closed-end questions by the other attorney that can usually only be answered "yes," "no," "I don't know," etc.

Here, Barbara Stark explains cross-examination more fully.

When the direct examination is over, the other lawyer gets up to cross-examine you. With a good cross examiner, you are the one who becomes less visible because the cross examiner is using what we call "leading questions."

The cross examiner is now telling the story and you are typically merely saying "yes or no" unless you are invited to explain.

Given the breakfast topic example from the previous section on direct examination, here's how the cross examination might sound.

Attorney Your name is Carol Ann Wilson, is it not?
You Yes.
A: Are you staying at the Sheraton Hotel?
Y: Yes.
A: The Sheraton Hotel is just across the street from The John Wayne Airport, isn't it?
Y: Yes, it is.
A: Now, Ms. Wilson, when you got up this morning, you went down to the cafe?
Y: Yes.
A: That cafe is on the first floor of the hotel?
Y: Yes.
A: And you sat down and you had breakfast?
Y: Yes.
A: When you had that breakfast, you ordered eggs, didn't you?
Y: Yes.
A: As a matter of fact, you had sausage with those eggs?
Y: Yes, I did.
A: And then you walked out of the restaurant without paying, DIDN'T you?

Do you see the difference? Cross-examinations are uncomfortable because you sense a loss of control. It is like you are being pulled here and there, and you don't know where you will end up. If it is done right, a cross-examination puts words in the witness's mouth.

* * * *

There are many different approaches to cross-examination. The cross examiner will try to attack the expert in various ways. Here are some things to watch for.

- Attacking the expert's qualifications
- Attacking the expert's objectivity
- Attacking the expert's methodology
- Attacking the expert's assumptions
- Trying to establish that the expert has bias toward the client who hired him or her.

Helen Stone adds this opinion.

Cross-examination is when the lawyer essentially gets to testify. The lawyer takes control and tries to put words in your mouth. The most common kinds of questions that the lawyer uses are those which require only a yes or no answer. If you try to add more explanation, the lawyer is going to cut you off. The lawyer wants to show the judge that there is a different slant on this topic other then the one that you have given in your direct testimony. So, on cross-examination you will probably not be asked any questions that start with "why." Only a less-experienced or sloppy lawyer will ask you "why" and will usually get tripped up on it. The cross-examining lawyer wants to show the limits of what you have done, show whatever deficiencies there are, and show any mistakes.

Practical Pointers for Cross Examination.

1. Keep your responses brief and do not volunteer information. Remember that on direct examination, you can explain fully anything that you want. On cross-examination, however, limit your answer to the narrow question asked. Then *stop talking.* Never volunteer information or answers.
2. Listen to your lawyer's objections. They are usually meant to alert you to a problem area, or if the objection is overruled, will help you to understand the question.
3. Don't answer too quickly or you risk answering while your attorney is preparing to object. Take a breath before each answer.
4. Appear briskly self-confident. If the cross examiner asks, "Did you consider that the husband might be disabled at work?" answer, "No, I did not." You cannot take into account everything.
5. Bring only essential documents to the witness stand unless other

documents, or your entire file is subpoenaed. Your file is subject to examination.

6. Do not render opinions on matters of law. Even if, on the stand, the cross examiner asks you about a legal issue, do not attempt to answer if you are not an attorney. You cannot render opinions on matters of law.
7. Understand the question, and if you do not understand the question, ask to have it repeated. Do not guess if you don't know the answer.
8. Do not be pushed to answer yes or no. Many times, they will ask you a question that you know is not a yes or no question. You could say, "That cannot be answered yes or no."
9. Avoid such phrases as "I think," "I guess," "I believe," or "I assume."
10. Remain silent if attorneys object during the examination.
11. Avoid mannerisms that signal nervousness.
12. Do not get overconfident.
13. Do not drop your voice or head. Even if they point out a mistake, stay confident. When you start dropping, it makes everybody think you really do not know what you are talking about.
14. Tell the truth.

Barbara Stark offers these additional tips for controlling cross-examination.

1. Listen for open-ended questions and limit your answer to the narrow question asked. . You usually won't get many such opportunities during a cross examination, so take advantage of them.
2. Never forget that after the other lawyer completes cross-examination, your lawyer gets up and does "redirect." You know cross-examination is putting words in your mouth and you are just dying to explain why you said yes to a cross-examination question. If you try to explain it during cross, that is considered "non responsive" and it may annoy the judge or subject you to a non-responsive objection. So just say yes or no and remember that your lawyer will later get up and say, "Now, you said on cross examination that you used a 4 percent inflation rate. Can you explain to us why you did that?" This is your chance to give all the explanation that you want.
3. Do not, under any set of circumstances, get angry. This case is not

about you. If you get angry, you may well lose your credibility. When you are angry, you do not look good to the judge. This increases the chance that the judge is not going to like you. Secondly, when you are angry, you are not listening to the question because you are thinking about yourself and how much you hate the cross-examiner. If you take it personally and you get angry, you are in trouble.

4. Answer tough questions head-on. If it is a tough question think about it and answer it directly.
5. No matter what you do, remember that the truth is never a problem. You may hate to admit to something on cross-examination that is not in your client's favor, but your job is to tell the truth on the witness stand. That is your entire job.
6. Remember that court is, in some ways, a game. Attorneys may be at each other's throat but at the end of the day they may socialize. They may be friendly to each other. But in court, they are doing their job for their client and you should not take it personally.
7. You may be asked about the speculative nature of your reports. You may want to address that in the following way: "I make certain assumptions based on historical data and I show financial results based on certain settlement options. When financial planners work with clients concerning their retirement issues, we make certain assumptions about their current income, expenses, and assets and make assumptions about future inflation and investment rates. From those assumptions, we have an idea about what they can save to meet their future needs. We know from past performances of certain investment vehicles, which ones are conservatively safe and what the yields on those will be."

FINAL WORDS FOR THE EXPERT WITNESS

Helen Stone gives these additional tips to the expert witness.

One thing is common to both juries and judges. They are going to pay more attention to your testimony if it is interesting. Many witnesses are tediously boring, either because they speak in a monotone or because they present information in an ineffective way. For example, they may have a chart and they merely read all the figures to the jury without adding any other detail. It's deadly boring.

Contrast this with witnesses who can really tell a story. They are linear, they present the information in a logical fashion, and they are interesting. Keep this in mind when you are making your presentation on direct examination—the more interested the judge is, the more the judge is going to pay attention to you and follow what you have to say. That becomes important as your testimony proceeds, because as soon as the judge is hooked into your testimony and what it is you are saying, then the judge is going to be focusing on you and really trying to understand. That, of course, is your purpose and goal as an expert witness.

You may have to explain to the judge what you do as a Certified Financial Planner and why you are before the court. Take as much time as possible to explain yourself and, more importantly, take as much time and go into as much detail as you can explaining the method you used to establish your assumptions and scenarios. That really is the key to your testimony.

One thing to add to your methodology is a theory, or a theme, of the case. If you want to say, for example, that a 50/50 property division is really the perfect solution and explain why, then keep that in mind from the very beginning. Although it is probably not necessary to state it in your direct examination at the outset, at some point you are going to want to have that as your conclusion. It gives you a focus—it is sort of your road map.

REPORT FROM THE COLORADO LAWYER, December 1999

The Colorado Bar Association sent nine-page questionnaires covering domestic law issues to ninety judges. Forty-one judges responded with useful comments. Following is a summation of some of the pertinent points for Certified Divorce Planners.

Charts

The judges really like charts if they are "comprehensive and comprehensible." The best ones are simple, easy to read, and realistic. All charts should include property that has been stipulated to as to value or as to division and any nonmarital property.

Experts

The judges said they liked experts' credentials to be established by resume or vitae, and they expected the attorneys to stipulate to the experts' credentials. If there is no stipulation, very brief testimony highlighting that which is critical will be tolerated, but, for the most part, resumes and *vitaes* should be the primary means of establishing expertise.

Under direct examination, the expert should identify the data used in forming the opinion, what the opinion is, and the underlying rationale for the opinion. If opposed, the expert should delineate disagreement with the other expert, critique the opposing opinion, and provide the reasons for disagreeing with the other expert. Complex matters must be explained as simply as possible.

The cross-examining attorney should be brief. The court should hear the differences in the data used or not used compared to the other expert; the differences in underlying assumptions; the differences in time spent and differences in credentials. Any error, bias, or relevant defects in the expert's opinion should be pointed out without showing disrespect for or arguing with the expert. "Get to the bottom line so we can see the outer limits of reason and common sense; usually there is a range and darn few absolutes."

Property and Debt Divisions

Judges need to see a complete list of assets, debts, and the value of such assets and debts. Additional information that is needed includes: mortgage balances; the amount of each debt; and the value of pensions, retirement plans, personal property, and fringe benefits.

In addition, they do not need to know how much the parties dislike each other; too much detail, such as all of the check registers; money spent or property depleted during the marriage; and anything said more than twice. Also stated were "grossly unfair demands which are not useful before a court in equity."

They like charts that had itemized proposals for the allocation of property and debt. Some had attached documents or references to admitted exhibits showing source of value; and some showed acquisition origin, value at the time of marriage in addition to current value, whether the asset was to be sold or retained, and by whom.

Experts who have knowledge of the law and its application to the circumstances the court is considering are very helpful. Expert testimony on pension divisions or valuations is helpful. Without expert testimony, the tax consequences may not be considered unless the court has acquired expertise outside of the case being presented and is willing to use it.

Most of the judges said that property and debt divisions were equal because it was "the most fair" where both had contributed time and energy to the marriage, it was the "intent going into the marriage," and "marriage is an equal responsibility, divorce an equal loss." Several reported an equal division of assets, with debts divided pro rata according to income. Yet, some judges stated that an equal division is simply the starting point and that equity could be achieved only when all of the statutory factors had been considered. Of this group, equal property or equal property and debt divisions were not the rule.

A few of the judges said that whether the property and debt division was equal depended on a number of factors such as differences in income, especially in longer marriages. In these cases, the judge may award more property to the spouse who earned less, particularly if it would change the amount or duration of maintenance. Multiple variables may have to be considered: responsibility for children, earning capacities, nature of the assets and debts, the type of property or debt, and the tax impact of particular divisions.

When asked about the impact of significant separate property on the partial property divisions, only one-fourth of the judges would not consider the separate property at all. The remaining majority would consider the separate property as a factor for a potential unequal property division based on the nature of, liquidity of, and income from the separate property; whether separate property had been used during the marriage; whether each party's pre-separation standard of living could be restored; what the length of the marriage had been and "other common sense considerations."

Maintenance

The judges were asked about information needed and not needed when awarding maintenance, the helpfulness of experts, and whether there were factors in addition to the statutory ones that may be considered when determining the amount and duration of maintenance. .

They answered that they want better information on why maintenance was needed, how long it would be needed, and the expectations during the marriage. Some wanted more extensive information on the tax ramifications and the parties' relative financial positions under different hypotheticals. More realistic proposals that take into account both parties' needs were requested. If health is an issue, the nature of the health problem and its impact on that person's ability to work must be fully explained, preferably by independent expert testimony. The information the courts did not need included marital misconduct or fault or either party, "extreme figures" for expenses, why divorcing, the income of any new boyfriend or girlfriend, and "vocational experts."

Experts on maintenance issues received very mixed reviews. Experts who provided information on income from assets, tax impacts, or the effect of a particular award were sought by about half of the judges; the other half thought such experts were full of assumptions and speculations that were not helpful.

When asked what factors a court might consider in addition to the statutory ones in determining the *amount* of maintenance, the following were included:

- the local economy
- the future financial outlook for each spouse in five, ten, or fifteen years
- reasonable expectations during the marriage
- tax factors
- contributions to the other's earning capacity
- whether marital resources have been wasted, particularly during separation
- the need to sacrifice economic advancement due to the age of the children

When asked what factors a court might consider in addition to the statutory ones in determining the *duration* of maintenance, the following were included:

- expectations during the marriage
- the future financial outlook for each spouse
- when either party might retire and have reduced income
- whether the duration equals half the length of the marriage after ten years
- expectations of future change
- the availability of insurance

NOTES

1. Devitt and Blackmar, Federal Jury Practice and Instructions, 3rd ed., Vol. 1, (West Publishing Company, 1977), 15.22, p.482.)

CHAPTER 15

Divorce Procedures

I. Divorce in general

The laws about divorce are very different from state to state. You must familiarize yourself with the divorce laws and procedures in your own state. There are three ways to accomplish this.

1. Divorce law is written in a book called Statutes, sometimes called Dissolution of Marriage Statutes. Contrary to public opinion, these laws are written in English. Most Statute books will give you the law on a topic, and then they will give you little paragraph bullet entries about the cases that have come down from Appellate Court to interpret that law. It is a real nice way to get the flavor of how the law is applied in your state.

   For instance, the divorce statute may list factors that the judge considers when dividing property in a divorce. The statute does not say that those same factors must be considered and weighted the same way when the spouses divide the property themselves. What the judge must consider is the fall-back position if the spouses cannot agree. For example, the statute defines *marital* and *separate* property. The spouses may agree to define these terms the way the statute does, but they are free to define them in their own way (subject to the judge's approving the settlement).

2. We recommend you contact the State or local Bar Association of your state. Every state has Continuing Legal Education programs on divorce law—everything from the basics for beginning lawyers, to advanced for long-time lawyers. Lawyers take classes on the different aspects of family law. If you pay the fee, you will probably be able to take the seminar or buy the tapes and materials.
3. You may want to go to the courtroom and watch a case which will increase your knowledge base.

A. Grounds
   1. In every state in this country, divorce is "no fault." That means that either spouse can get a divorce even if the other spouse doesn't want the divorce. It does not need to be proven that the other spouse was a bad person in order to get a divorce. The language is typically that the marriage is "irretrievably broken" with no chance for reconciliation.
   2. In some states, "fault" could play a role in the division of property, award of custody, award of alimony or child support. It's an intimidating factor in settling a case if one spouse has to testify regarding his or her bad acts.

B. Most people who go through divorce have lawyers. But there is a trend in this country that people not retain lawyers. People who go through divorce without a lawyer are called "pro se." The statistics are that at least 50% of the people who go through divorce or sue each other after the divorce have no lawyer.

Problems with "pro se" divorces
1. Income taxes. Many people do not understand the tax consequences of transferring certain property, such as the house, or stock with a low basis. One of them may be stuck with a huge tax bill.
2. Missed assets. If the parties don't completely understand the difference between marital and separate property, some property may be transferred without fully understanding the legal options.
3. Pensions. Sometimes, retirement accounts are the most valuable marital asset. If the parties do not fully understand the retirement plans, they could grossly undervalue what is to be divided. Some also fail to understand the consequences of the death of the em-

ployee or the nonemployee. In these cases, benefits could revert to the company rather than the beneficiaries the parties intended.

II. Waiting periods

A. Residency

In all states, one spouse needs to have been a resident for a certain period of time for the court to have jurisdiction to divorce the couple. The typical length of time is 90 days.

B. "Cooling off" period

The other time period that states have is the "cooling off" period" intended to prevent people rushing through the divorce. In many states the period of time from when you start the case to when you end the case is typically 90 days. Even though that period is relatively short, the average divorce case takes about a year. About 90-95% of divorce cases reach a settlement. If no settlement is reached, the parties go to court and the judge makes the final decision.

III. Temporary Orders

Whether the case takes 90 days or it takes 5 years, the period of time between the beginning and the end of the case, is a time when the financial and emotional life of the family goes on. There are children to feed, there are mortgages to pay, there are insurances to deal with. This is the temporary period. It's during this temporary period that people usually reach settlement about how to manage their lives while they are waiting for the case to be over. If they can't settle, they go to a judge to have a Temporary Orders trial.

A common temporary order is one that orders one spouse to pay support to the other until the divorce trial takes place. Before the judge can grant the motion, it must be shown that support is needed and that the spouse is capable of paying the amount requested.

To show the need and the ability to pay, most states require that a sworn statement (the Financial Affidavit) be prepared, detailing both spouse's living expenses and incomes.

IV. Permanent Orders

Permanent Orders are the final divorce orders which dissolve the marriage and enters permanent financial and child based orders.

Couples reach the permanent order stage by resolving their situation one of two ways; they either settle or they go to trial.

Some states, but not all, allow divorce by mail in some cases.

The tax filing status for each spouse is determined by the legal status (divorced or married) on December 31. If the couple doesn't get divorced until Dec 31, they are divorced for the entire year. If they don't get divorced until Jan 1, they are married for the entire prior year. This creates financial planning opportunities. Taxes can be figured for the couple based on Married, Filing Separately or Head of Household versus a joint return to see which would give the greatest tax benefit.

V. Approaches to settlement

A. Parties direct the negotiation
Most people who are getting divorced can't talk to each other so this approach doesn't always work. The "pro se" population is generally more able to talk to each other. They are working without lawyers and are trying to settle.

B. Lawyers direct the negotiation
One lawyer represents the husband and one represents the wife
1. Settlement letters—the lawyers send letters back and forth
2. Four-way meetings—these are meetings with both lawyers and both spouses to try to reach a settlement.

C. Alternative dispute resolution (Mediation)
This is a great growth industry and is a natural complement for the work of a CDP.
1. Court-based programs
Someone is appointed by the court to sit down with the parties to try to settle.
2. Private mediation
The parties pay a divorce mediator to help them reach an agreement. It could be a trained financial planner or mediator. The mediator is neutral and doesn't give advice to either party. He/she helps the parties understand the issues and the facts and creates an environment where the parties can settle. The mediator (even a lawyer mediator) provides information, but does not give legal advice. People can make quality decisions when they have infor-

mation. The parties may or may not have lawyers giving them legal advice during the mediation.

IV. Trials

If the parties don't settle, then they go to trial and have a judge decide their future. Only about 5% of divorce cases actually go to trial. Whether they settle "on the courthouse steps" or earlier is impossible to ascertain. That fact that about 95% of them settle is good because if they have come to an agreement on their own, they are more likely to honor that agreement than one handed down to them by "the person in the black robe." In one sense, they have taken charge of their own future and it gives them a feeling that they are in control. Going to court takes all control away from them.

All divorce cases are decided by a judge and not a jury (although a couple of states have limited jury trials).

If one or the other of the divorcing couple strongly opposes the judge's decision, they can appeal for either of the following reasons:

1. Error of law
   A judge's decision can be appealed if one of the parties feels there was an error in the interpretation of the law or if the judge handed down the decision incorrectly.
2. Abuse of discretion
   A judge's decision can be appealed if one of the parties feels there was an abuse of discretion.

DISCOVERY

Discovery is the process of gathering information about the nature, scope, and credibility of the opposing party's claim. Discovery procedures include depositions, written interrogatories, and notices to produce various documentation relating to issues which are decided in the case. Many cases are won or lost at the discovery stage.

The theory is that justice is best served if both sides have access to the same facts and evidence. But with a spouse who is knowledgeable about financial affairs and willing and able to manipulate records, discovery can turn into a struggle.

If your client's spouse works for someone else, be thankful, because tracking down accounts and investments will be easy compared to the situation if the spouse is a self-employed professional or runs his or her own business. Manipulation of financial data may be relatively easy for the self-employed people such as doctors, dentists, lawyers, accountants, financial consultants, stockbrokers, real estate agents, store or factory owners, independent contractors, or someone who runs a cash business.

The law gives your client's lawyer wide discretion to review tax returns, business and personal records, contracts, canceled checks, credit card receipts, and other documents; and to question the spouse, his or her friends, relatives, and business associates about the spouse's financial dealing. And it gives you, as the expert witness, liberal access to inspect and evaluate the books of any enterprise the spouse owns, controls, or profits from. This is the time when you can verify errors on the Financial Affidavit.

TYPES OF DISCOVERY

There are two types of discovery; informal and formal.

Formal Discovery

Formal discovery includes legal procedures such as **depositions, interrogatories** and requests for production of documents.

A **deposition** is the sworn testimony of a witness taken outside the court in the presence of lawyers for each side. There is also a court reporter present to record the proceedings and testimony has to be given under oath. Because it is a sworn statement, it becomes part of the record of the case. If you say one thing in the discovery deposition, and another thing at the trial, you will have to explain why your answer changed. The parts of the discovery deposition that are in conflict can be read to the witness at trial, and if the change is substantial and unexplained, the overall testimony of the witness is less believable.

Depositions are used for many purposes—for example, to gather information that the witness may have that would be difficult to obtain in a written exchange of questions (interrogatories), to compel a reluctant witness to share information, or to test the competence and reliability of an expert witness, and generally to tie down information given under oath.

Interrogatories are a series of written questions submitted to the other party. Because interrogatories are in writing and do not require the "live" presence of the attorneys and the court reporter, they are used more frequently than depositions. The answers to interrogatories must be under oath and filed within a prescribed period of time.

Interrogatories are commonly used to obtain more information or details about a particular item such as an employment contract or pension plan information.

Requests for Production of Documents require the spouses and third parties to produce documents necessary to understand the issues in the case.

Informal Discovery

Informal discovery can be as simple as one lawyer calling the other lawyer and saying, "Send over to me everything you've got about the Smith case including financial affidavits, tax returns, check stubs, investment statements, list of assets, and anything else we might need to see." And the other lawyer responds, "Okay, you'll have it by Friday."

Well, it might not be *quite* that simple but if the spouse's lawyer is cooperating, he/she adds to the informal discovery by *voluntarily* providing requested information and documentation. The best lawyers do this without hesitation and give complete relevant financial facts. The lawyer knows he will be required to provide this information anyhow, and he can save time for the client and himself, as well as the expense of formal discovery.

The lawyer is within his rights not to disclose information that is not requested, but he cannot go along with intentional deception.

LEGAL ADVICE VS. LEGAL INFORMATION

Practicing law without a license is a criminal offense!

Now that we have your attention, let's look very closely at this situation. If you do not have a license to practice law, you may not give legal advice or in any other way practice law. While you are going to be on the edges of the law working with divorcing clients and their attorneys, stick to your financial expertise and leave the legal interpretation to the attorneys.

What is the difference between giving legal advice and giving legal information? Let's look at two different areas:

1. If you say, "You should ask for more maintenance." or "You should sell the house." or "You should take the savings account because....", you are giving legal advice. Did you notice the words "should"? Only an attorney or a judge can tell a divorce client what they "should" do.

Your proper language is, "If you get more maintenance, this is the financial result." or "If you sell the house, this would be the capital gains tax." or "If you take the savings account, this is the financial result."

Remember, we are taking numbers *provided to us by the client* (or attorney), putting them in a spreadsheet, and showing them the result. We are showing the financial results of different settlement options that are given to us by the client and/or the attorney. It is only after the divorce is final and we are talking to them as a financial planner, that we can give them investment advice.

2. We have had graduates of this program write in their promotion material that they will help clients "achieve an equitable settlement". But *only a judge* can determine what an "equitable settlement" is. It is better to say, "...help in achieving a financially fair settlement." or "We examine the financial issues of your divorce—and provide you and your attorney with powerful data to support your case."

   We have had graduates write, "I will help you get adequate maintenance." But *only a judge* can determine what "adequate" or "equitable maintenance" is. It is better to say, "I can show you the financial issues of dividing property, alimony..." or "My work shows the after-tax results of alimony, dividing property,...."

   These promotions have been challenged by some state Bar Associations. Don't let yourself get into this uncomfortable position.

   Be very careful about how you talk to your clients and how you promote yourself and your services. Just keep remembering to use the word "financial" as a qualifier because after all, you are a financial expert.

   We at ICDP are your compliance officers in this area. We ask that you fax us any promotional material before you print it so we can save you the trouble of having to re-do it.

LEGAL DEFINITIONS

Affidavit: A written statement of facts made under oath and signed before a notary public or other officer who has authority to administer oaths.

Alimony: Periodic or lump sum support payments to a former spouse. Also referred to as spousal support. Same as maintenance.

Alternative Dispute Resolution: Ways for parties in a divorce to resolve their disagreements without a trial; usually defined to include negotiation, mediation and arbitration.

Appeal: The process whereby a higher court reviews the proceedings in a lower court and determines whether there was reversible error. If so, the appellate court amends the judgment or returns the case to the lower court for a new trial.

Appraisal: Procedure for determining the fair market value of an asset when it is to be sold or divided as part of the divorce process.

Arbitration: Submitting a disputed matter for decision to a person who is not a judge. The decision of an arbitrator is usually binding and final.

Assets: Cash, property, investments, goodwill, and other items of value (as defined by state law) that appear on a balance sheet indicating the net worth of an individual or a business.

"Best interests of the child": A discretionary legal standard used by judges when making decisions about custody, visitation, and support for a child when the parents are divorcing.

Change of Venue: A change of judges or geographical location, requested by a party to the action who feels that the change is justified by state law.

Child support: The amount of money paid by a non-custodial parent to the custodial parent for a child's day-to-day expenses and other special needs.

Child support guidelines: A series of mathematical formulas that calculate the amount of child support to be paid in some cases. Congress has mandated that states adopt child support guidelines and support enforcement procedures.

Community property: A form of co-ownership of property by a husband and wife who reside in one of the eight states where community property is recognized. Currently, these eight states follow the community property method: Arizona, California, Idaho, Louisiana, Nevada, New Mexico, Texas and Washington. The Wisconsin system has similarities.

Complaint: A legal document filed by the plaintiff stating that the marriage has ended and listing the grounds and claims of the divorce. Also known as a petition.

Contempt of court: The willful failure to comply with a court order, judgment, or decree by a party to the actions. Contempt of Court may be punishable by fine or imprisonment.

Contested Divorce: Any case where the judge must decide one or more issues that are not agreed to by the parties. All cases are considered contested until all issues have been agreed to.

Court order: The court's written ruling.

Cross-examination: The questioning of a witness presented by the opposing party on trial or at a deposition. The purpose is to test the truth of that testimony.

Custody: Usually refers to the parent's right to (1) have a child live with that parent and (2) make decisions concerning the child. Exact meaning varies greatly in different states.

Decree: The final ruling of the judge on an action for divorce, legal separation, or annulment. Same as judgment.

Defendant: The partner in a marriage against whom a divorce complaint is filed. Same as respondent.

Deposition: The testimony of a witness taken out of court under oath and reduced to writing. The most common depositions are discovery depositions taken for the purpose of discovering the facts upon which a party's claim is based or discovering the substance of a witness's testimony prior to trial. The deposition may be used to discredit a witness if he changes his testimony.

Direct examination: The initial questioning of a witness by the attorney who called him to the stand.

Discovery: Procedures followed by attorneys in order to determine the nature, scope, and credibility of the opposing party's claim. Discovery procedures include depositions, written interrogatories, and notices to produce various documentation relating to issues which are decided in the case.

Dissolution of Marriage: The legal process of ending a marriage. In most states, the legal term for divorce.

Emancipation: The point at which a minor child comes of age. Children are emancipated in most states upon reaching the age of either 18, 19, or 21, or upon marriage, full-time employment, graduation from high school, or entering the armed services. Emancipation is the point where parents have no further legal or financial obligations for a child's support.

Equitable division of property: Method of dividing property based on a number of considerations such as length of marriage, differences in age, wealth, earning potential, and health of partners involved that attempts to result in a fair distribution, not necessarily an equal one.

Evidence: Proof presented at a hearing, including testimony, documents or objects.

Exhibits: Tangible things presented at trial as evidence.

Expert witness: In court proceedings, professional whose testimony helps a judge reach divorce decisions.

File: To place a document in the official custody of some public official. Also used to mean start a case.

Foundation: The evidence that must be presented before asking certain questions or offering documentary evidence on trial.

Goodwill: The value of a business beyond its sales revenue, inventory, and other tangible assets; includes prestige, name recognition, and customer loyalty.

Guardian ad litem: An individual, usually an attorney, appointed by the court to advocate the rights and interests of the children in a divorce—most often when the parents are unable to arrange a custody agreement.

Grounds for divorce: Reasons for seeking a divorce, such as incompatibility, mental cruelty, physical abuse, or adultery. While some states allow fault grounds for divorce, all states have some form of no-fault divorce.

Guardian-ad-Litem: A person appointed by a judge to prosecute or defend a case for a person legally unable to do so, such as a minor child.

Hearing: Any proceeding before a judicial officer.

Interrogatories: A series of written questions served upon the opposing party in order to discover certain facts regarding the disputed issues in a matrimonial proceeding.

Joint Custody: Any arrangement which gives both parents legal responsibility for the care of a child. In some states, also means shared rights to the child's companionship.

Joint property: Property held in the name of more than one person.

Judgment: The order of the court on a disputed issue; same as decree.

Jurisdiction: The power of the court to rule upon issues relating to the parties, their children or their property.

Legal separation: Court ruling on division of property, spousal support, and responsibility to children when a couple wishes to separate but not to divorce. A legal separation is most often desired for religious or medical reasons. A decree of legal separation does not dissolve the marriage and does not allow the parties to remarry.

Maintenance: Spousal support; same as alimony.

Marital property: Accumulated income and property acquired by the spouses during the marriage, subject to equitable division by the court. States will vary on their precise definition of what is to be included in marital property, sometimes excepting property acquired by gift or inheritance. (See *community property* and *equitable division of property.)*

Mediation: A non-adversarial process in which a husband and wife are assisted in reaching their own terms of divorce by a neutral third party trained in divorce matters. The mediator has no power to make or enforce decisions.

Modification: A change in the judgment, based on a change of circumstances.

Motion: An application to the court for an order. May be written or oral.

No-fault divorce: A marriage dissolution system whereby divorce is granted without the necessity of proving one of the parties guilty of marital misconduct.

Order: A ruling by the court.

Petition: A written application for particular relief from the court. In some jurisdictions complaint for divorce is entitled "petition for dissolution."

Petitioner (Plaintiff): The party who filed the Petition (Complaint).

Plaintiff: The spouse who initiates the legal divorce process by filing a complaint stating that the marriage is over and listing the grounds and claims against the other spouse. Same as petitioner.

Privilege: The right of a spouse to make admissions to an attorney, clergyman, psychiatrist or others as designated by state law that are not later admissible in evidence.

Pro Se: A party who is representing him or herself in a lawsuit.

Marital agreement: A contract signed by a couple usually before marriage that lists the assets and liabilities each partner is bringing into the marriage and provides a framework for financial limits to rights of support, property, and inheritance after the marriage and in the event of a divorce or death. Also called prenuptial or antenuptial agreement.

Pro se divorce: A divorce wherein the divorcing partners represent themselves in court (with or without a mutually agreeable separation agreement) without the assistance of attorneys.

Qualified Domestic Relations Order (QDRO): A court ruling earmarking a portion of a person's retirement or pension fund payments to be paid to his/her ex-spouse as part of a division of marital assets. Payments are made directly to the non-employee ex-spouse by the fund administrator at the time of divorce or at the time the employee's retirement payments are to begin.

Rebuttal: The introduction of evidence at a trial that is in response to new matter raised by the defendant at an earlier stage of the trial.

Respondent (Defendant): The party defending against a divorce Petition (Complaint).

Retainer: Money paid by the client to the lawyer or expert witness to obtain a commitment from the lawyer or expert witness to handle the client's case. A retainer can be a deposit against which the lawyer or expert witness charges fees as they are earned.

Rules of evidence: The rules that govern the method of presentation and admissibility or oral and documentary evidence at court hearings or depositions.

Separate property: Generally considered any property owned before marriage (earned or acquired by gift or inheritance), acquired during marriage by one partner using only that partner's separate property, or earned after a formalized separation. This definition will vary from state to state.

Separation agreement: The legal document listing provisions for peace between the divorcing couple, division of property, spousal support, and responsibility for children of the marriage. The couple's agreement or court-ordered terms are part of the divorce decree.

Settlement agreement: Same as Separation agreement.

Spousal support: Money paid by one partner to the other for the recipient's support following a divorce. Support may be mandated for a specific period of time (long-term or short-term) and is based on the needs of the recipient, ability to pay, and economic differences between the partners. Also called alimony or maintenance.

Stipulation: An agreement between the parties or their counsel, usually relating to matters of procedure.

Subpoena: A court order requiring a person's appearance in court or deposition as a witness or to present documents or other evidence for a case.

Temporary Orders: Orders granting relief between the filing of the lawsuit and the judgment. Automatic in some states. Also called Pendente Lite Orders.

Testimony: Statements under oath by a witness in a court hearing or deposition.

Trial: The time when a judge hears the contested permanent or temporary issues, with supporting evidence and witnesses, in a couple's divorce decisions. The judge may take a few hours or a few weeks to review the information presented and issue a court opinion.

(Special thanks for contributions to this chapter go to Barbara K. Stark, J.D., a fellow of the American Academy of Matrimonial Lawyers, New Haven, CT)

CHAPTER 16

Forms and Information Needed

CHECKLIST OF INFORMATION TO GATHER FOR ATTORNEY

__ Name, address, and phone number of client
__ Business address and phone number
__ Name, address, and phone number of other party
__ Name and address of lawyer representing other party
__ Dates of birth of each party
__ Date and place of marriage
__ Names and dates of birth of children
__ Prior marriages of each party and details of termination
__ Children of prior marriages and custodial arrangements
__ Length of time lived in this state
__ Existence of prenuptial agreement
__ Grounds for divorce
__ Objectives of each party
__ Date of separation
__ Current employment and place of employment
__ Income of each parties
__ Social Security numbers of each party
__ Education/degrees/training of each party

__ Job history and income potential of each party
__ Employee benefits of each party
__ Details of pension and profit-sharing plans for each party
__ Joint assets of the parties, including:
  __ Real estate
  __ Stocks, bonds, and other securities
  __ Bank and savings accounts
  __ IRAs
__ Liabilities or debt of each party
__ Life insurance of each party
__ Separate or personal assets of each party
__ Incidences of domestic abuse or threats
__ Financial records which include:
  __ Bank statements
  __ Tax returns
  __ Applications for loans
  __ Investment statements
__ Family business records which include:
  __ Type of business
  __ Shareholders
  __ Percent of ownership of business
  __ Bank statements of business
  __ Tax returns of business
  __ Applications for loans
  __ Income and balance sheets
  __ Financial reports
__ Furniture
__ Patents, royalties, and copyrights
__ Collections, artwork, and antiques
__ Trust funds, annuities, and inheritances
__ Career assets (Allowed in some states.) Includes education, license or degree, benefit packages, stock options, deferred compensation, vacation, sick leave, bonuses, etc.

FINAL DIVORCE DECREE

After the divorce is final is too late to find out that additional items should have been negotiated and covered in the final settlement. To make sure that the final divorce decree gives the protection wanted, use this checklist to include those items that pertain to your client's case.

1. The Divorce Process
   - Who pays the legal fees?
   - If the ex-wife must take the ex-husband to court for non-support or for not complying with the divorce decree, will the husband pay the legal fees and court costs? Will there be interest charges?
   - Does the wife want to take back her maiden name?
2. Property
   - Who gets which property?
   - Who gets which debt?
   - If the pension is to be divided, has the proper paperwork been prepared?
   - If there is a property settlement note, is it collateralized? Is there interest on it?
   - Does the spouse who gets the house get the whole basis in the house?
   - If the spouse who gets the house needs to sell it immediately, will that person be responsible for the entire capital gains tax?
3. Maintenance
   - How much maintenance for how long?
   - If maintenance is not awarded now, can it be awarded later?
   - Will there be life insurance to cover maintenance in the event of the payor's death?
4. Child Support
   - How much child support for how long?
   - Will the child support change during college or when visitation times change?
   - Who has custody of the children?
   - What is the visitation schedule?

- Who pays related expenses for school (transportation, books, etc.) and unusual expenses (lessons, camp, teeth, etc.)?
- Who will deduct the children on income tax forms?

FORMS

Basic Information

The Basic Information form is for the purpose of data gathering. Many times, some of these pieces of information are missed or overlooked when meeting with the client for the first time. This form will help you to be more thorough.

BASIC INFORMATION

1. Wife's name ______________________
   Address ______________________
   ____
   Age __________
   Phone (____) __________ day (____) __________ evening
   Wife's attorney ______________________
   Phone ______________________
   Occupation & no. of years ______________________

2. Husband's name ______________________
   Address ______________________
   ____
   Age __________
   Phone (____) __________ day (____) __________ evening
   Husband's attorney ______________________
   Phone ______________________
   Occupation & no. of years ______________________

3. Length of marriage—yrs ______________________

4. Number of children ______________________
   Name Birthdate
   ____
   ____
   ____
   ____

5. Will wife work after divorce? ______________________
   Projected gross income ______________________
   Projected net income ______________________

6. Husband's projected gross income ______________________
   Husband's projected net income ______________________

7. Husband's settlement proposal (attach additional pages as necessary)
   Asset division ______________________
   Monthly maintenance ______________________
   How long maintenance will continue ______________________
   Monthly child support (per child) ______________________
   How long child support will continue ______________________
   Contribution to children's college expenses ______________________

8. Wife's settlement proposal (attach additional pages as necessary)
   Asset division ______________________
   Monthly maintenance ______________________
   How long maintenance will continue ______________________
   Monthly child support (per child) ______________________

How long child support will continue ____________________
Contribution to children's college expenses ____________________

9. Residence
    Fair market value of home ____________________
    Remaining balance of the mortgage ____________________
    Years remaining to pay ____________________
    Interest rate ____________________
    Monthly payment (PITI) ____________________
    Basis in the house ____________________
    Will the house be sold? ____________________
    If not, who wants to stay in the house? ____________________

10. Please provide the following information:
    - List of assets (Provide information on each that applies)
        - Checking and Savings accounts
        - CD's
        - Annuities
        - Stocks and Bonds
        - Mutual Funds
        - Real estate (Rentals, second home, land, etc.)
        - Limited partnerships
        - Life Insurance policies
        - Family Business
            - Percent of ownership
            - Tax returns
            - Financial statements
        - IRAs
        - 401K or other retirement plans
        - Defined Benefit pension plan (future payments at retirement)
        - Debt (credit card, loans, etc.)
        - Vehicles
        - Personal possessions
        - Antiques & collectibles
        - Personal or separate property
    - Last 3 years tax returns
    - Paycheck stubs
    - Financial affidavit for husband & wife (shows income & expenses)
    - Information on pension and retirement plans

ALL INFORMATION IS STRICTLY CONFIDENTIAL

Financial Affidavit

You saw examples of errors in the financial affidavit in Chapter 7. The following format will help gather all pieces of information that goes into putting the numbers of your case together.

FINANCIAL AFFIDAVIT

Name ______________________________

1. Job Title or Occupation ______________________________

2. Primary Employer's name ______________________________
   Hours worked per week ______________________________

3. I am paid ☐ weekly ☐ (every other week ☐ twice each month ☐ (monthly
   Amount of each check (gross) ______________________________

4. Month gross income ______________________________

5. Monthly payroll deductions
   (Number of exemptions being claimed: ____)
   Federal Income Tax ______________
   Social Security ______________
   Medicare ______________
   State Income Tax ______________
   Health Insurance Premium ______________
   Life Insurance Premium ______________
   Dental Insurance Premium ______________
   401(k) ______________
   Total deductions from this employment ______________

6. Net Monthly Take Home Pay from primary employer ______________

7. Other Sources and Amounts of Income

SOURCE	AMOUNT
______________	________
______________	________

8. Deductions from Other Income Sources Listed in Part 7

DEDUCTIONS	AMOUNT
______________	________
______________	________

9. Net Monthly Income from Other Sources ______________

10. NET MONTHLY INCOME from ALL sources ______________

11. Net Monthly Income of Children ______________________________

12. Income Reported on Last Federal Return ______________________________

13. Monthly Gross Income of Other Party ______________________________
Monthly Net Income of Other Party ______________________________

14. MONTHLY EXPENSES for _____ adult and _____ children:

A. HOUSING
Rent ______________________
First Mortgage ______________
Second Mortgage ____________
Homeowners Fee ____________
TOTAL HOUSING ______________

B. UTILITIES
Gas and Electric ______________
Telephone __________________
Water and Sewer _____________
Trash Collection _____________
Cable TV ___________________
TOTAL UTILITIES ______________

C. FOOD
Grocery Store Items ___________
Restaurant Meals _____________
TOTAL FOOD ________________

D. MEDICAL (after insurance)
Doctor _____________________
Dentist _____________________
Prescriptions ________________
Therapy ____________________
TOTAL MEDICAL _____________

E. INSURANCE
Life Insurance _______________
Health Insurance _____________
Dental Insurance _____________
Homeowners ________________
TOTAL INSURANCE ____________

F. TRANSPORTATION
Vehicle #1
Payment ___________________
Fuel ______________________
Repair & Maintenance _________
Insurance __________________
Parking ____________________

Vehicle #2
Payment ____________
Fuel ____________
Repair & Maintenance ____________
Insurance ____________
Parking ____________
TOTAL TRANSPORTATION ____________

G. CLOTHING TOTAL CLOTHING ____________

H. LAUNDRY TOTAL LAUNDRY ____________

I. CHILD CARE (and related)
Child care ____________
Allowance ____________
TOTAL CHILD CARE ____________

J. EDUCATION (and related)
For children
School costs ____________
Lunches ____________
Sports ____________
For spouse
Tuition ____________
Books and fees ____________
TOTAL EDUCATION ____________

K. RECREATION
Entertainment ____________
Hobbies ____________
Vacations ____________
Memberships/Clubs ____________
TOTAL RECREATION ____________

L. MISCELLANEOUS
Gifts ____________
Hair care/nail care ____________
Pet care ____________
Books/newspapers ____________
Donations ____________
TOTAL MISCELLANEOUS ____________

M. TOTAL REQUIRED MONTHLY EXPENSES ____________

15. DEBTS

	Creditor	Unpaid Balance	Monthly Payment
A.	____________	$____________	$________
B.	____________	$____________	$________
C.	____________	$____________	$________
D.	____________	$____________	$________
E.	____________	$____________	$________

16. ASSETS

A. Real Estate

Location ______________________
Market Value __________________
Loan __________________________
Net Equity ____________________

Estate
Location ______________________
Market Value __________________
Loan __________________________
Net Equity ____________________

TOTAL REAL ESTATE (NET) __________

B. FURNITURE

Location ______________________
Market Value __________________

Location ______________________
Market Value __________________

TOTAL FURNITURE ______________

C. MOTOR VEHICLES

Year/Make _____________________
Market Value __________________
Loan __________________________
Net Equity ____________________

Year/Make _____________________
Market Value __________________
Loan __________________________
Net Equity ____________________

TOTAL VEHICLES ________________

D. BANK ACCOUNTS

Name of Bank __________________
Current Balance _______________

Name of Bank __________________
Current Balance _______________

Name of Bank __________________
Current Balance _______________

TOTAL BANKS ___________________

E. STOCKS AND BONDS

Stock Name ______________
No. of Shares ______________
Market Value ______________

Stock Name ______________
No. of Shares ______________
Market Value ______________

TOTAL STOCKS/BONDS ___________

F. LIFE INSURANCE

Company Name ______________
Policy Number ______________
Owner's Name ______________
Insured's Name ______________
Beneficiary's Name ______________
Face Value ______________
Cash Surrender Value ______________

Company Name ______________
Policy Number ______________
Owner's Name ______________
Insured's Name ______________
Beneficiary's Name ______________
Face Value ______________
Cash Surrender Value ______________

Company Name ______________
Policy Number ______________
Owner's Name ______________
Insured's Name ______________
Beneficiary's Name ______________
Face Value ______________
Cash Surrender Value ______________

TOTAL INSURANCE ______________

G. PENSION, PROFIT SHARING, RETIREMENT FUNDS

Plan Name ______________
Participant Name ______________
Value ______________

Plan Name ______________
Participant Name ______________
Value ______________

TOTAL PENSION ______________

TOTAL ASSETS ______________

CHAPTER 17

The Final Word

At the start of this book, my objective was to illustrate that divorce could be fair to both parties. In the process, it is also obvious that divorce is rarely easy. Perhaps people should look at what it takes to get divorced before they get married. With all the time and money and emotion involved, it might make potential spouses think hard about whether they are getting married for the right reason. If they're not, it would allow them to reconsider getting married in the first place.

However, even this knowledge won't stop many from getting married—and then, unfortunately, divorced. There is a type of insanity that seems to surface when a divorce is imminent. Otherwise, why would rational people divorce? Men and women say, and do, things to each other that are horrible - things that they would never have imagined they would say and do to someone they loved and cared for at one time.

Someone once said that the cost of divorce averages $20,000 per couple. If this is true, Americans are needlessly spending $28 billion dollars on divorce *every year*! And the work force suffers because it's not easy to leave the emotions outside the door of the office. Added to that are the anger and bitterness and vindictiveness that tear families apart.

Well-informed financial advisors can do a lot toward helping people achieve equitable settlements and minimize the negative, destructive forces of divorce. In fact, the wave of the future is having teams of experts who can help people through the difficult times of breaking up a family. This team can help the divorcing couple stay out of court.

Who makes up this team?

1. The attorney is critical to the team. Legal documents need to be drawn up. New wills need to be made. Pensions need to be divided via a legal document.
2. The financial expert—whether it be a Certified Public Accountant (CPA), Certified Divorce Planner (CDP), Certified Financial Planner (CFP), or other financial planner—can help the attorney look at basis in property, how assets will be taxed, how pensions are valued, the long term effect of dividing property and maintenance, and how inflation assumptions will affect these decisions.
3. Real estate appraisers, business appraisers, and other asset appraisers are needed to place values on different pieces of property so that property settlement negotiations can take place.
4. Mediators can work with the couple in the beginning to get as many agreements as they can and possibly reach a settlement.
5. Therapists are needed when the emotions are so strong that the issues are clouded. Each person needs to know of their worth and each person also needs to take responsibility for themselves as much as is possible.
6. Career counselors can test and evaluate a spouse who has been out of the workplace for a long time to see what the future might hold for this person and where he or she might best concentrate job skills or talents.

It is well known among judges, attorneys and other professionals in the divorce arena, that people in this area burn out faster than in any other legal career. Divorce judges change venue when they can't take the negative emotional atmosphere in the court anymore. Criminal court becomes more desirable than divorce court! Divorce attorneys retire early or become mediators or maybe even open a cooking school!

My vision is that all the professionals work together to minimize the negative impact of divorce. Attorneys help their clients settle out of court. Judges hand down more equitable settlements. Financial advisors provide the essential information to help in the decision making. And in the end, Americans will have more money available to keep them on the positive side of cash flow instead of being in debt, and children in divorced families will have fewer deep emotional scars. Who knows, maybe the crime rate will even decrease!

I believe the key to all this lies with you, the financial advisor. Laws change. The economic environment changes. You must have the tenacity and experience to flow with these changes.

Simple? No, but then, when is anything worthwhile simple? Do what makes common sense. Have patience. Keep learning. I believe in your ability to put it together. Now it's your turn.

CHAPTER 18

Resources

BOOKS ON DIVORCE

After Marriage Ends: Economic Consequences for Midlife Women. Leslie A. Morgan. Newbury Park, CA. Sage Publications, Inc. 1991.

Between Love and Hate: A Guide to Civilized Divorce. Lois Gold. New York. A Plume Book. 1992.

The Boys and Girls Book About Divorce. Richard Gardner. New York. Science House, Inc.

The Complete Guide for Men and Women Divorcing. Melvin Belli and Mel Krantzler. New York. St. Martin's Press, Inc. 1990.

The Consequences of Divorce: Economic and Custodial Impact on Children and Adults. Craig A. Everett. Binghamton, NY. Haworth Press, Inc. 1991.

Creative Divorce: A New Opportunity for Personal Growth. Mel Krantzler. New York. A Signet Book. 1974.

The Dollars and Sense of Divorce: The Financial Guide for Women. Judith Briles. New York: Ballantine Books. 1991.

Divorce and Money: Everything You Need to Know About Dividing Property. Violet Woodhouse & Victoria Felton-Collins. Berkeley, CA. Nolo Press.

Divorce and New Beginnings: An Authoritative Guide to Recovery and Growth, Solo Parenting, and Step Families. Genevieve Clapp. John Wiley & Sons, Inc. 1992.

Divorce: A Woman's Guide to Getting a Fair Share. Patricia Phillips and George Mair. New York. Macmillan. 1995.

Divorce Decisions Workbook: A Planning and Action Guide. Margorie L. Engel & Diana D. Gould. New York. McGraw Hill, Inc. 1992.

The Divorce Handbook: Your Basic Guide to Divorce. James T. Friedman. New York. Random House. 1984.

Divorce Help Sourcebook. Margorie L. Engel. Detroit, MI. Visible Ink Press. 1994.

The Divorce Revolution: the Unexpected Social and Economic Consequences for Women and Children in America. Lenore Weitzman. New York. The Free Press (A Division of Macmillan, Inc.). 1985.

Divorcing. Mel Krantzler & Melvin M. Belli, Sr. New York. St. Martin's Press. 1988.

Dollars and Sense of Divorce: Judith Briles, Ed Schilling III, and Carol Ann Wilson. Chicago. Dearborn Financial Publishing, Inc. 1998.

Fair Share Divorce For Women. Kathleen Miller. Bellevue, WA. Miller, Bird Advisors. 1995.

The Financial Guide to Divorce: Everything You Need to Know for Financial Strategies During and After Divorce. Frances Johansen. Irvine, CA. United Resources Press. 1991.

Financial Fitness Through Divorce: A Guide to the Financial Realities of Divorce. Elizabeth S. Lewin. New York. Facts On File Publications. 1987.

Financial Planning From We to Me: Divorce Strategies to Help You Get More of What You Want. Kathleen L. Cotton. Lynwood, WA. Wealth Books. 1996.

The Five-Minute Lawyer's Guide to Divorce. Michael Allan Cane. New York. Dell Publishing. 1995.

Friendly Divorce Guidebook for Colorado: M. Arden Hauer & S.W. "Wendy" Whicher. Denver, CO. Bradford Publishing Co. 1994.

The Expert Witness Handbook: Tips and Techniques for the Litigation Consultant. Dan Poynter. Santa Barbara, CA. Para Publishing. 1987.

The Good Divorce: Keeping Your Family Together When Your Marriage Comes Apart. Constance Ahrons. New York. Harper Perennial. 1994.

A Guide To Divorce Mediation: How to Reach a Fair, Legal Settlement at a Fraction of the Cost. Gary J. Friedman. New York. Workman Publishing. 1993.

Handbook of Financial Planning for Divorce and Separation: 1993 Cumulative Supplement. D. Larry Crumbley. New York. John Wiley & Sons, Inc. 1993.

In Defense of Children: Understanding the Rights, Needs and Interests of the Child. Thomas A. Nazario. New York. Charles Scribner's Sons, Bennett Publishing Co. 1988.

Money Sense: What Every Woman Must Know To Be Financially Confident. Judith Briles. Chicago. Moody Press. 1995.

Rebuilding: When Your Relationship Ends. Dr. Bruce Fisher. San Luis Obispo, CA. Impact. 1995.

Smart Ways to Save Money During and After Divorce. Victoria Felton-Collins & Ginita Wall. Berkeley, CA. Nolo Press. 1994.

Succeeding As An Expert Witness: Increasing Your Impact and Income. Harold A. Feder. Glenwood Springs, CO. Tageh Press. 1993.

Survival Manual For Men In Divorce. Edwin Schilling III & Carol Ann Wilson. Boulder, CO. ICDP Press. 2000.

Survival Manual For Women In Divorce. Carol Ann Wilson & Edwin Schilling III. Boulder, CO. ICDP Press. 1999.

Tax Strategies in Divorce: 1992 Supplement. Dennis C. Mahoney. New York. John Wiley & Sons, Inc. 1992.

A Woman's Guide to Divorce and Decision Making. Christina Robertson. New York. Simon & Schuster Inc. 1989.

You're Entitled: A Divorce Lawyer Talks to Women. Sidney M. DeAngelis. Chicago. Contemporary Books. 1989.

DIVORCE SOFTWARE

DIVORCE PLAN™
Institute for Certified
Divorce Planners
6395 Gunpark Drive, Suite W
Boulder, CO 80301
800-875-1760
Available through the Institute only

Spreadsheets, graphs,
net-worth comparisons

FinPlan's DIVORCE PLANNER™
FinPlan Co.
100 E. Cuttriss Street
Park Ridge, IL 60068
800-777-2108
$500

Tax and support
planning for divorce

LEGAL AND MEDIATION ASSOCIATIONS

American Academy of Family Mediators
5 Militia Drive
Lexington, MA 02173
781-674-2663

American Academy of Matrimonial Lawyers
150 N. Michigan Ave., Suite 2040
Chicago, IL 60601
312-263-6477

American Bar Association
750 N. Lake Shore Drive
Chicago, IL 60611
312-988-5000
800-621-6159

STATE RESOURCES

Alabama

Alabama State Bar
415 Dexter Street
PO Box 671
Montgomery, AL 36104
205-269-1515

Alaska

Alaska Bar Association
510 L Street, No. 602
PO Box 100279
Anchorage, AK 99510
907-272-7469

Arizona

American Arbitration Association
Phoenix Regional Office
333 E. Osborn Road, Suite 310
Phoenix, AZ 85012
602-234-0950

State Bar of Arizona
363 N. 1st Avenue
Phoenix, AZ 85003
602-252-4804

Arkansas

Arkansas Bar Association
400 W. Markham
Little Rock, AR 72201
501-375-4605

California

American Arbitration Association
Los Angeles Regional Office
443 Shatto Place
PO Box 57994
Los Angeles, CA 90020
213-383-6516

American Arbitration Association
Orange County, CA Regional Office
2601 Main Street, Suite 240
Irvine, CA 92714
714-474-5090

American Arbitration Association
San Diego Regional Office
525 C Street, Suite 400
San Diego, CA 92101
619-239-3051

American Arbitration Association
San Francisco Regional Office
417 Montgomery Street, 5th Floor
San Francisco, CA 94101
415-981-3901

State Bar of California
180 Howard Street
San Francisco, CA 94105-1639
415-538-2000

Colorado

American Arbitration Association
Denver Regional Office
1660 Lincoln Street, Suite 2150
Denver, CO 80264
303-831-0823

Colorado Bar Association
1900 Grant Street, Suite 950
Denver, CO 80203
303-860-1115

Connecticut

American Arbitration Association
Hartford Regional Office
11 Founders Place, 17th Floor
Hartford, CT 06108
203-289-3993

Connecticut Bar Association
101 Corporate Place
Rocky Hill, CT 06067
203-721-0025

Delaware

Delaware State Bar Association
1225 King Street
Wilmington, DE 19801
302-658-5279

District of Columbia

American Arbitration Association
Washington, DC Regional Office
1150 Connecticut Avenue NW, 6th Floor
Washington, DC 20036
202-296-8510

Bar Association of the District of Columbia
1819 H Street NW, 12th Floor
Washington, DC 20006
202-223-6600

District of Columbia Bar
1250 H Street NW, 6th Floor
Washington, DC 20005
202-737-4700

Florida

American Arbitration Association
Miami Regional Office
99 SE 5th Street, Suite 200
Miami, FL 33131
305-358-7777

American Arbitration Association
Orlando Regional Office
201 E. Pine Street, Suite 800
Orlando, FL 32801
407-648-1185

Florida Bar
The Florida Bar Center
650 Apalachee Parkway
Tallahassee, FL 32399
850-561-5600

Georgia

American Arbitration Association
Atlanta Regional Office
1360 Peachtree Street NE, Suite 270
Atlanta, GA 30361
404-872-3022

State Bar of Georgia
800 The Hurt Building
50 Hurt Plaza
Atlanta, GA 30303
404-527-8700

Hawaii

American Arbitration Association
Honolulu Regional Office
810 Richards Street, Suite 641
Honolulu, HI 96813
808-531-0541

Hawaii State Bar Association
Penthouse, 9th Floor
1136 Union Mall
Honolulu, HI 96813
808-537-1868

Idaho

Idaho State Bar
PO Box 895
Boise, ID 83701
208-342-8958

Illinois

American Arbitration Association
Chicago Regional Office
225 N. Michigan Avenue, Suite 2527
Chicago, IL 60601
312-616-6560

Illinois State Bar Association
424 S. 2nd Street
Springfield, IL 62701
217-525-1760

Indiana

Indiana State Bar Association
230 E. Ohio Street, 4th Floor
Indianapolis, IN 46204
317-639-5465

Iowa

Iowa State Bar Association
521 E. Locust
Des Moines, IA 50309
515-243-3179

Kansas Bar Association
1200 Harrison Street
Topeka, KS 66612
913-234-5696

Kentucky

Kentucky Bar Association
514 W. Main Street
Frankfort, KY 40601
502-564-3795

Louisiana

American Arbitration Association
New Orleans Regional Office
650 Poydras Street, Suite 1535
New Orleans, LA 70130
504-522-8781

Louisiana State Bar Association
601 St. Charles Avenue
New Orleans, LA 70130
504-566-1600

Maine

Maine State Bar Association
124 State Street
Box 788
Augusta, ME 04330
207-622-7523

Maryland

Maryland State Bar Association Inc.
520 W. Fayette Street
Baltimore, MD 21201
410-685-7878

Massachusetts

American Arbitration Association
Boston Regional Office
133 Federal Street
Boston, MA 02110
617-451-6600

Massachusetts Bar Association
20 West Street
Boston, MA 02111
617-542-3602

Michigan

American Arbitration Association
Southfield, MI Regional Office
10 Oak Hollow Street, Suite 170
Southfield, MI 48034
313-352-5500

State Bar of Michigan
306 Townsend Street
Lansing, MI 48933
517-372-9030

Minnesota

American Arbitration Association
Minneapolis Regional Office
514 Nicollet Mall, Suite 670
Minneapolis, MN 55402
612-332-6545

Minnesota State Bar Association
514 Nicollet Mall, Suite 300
Minneapolis, MN 55402
612-333-1183

Mississippi

Mississippi State Bar
643 N. State Street
Jackson, MS 39202
601-948-4471

Missouri

American Arbitration Association
Kansas City Regional Office
1101 Walnut Street, Suite 903
Kansas City, MO 64106
816-221-6401

American Arbitration Association
St. Louis Regional Office
1 Mercantile Center, Suite 2512
St. Louis, MO 63101
314-621-7175

Missouri Bar
326 Monroe
Jefferson City, MO 65102
314-635-4128

Montana

State Bar of Montana
46 N. Last Chance Gulch
Box 577
Helena, MT 59624
406-442-7660

Nebraska

Nebraska State Bar Association
635 S. 14th Street, 2nd Floor
Lincoln, NE 68508
402-475-7091

Nevada

State Bar of Nevada
201 Las Vegas Blvd., Suite 200
Las Vegas, NV 89101
702-382-2200

New Hampshire

New Hampshire Bar Association
112 Pleasant Street
Concord, NH 03301
603-224-6942

New Jersey

American Arbitration Association
Somerset Regional Office
265 Davidson Avenue, Suite 140
Somerset, NJ 08873
908-560-9560

New Jersey State Bar Association
New Jersey Law Center
1 Constitution Square
New Brunswick, NJ 08901
908-249-5000

New Mexico

State Bar of New Mexico
121 Tijeras Street, NE
Albuquerque, NM 87102
505-842-6132

New York

American Arbitration Association
Garden City, NY Regional Office
666 Old Country Road, Suite 603
Garden City, NY 11530
516-222-1660

American Arbitration Association
New York Regional Office
140 W. 51st. Street
New York, NY 10020
212-484-4000

American Arbitration Association
Syracuse Regional Office
205 S. Salina Street
Syracuse, NY 13202
315-472-5483

American Arbitration Association
White Plains, NY Regional Office
34 S. Broadway
White Plains, NY 10601
914-946-1119

New York State Bar Association
1 Elk Street
Albany, NY 12207
518-463-3200

North Carolina

American Arbitration Association
Charlotte Regional Office
428 E. 4th Street, Suite 300
Charlotte, NC 28202
704-347-0200

North Carolina Bar Association
1312 Annapolis Drive
Box 12806
Raleigh, NC 27608
919-828-0561

North Carolina State Bar
208 Fayetteville Street Mall
Raleigh, NC 27611
919-828-4620

North Dakota

State Bar Association of North Dakota
515 1/2 E. Broadway, Suite 101
Bismark, ND 58502
701-255-1404

Ohio

American Arbitration Association
Cincinnati Regional Office
441 Vine Street, Suite 3308
Cincinnati, OH 45202
513-241-8434

American Arbitration Association
Middleburg Heights Regional Office
17900 Jefferson Road, Suite 101
Middleburg Heights, OH 44130
216-891-4741

Ohio State Bar Association
1700 Lake Shore Drive
Columbus, OH 43216
614-487-2050

Oklahoma

Oklahoma Bar Association
1901 N. Lincoln
Oklahoma City, OK 73105
405-524-2365

Oregon

Oregon State Bar
5200 SW Meadows Road
Box 1689
Lake Oswego, OR 97035
503-620-0222

Pennsylvania

American Arbitration Association
Philadelphia Regional Office
230 S. Broad Street
Philadelphia, PA 19102
215-732-5260

American Arbitration Association
Pittsburgh Regional Office
4 Gateway Center, Room 419
Pittsburgh, PA 15222
412-261-3617

Pennsylvania Bar Association
100 South Street
Box 186
Harrisburg, PA 17108
717-238-6715

Rhode Island

American Arbitration Association
Providence Regional Office
115 Cedar Street
Providence, RI 02903
401-453-3250

Rhode Island Bar Association
115 Cedar Street
Providence, RI 02903
401-421-5740

South Carolina

South Carolina Bar
950 Taylor Street
Box 608
Columbia, SC 29202
803-799-6653

South Dakota

State Bar of South Dakota
222 E. Capitol
Pierre, SD 57501
605-224-7554

Tennessee

American Arbitration Association
Nashville Regional Office
221 4th Avenue, N., 2nd Floor
Nashville, TN 37219
615-256-5857

Tennessee Bar Association
3622 West End Avenue
Nashville, TN 37205
615-383-7421

Texas

American Arbitration Association
Dallas Regional Office
2 Galleria Tower, Suite 1440
Dallas, TX 75240
214-702-8222

American Arbitration Association
Houston Regional Office
1001 Fannin Street, Suite 1005
Houston, TX 77002
713-739-1302

State Bar of Texas
1414 Colorado
Box 12487
Austin, TX 78711
512-463-1400

Utah

American Arbitration Association
Salt Lake City Regional Office
645 S. 200 E., Suite 203
Salt Lake City, UT 84111
801-531-9748

Utah State Bar
645 S. 200 E., Suite 310
Salt Lake City, UT 84111
801-531-9077

Vermont

Vermont Bar Association
Box 100
Montpelier, VT 05601
802-223-2020

Virginia

Virginia Bar Association
701 E. Franklin Street, Suite 1515
Richmond, VA 23219
804-644-0041

Virginia State Bar
707 E. Main Street, Suite 1500
Richmond, VA 23219
804-775-0500

Washington

American Arbitration Association
Seattle Regional Office
1325 4th Avenue, Suite 1414
Seattle, WA 98101
206-622-6435

Washington State Bar Association
500 Westin Building
2001 6th Avenue
Seattle, WA 98121
206-727-8200

West Virginia

West Virginia Bar Association
904 Security Building
100 Capitol Street
Charleston, WV 25301
304-342-1474

West Virginia State Bar
2006 Kanawha Blvd., E.
Charleston, WV 25311
304-558-2456

Wisconsin

State Bar of Wisconsin
402 W. Wilson Street
Madison, WI 53703
608-257-3838

Wyoming

Wyoming State Bar
500 Randall Avenue
Cheyenne, WY 82001
307-632-9061